MINNESOTA MEDAL OF HONOR
RECIPIENTS

FROM THE CIVIL WAR TO VIETNAM

Compiled by the members of the Minnesota State Society
Daughters of the American Revolution

ISBN-13: 978-1537723082

This book represents a compilation of bio sketches written by dedicated volunteers who worked with scarce, hard-to-find, and often-conflicting information in a diligent and good faith effort to honor Minnesota's Medal of Honor recipients. The information contained herein is accurate to the best of our knowledge, however, no one is infallible. Therefore, we welcome corrections with accompanying documentation, and will include the updated information in any subsequent editions.

Cover design by June Gossler-Anderson
Edited by June Gossler Anderson
Layout and design Todd Anderson

Printed in USA

DEDICATED TO THE MEMORY OF THOSE WHOSE BRAVERY AND SELF-SACRIFICE WENT BEYOND THE CALL OF DUTY.

In Flanders fields the poppies blow
Between the crosses row on row,
That mark our place; and in the sky
The larks still bravely singing, fly
Scarce heard amid the guns below.

We are the Dead. Short days ago
We lived, felt dawn, saw sunset glow,
Loved and were loved, and now we lie
In Flanders fields.

Take up our quarrel with the foe:
To you from failing hands we throw
The torch; be yours to hold it high.
If ye break faith with us who die
We shall not sleep, though poppies grow
In Flanders fields.

John McCraw

MEDAL OF HONOR MEMORIAL

DEDICATED OCTOBER 3, 2016

MINNESOTA STATE CAPITAL

ST. PAUL, MINNESOTA

FORWARD

The Medal of Honor Society

The history of the MOHS has been evolving since 1890 when the MOH Legion was formed by recipients in the effort to protect the dignity of the MOH. The Legion's actions thereafter involved lobbying to protect the integrity of the medal that eventually led to the creation of the MOH Society in 1946. At that time and since the society has been more concerned with the ideals embodied in medal. In 1958 President Eisenhower signed legislation chartering the MOH Society and establishing more specific and comprehensive principles and purposes that guide the MOHS to this day.

The mission of the MOHS is to preserve the history of the MOH recipients and to educate and inspire current and future generations in the character virtues necessary for success in life. Goals of the MOHS are to honor those who have served our country and promote those principles on which our nation was formed.

The Congressional Medal of Honor Society credits Medal of Honor recipients to the state of Minnesota based on the following criteria:

> Recipients born in Minnesota
>
> Recipients enlisted into service in Minnesota
>
> Surviving recipients who died in Minnesota
>
> Recipients who are buried in Minnesota

How the Memorial came to be

The genesis for the idea for a Medal of Honor Memorial on the State Capitol grounds dates back to 2013 with the realization that the State of Minnesota had not given prominent and commensurate recognition, honor, and respect to our state and nation's greatest, most revered heroes and cultural icons, our Medal of Honor recipients. A proposal was submitted for a Minnesota Medal of Honor Memorial soon thereafter that generated further impetus when it was realized that not all recipients with birth, death, and internment connections to Minnesota had been identified and so honored. Furthermore, a particular recipient was identified who had been formally credited to the State of Minnesota in error and the vital information on other recipients was found to be inaccurate and/or incomplete. There was also an obvious need to identify descendants of recipients as a source of needed biographical information and publicly recognize their association with the recipients. Accordingly, the Daughters of the American Revolution chapters throughout the State of Minnesota rose to the challenge and the time constraints to provide extensive biographies on Minnesota recipients and identify descendants in advance of the groundbreaking ceremony of the Minnesota Medal of Honor Memorial approved by the 2016 State Legislature. The DAR volunteers involved in writing biographies on the 72 Minnesota Medal of Honor recipients additionally published

this book in time to meet the demand for information on the Minnesota recipients in advance of the 2016 National Medal of Honor Society Convention, Twin Cities. The Medal of Honor Memorial project is destined to succeed and be successful because of such dedicated and all out volunteer efforts.
John Kraemer, Chairman of the Minnesota Medal of Honor Memorial

The Daughters of the American Revolution

The DAR, founded in 1890 and headquartered in Washington, D.C., is a non-profit, non-political volunteer women's service organization dedicated to promoting patriotism, preserving American history, and securing America's future through better education for children.

DAR members volunteer millions of service hours annually in their local communities including supporting active duty military personnel and assisting veteran patients, awarding thousands of dollars in scholarships and financial aid each year to students, and supporting schools for underserved children with annual donations exceeding one million dollars.

As one of the most inclusive genealogical societies in the country, DAR boasts 180,000 members in 3,000 chapters across the United States and internationally. Any woman 18 years or older-regardless of race, religion, or ethnic background-who can prove lineal descent from a patriot of the American Revolution, is eligible for membership. Encompassing an entire downtown city block, DAR National Headquarters houses one of the nation's premier genealogical libraries, one of the foremost collections of pre-industrial American decorative arts, Washington's largest concert hall, and an extensive collection of early American manuscripts and imprints.
(Taken from www.DAR.org)

The Anoka Chapter serves our local community through contributions to a drop in center for homeless youth a local women's shelter and various community emergency assistance providers including Project Linus.

We assist veterans by contributing to the Veterans Food Shelf in the Anoka County Government Center, and providing lap quilts for residents of veterans' homes. We are also participants in the Flag Day 5K Race benefiting the Fisher Houses in Minneapolis, Minnesota.
Lynne Yarbrough, Honorary State Regent, Past Anoka Chapter Regent

DAR Involvement with the Medal of Honor Convention

I have been a member of DAR since 1996. What attracted me to DAR is their mission of Historic Preservation, Education and Patriotism. (My father was a WWII veteran.) As a result, military events that show "patriotism and service to our veterans" have always been very special to me. Without the sacrifice and service of our veterans, our nation would not have the freedoms and liberties we enjoy today. In the spring of 2015, it came to my attention that the Medal of Honor Convention was going to be held in Minnesota during the fall of 2016. It became a priority for me to get DAR involved in this historic patriotic event! After all, our revolutionary ancestors were the very first veterans! With the help of Senator Carla Nelson who is a DAR member of the Rochester Chapter, I was able to make contact with Liz Dapp, Chairwoman of the Medal of Honor Committee.

At last in early February 2016, I was contacted by John Kraemer, Chairman of the Minnesota Medal of Honor Memorial asking for our participation in a project to write bios on the 72 MN MOH recipients. I was put in contact with the National Archivist of the Congressional Medal of Honor Society who provided me with an excel sheet on the 72 MN Medal of Honor recipients with basic information. In my own mind, I felt that I would need a minimum of 10 volunteers to do the research and write the bios on these heroic men and so I sent a letter to all the Chapter Regents asking for volunteers.

As a result of this request, twenty-eight DAR members stepped forward and volunteered to participate, completing all 72 bios by early August 2016. This project was a "natural" for our organization which is known for doing genealogy as well as DAR's focus on Patriotism & Service to our Veterans. These volunteers are so very special and as a result of their efforts, DAR will always be recognized for this patriotic project! One hundred years from now, these bios will still be available! I am so proud of the volunteers who made this project to honor these heroes a reality! "Thank You!"
Bonnie Kottschade, Honorary State Regent & Project Leader

(With the consent of John Kraemer Chairman of the Medal of Honor Memorial Committee as well as the MNSSDAR Executive committee, The Anoka Chapter NSDAR has published this book containing these bios. Profits from sales will be used to benefit veterans and veteran's organization throughout the State of Minnesota.)

A SALUTE TO THOSE WHO MADE THIS BOOK POSSIBLE

John Kraemer Chairman of the Minnesota Medal of Honor Memorial
Bonnie Kottschade Honorary Minnesota State DAR Regent and project leader
Senator Carla Nelson, Rochester Chapter NSDAR and Liz Dapp, Medal of Honor Committee for their help in getting this project off the ground
Rachael Sanisidro, Minnesota State Society DAR Regent and the Minnesota State Society DAR Executive Board for their enthusiasm, encouragement, and support
Anoka Chapter NSDAR for giving wings to this project

Those who compiled

And a big hats off to the twenty-eight Daughters from the twelve Minnesota DAR Chapters whose research, scholarship, and diligence made this book possible. Their original manuscripts, complete with footnotes and documentation, have been entrusted to John Kraemer, Minnesota Medal of Honor Society and Bonnie Kottschade, Minnesota State Society Daughters of the American Revolution. They are available upon request.

They include:

Anoka Chapter NSDAR: June Gossler Anderson, Cindy Jorgenrud, Laura Gallup; Anthony Wayne Chapter NSDAR, Mankato: Elizabeth Beck, Ruth Carlson, Joyce Rohloff Gardner, Susan Carleton Jirele, Leslie Hartz Sprott, Marilyn Wilkus, Beth Zimmer; Captain Robert Orr Chapter NSDAR, Brainard: DeAnn Cady, Susan Duff Erkel; Greysolon Daughters of Liberty, Duluth Chapter NSDAR: Karrie Louise Norenberg Kees, Royleen Newman; Keewaydin Chapter NSDAR, Minneapolis: Diana Myers; Lake Minnetonka Chapter NSDAR, Wayzata: Georgetta "Gigi" Hickey, Shirleen Ann Hoffman, Kathleen M. Barrett Huston; Maria Sanford Chapter NSDAR: Glynae Deschene, Beth Iseminger, Tracy Moore MacAllister, Linda Sugarman; Monument Chapter NSDAR, Edina: Diana Dickinson Lynch; Nathan Hale Chapter NSDAR, St. Paul: Merrilee Carlson; Josiah Edson Chapter DAR, Northfield: Dianne Lawson; Rochester Chapter NSDAR: Marilyn Burbank, Lorraine Hall Keith; St. Croix River Valley Chapter NSDAR, Stillwater: Jane Homme.

A special note of appreciation to the Anoka Chapter members of the Medal of Honor book committee: Jacqueline Cottingham-Zierdt, Regent; Laura Gallup; Cindy Jorgenrud; Glenda Meixell; Joannie Moses; Marijane Tessman; and Lynne Yarbrough for their advice, guidance, and help with this project.

And the biggest thank you of all goes to my son, Todd Anderson. Without his help and expertise this project could never have become a reality.

June Gossler Anderson, Editor

CONTENTS

The Congressional Medal of Honor

The Medal of Honor is the United States of America's highest military honor, awarded for personal acts of valor above and beyond the call of duty. The medal is awarded by the President of the United States in the name of the U.S. Congress to U.S. military personnel only. There are three versions of the medal, one for the Army, one for the Navy, and one for the Air Force. Personnel of the Marine Corps and Coast Guard receive the Navy version.

On December 9, 1861 Iowa Senator James W. Grimes introduced S. No. 82 in the United States Senate, a bill designed to "promote the efficiency of the Navy" by authorizing the production and distribution of "medals of honor." On December 21st the bill was passed, authorizing 200 such medals be produced "which shall be bestowed upon such petty officers, seamen, landsmen and marines as shall distinguish themselves by their gallantry in action and other seamanlike qualities during the present war (Civil War)." President Lincoln signed the bill and the (Navy) Medal of Honor was born.

The 3 Present Day Variations of the Medal Of Honor

| Army | Navy | Air Force |

Two months later on February 17, 1862 Massachusetts Senator Henry Wilson introduced a similar bill, this one to authorize "the President to distribute medals to privates in the Army of the United States who shall distinguish themselves in battle." Over the following months wording changed slightly as the bill made its way through Congress. When President Abraham Lincoln signed S.J.R. No. 82 on July 12, 1862, the Army Medal of Honor was born. It read in part:

Resolved by the Senate and House of Representatives of the United States of America in Congress assembled, That the President of the United States be, and he is hereby, authorized to cause two thousand "medals of honor" to be prepared with suitable emblematic devices, and to direct that the same be presented, in the name of the Congress, to such non--commissioned officers and privates as shall most distinguish themselves by their gallantry in action, and other soldier-like qualities, during the present insurrection (Civil War).

With this simple and rather obscure act Congress created a unique award that would achieve prominence in American history like few others.
Taken from the Congressional Medal of Honor Society Website; CMOHS.org

THE CIVIL WAR

The Civil War is the central event in America's historical consciousness. While the Revolution of 1776-1783 created the United States, the Civil War of 1861-1865 determined what kind of nation it would be. The war resolved two fundamental questions left unresolved by the revolution: whether the United States was to be a dissolvable confederation of sovereign states or an indivisible nation with a sovereign national government; and whether this nation, born of a declaration that all men were created with an equal right to liberty, would continue to exist as the largest slaveholding country in the world. ...*Dr. James McPherson*

In terms of American deaths, this was the costliest war in U.S History. The commonly cited figures are 360,000 Union Army deaths; 260,000 for the Confederacy. The Union Army dead amounted to 15 percent of the over two million who served.

Minnesota was the first state to respond to President Lincoln's request for volunteer regiments to defend the Union. According to the Minnesota Historical Society, "Minnesota sent 25,000 men, or about half of the state's eligible male population, to war. More than 100 black men, a number of American Indians, and at least one woman also served."

On the second day of the battle at Gettysburg, July 2, 1863, eight companies of the First Minnesota were ordered to make a suicide charge against a vastly superior in number regiment of Alabamans to buy time for the Union Army. The casualty count was the highest ever recorded in military history costing the 1st Minnesota 262 men. Fifteen percent of their number survived. In self sacrificing desperate valor this charge has no parallel in any war.

Ironically, out the 27 Medals of Honor awarded to Minnesotans during the Civil War, only one went to a participant in this battle. Another curious fact is that most of the Medals of Honor were awarded thirty years after the fact; none of them posthumously.

CIVIL WAR
1861-1865

James Allen 1843-1913

Medal of Honor
Action: Crampton Pass, Maryland
Date: September 14, 1862

Early Years

Mr. James Allen was born in Ireland on May 5, 1843. As a child his parents immigrated to the United States settling in New York sometime around 1850 according to information on Federal census records in 1900 and 1910. Information regarding his family is sparse. It is known he had at least one brother, Henry, and other siblings.

Civil War Years

On May 15, 1861 in Potsdam, St. Lawrence County, New York, nineteen year old James Allen enlisted in the service. He entered as a private in the United States Army serving in

JAMES ALLEN.

the F Company 16th New York Infantry. During his time of service Mr. Allen "participated in all the battles in which the Army of the Potomac was engaged, from the first Bull Run to Chancellorsville."

While we have limited information on Mr. Allen years prior to his military service, we have the great fortune of having Mr. Allen give his own recollection of his heroic act. In 1897 a book was published titled, *The Story of American Heroism* described as "thrilling narratives of personal adventures during the Great Civil War as told by the Medal Winners and Roll of Honor Men." Mr. Allen received a letter from the commander of the Garfield Post #8 of St. Paul requesting his written response to describe the events that took place on September 14, 1862 at South Mountain, Maryland against the 16th Georgia regiment. Here, in his own words, is what Mr. Allen wrote:

"I won a medal of honor at the battle of Crampton's Pass, when our division made a charge. My regiment was in the 2nd brigade, 1st division, sixth corps, which was composed of the 16th and 27th New York, 5th Maine, and 96th Pennsylvania. The charge was conducted by General J. J. Bartlett. The charge was made through a cornfield of large growth, and ongoing in our color-sergeant was killed by a bullet in the forehead. After entering the corn a comrade and myself by mistake became detached from the company, and when near a stone wall at the base of the mountain we learned that we were alone with a large squad of the enemy directly in our front. Turning to me my comrade said with a grimace: 'Now what have we to do, Jim?' 'Charge the wall, I reckon. That was what we came for.'

"He was willing, and the two of us represented the Second Brigade at this particular point, being so fortunate as to drive the enemy from cover. After gaining a few rods beyond the wall, my comrade had his left leg broken above the knee by a bullet, from which wound he afterward died. I helped the poor boy to a tree which would shelter him somewhat, and continued the charge alone up the rugged side of the mountain only a few rods behind the enemy, until they reached the road which led through the pass, where was a wall about seven feet high on the lower side, over which they went, leaping down into the highway. Then one of them turned and fired at me, cutting my coat and shirt, and grazing the skin under my right arm. I stopped to load my gun, and while doing so came to the conclusion that it wasn't safe to stay there alone, when only about five rods separated me from the squad, so I did my level best to get under cover of the wall. Once there, I was at a loss to decide what would be the next best move. To beat a retreat now would simply be to invite death, for the Confederates evidently thought there were more behind me, otherwise they never would have run from one man, and it seemed as if my wisest course was to let them continue in the same train of thought.

"I made a sudden dash over the wall, and landed in the road in the midst of fourteen members of the 16th Georgia Regiment, one of whom was the color-sergeant, and seeing the flag I made up my mind to get it if possible. I ordered them to surrender as boldly as if the entire division was at my back, and after some little hesitation, induced by my threats of what might happen; they complied. I took the colors from the sergeant, ordered the men to stack their arms, hang the cartridge boxes on the guns, and you can fancy I got between them and the weapons without loss of time. I was having quite an interesting conversation with them when my colonel rode up the road, for I had gained a position far in advance of the regiment, and I told him he had better take charge of the prisoners; but he ordered me to hold on until he sent a detachment to carry them to the rear.

"In a few moments I was relieved of what might have proved a troublesome charge if they had taken it into their heads to overpower me before the colonel came, and, retaining the colors, proceeded up the mountain. On reaching the summit I rejoined my company and reported to the captain, showing the flag as proof of what I had done. A detail was sent out for my wounded comrade, and he was cared for as well as possible under the circumstances. In this engagement my company lost one third of its members, and it was a small party of us that marched to Antietam next day to take part in that action."

On the 22nd of May in 1863 in Albany, Albany County, New York after expiration of his enlistment, Mr. Allen was honorably discharged. Mr. Allen added in his account that he "served in the military railroad service from September, 1863, until October 1, 1865, always at the front." Completing his military service, Mr. Allen had achieved the rank of Corporal.

On September 11, 1890 Mr. Allen was awarded his Congressional Medal of Honor for taking captive 14 members and the flag of the 16th Georgia Infantry. An interesting footnote to Mr. Allen's story is that an article in the St. Paul Globe on September 4, 1896 stated that Mr. Allen had petitioned Congress for return of the captured flag from the color guard so that he could pass it on to his heirs...

Post War Years

A carpenter by trade, by 1870 Mr. Allen had travelled west and was now living in McGregor, Clayton County, Iowa with his wife, Susan and a son Burton E. born November 26, 1866 in Iowa. Susan Blanchard Morgan Allen was born in Vermont on January 22 1844. Where she met James or when and where she married him is unknown. From Iowa the family moved north settling in Minnesota. By 1880 the Federal Census listed Mr. Allen as living in Farmington, Dakota County, Minnesota with another son joining the family. Benton O. was born in Iowa on August 18, 1876. In 1885 the family was living in Mankato, Blue Earth County, Minnesota. The family moved once again this time to St. Paul, Ramsey County, Minnesota by 1900. On October 23, 1912, Susan Allen died. She was survived by her husband and her two sons, one child dying in infancy. Less than a year later, on August 31, 1913, Mr. Allen passed away, not at the Soldiers' Home in St. Paul where he had been living, but back east while on a trip. Mr. Allen had traveled to Gettysburg to attend a reunion and on to New York to meet siblings he had never met.

Of his children James Allen died at 12:30 AM on August 31, 1913 at the home of his brother Henry in Carthage, New York. Burton Allen, a Ramsey County Sherriff, would pass away in St. Paul on January 23, 1937 without issue. Benton Allen would die February 6, 1942 in Ramsey County, a Veteran of the Spanish American War also without descendants. James Allen and his wife are both buried at Oakland Cemetery in St Paul, Minnesota.

Compiled by Laura Gallup
Anoka Chapter NSDAR

Jesse T. Barrick 1841-1923

Medal of Honor
Action: Duck River, Tennessee
Date: March, 1863

Early Years

Jesse T Barrick was born in Columbiana, Columbus County Ohio on January 18, 1841 to Isaac & Mary Barrick. Jesse's father was a wheelwright according to the 1850 US Census. His two older brothers had already left the family home by the time Jesse was born, but he had two older sisters, Eliza and Nancy. His third sister, Rachel, was born five years later.

Civil War Years

In 1861, Jesse married Sarah Ann Strang on August 24, in Faribault, Minnesota. When Jesse enlisted in the US Army Company H Third Minnesota Infantry on October 25, at Fort Snelling, Minnesota 1861, Sarah enlisted as an Army nurse a couple of months later.

The Third Regiment left Fort Snelling for Louisville, Kentucky in November of 1861, assigned to guard the Louisville and Nashville Railroads until March of 1862. After that they were assigned garrison duty at Murfreesboro until Forest's attack there on July 13. The regiment surrendered, was paroled, and sent to Benton Barracks, Missouri. In late August, the Regiment was declared exchanged and moved to Minnesota to join Sibley's campaign against hostile Sioux Indians.
In January of 1863 it moved on to Cairo, Illinois, then on to Columbus, Kentucky. The Expedition to Fort Heiman, Tennessee and operations against area guerrillas began in early March. It was during this campaign that Jesse showed his outstanding bravery, winning him his Medal of Honor near the Duck River in Tennessee.

In his action report on June 4, 1863, Major Hanz Mattson wrote, " The conduct of Corporal Jesse Barrick, Company H, Third Minnesota Infantry is particularly worthy of mention. He captured, single handed, the two desperate guerrilla officers, Major Algee and Captain Grizzel, both of whom were together and well armed"

Another report mentioned that Barrick had tracked the two officers from the main road and found them having lunch. Catching them off guard and aiming his gun as if to shoot, they shouted, "for God's sake don't shoot, we'll surrender."

On July 10, 1864, Jesse mustered out of the Third Infantry and the following day reenlisted as Second Lieutenant Company G, US Colored Troops 57 Infantry. However, he mustered out a few months later due to an unknown injury, on October 15, 1864.

Post War Years

Jesse and Sarah had a son, Harvey, born during the war in 1862. They returned to Rice County Minnesota after the war and continued to grow their family. Dorothy was born in 1866, son Lewis was born in 1869, and Alice was born in 1874. The family then moved to Unk, Minnesota where son Jesse I was born in 1877, followed by Harry in 1884. The 1900 US census listed the family in Alexandria, Minnesota.

After the war, Jesse was involved in the fur trade and eventually migrated further west to Suquamish, Kitsap County, Washington in 1909. He was finally awarded his Medal of Honor on March 3, 1912.

Jesse Barrick died November 3, 1923, at the age of 82, in Pasco, Franklin County Washington and was buried in an unmarked grave in the City View Cemetery in Pasco. It is unknown why he was buried in an unmarked grave.

Some believe he was indigent. Others assume that there was no one left to oversee his burial. Wife Sara died in 1928. It is believed she is buried in Mukilteo, Washington.

Due to the efforts of Dwight Davison, a Navy Veteran and a Pasco Police Officer, and his "Barrick's Brigade," they were able to move and reinter Jesse's remains to his final resting place in the Tahoma National Cemetery in Kent, Washington.

Great-great grandnephew, Eugene Barrick, a farmer near Darwin, Minnesota, speaking at the ceremony, recalls family stories about "Uncle Jesse," the family's Civil War hero, which brought smiles to those in attendance. It is good to know that Jesse Barrick will not be forgotten.

Compiled by Cynthia Jorgenrud
Anoka Chapter NSDAR

Joseph Burger 1848-1921

Medal of Honor
Action: Nolensville, Tennessee
Date: February 15, 1863

Early Years

Joseph Burger was born on April 16, 1848 in Bludenz, Voralberg, Tyrol Austria. His family immigrated to the United States when he was a toddler and settled in Chicago. His parents both died from cholera in 1854, making him an orphan at age six. He was then sent on an orphan train to a foster home in New Ulm, Minnesota.

At age nine, he began work as a farm hand in New Ulm, but he grew restless. When Fort Sumter was fired upon on April 12, 1861, Joseph began thinking about becoming a soldier. But he was only 13 years old!

Civil War Years

Then when the Second Minnesota Regiment was being organized in July, 1861, Joseph wrote in his diary that he thought he could join "maybe as a drummer" even though he was only 13 years and 3 months. He ran away from home at that point to join the army. As he was tall for his age, he convinced the recruiter that he was eighteen, and it was official; Joseph was a volunteer in Minnesota Second Regiment as a drummer. He excitedly wrote in his diary that he received "drumsticks, a new uniform, boots, et al"

Until the Second Minnesota left the state on October 14, 1861, Joseph worked on his drumming and his marching. He also did a lot of water carrying, road building, trench digging, wood gathering, and tending horses – normal soldier activities. However, he learned that the drummers were special targets for the enemy – "we were vital to the signaling of troop movements".

Before the Second Minnesota reached its intended destination of Washington, they were diverted to Louisville, Kentucky for guard and picket duty in and around Lebanon Junction. In January 1862, the Second took part in the Mill Springs Campaign, driving a Confederate regiment back in disorder and capturing their supplies.

The regiment then moved on to Shiloh, arriving on April 9, 1862, missing that famous battle by two days (July 6-&7). They camped in Corinth, Mississippi until late June when they moved on to Perryville. Here they were held in reserve at the Battle of Perryville in October. The remainder of 1862 was spent on short expeditions and various guard duties, finally making camp near Gallatin, Tennessee.

In early February, the regiment was located near the Battle Farm along Nolan Pike. On February 15, 1863, Burger was assigned, with 16 others, the task of guarding foraging wagons. Leading the squad was Sgt. Lovilo Holmes from Mankato, Minnesota. It was later that day that the squad ran into a company of Confederate cavalrymen, numbering about 125. Joseph and his squad were defiant and held the Southern men off until the remaining Second Minnesota, back at camp, heard the sound of the distant fighting and came to the rescue. Sgt. Holmes and two other privates were wounded. This brave and defiant action by this squad of 16 earned them all the Medal of Honor. Joseph was then just 14 years old.

The Second Minnesota fought again later at Chickamauga, Missionary Ridge, and Kennesaw Mountain. As his enlistment term was up in late 1863, Joseph Burger reenlisted into the Second Minnesota on December 12, 1863.

On July 9, 1864, Burger was guarding Confederate prisoners being moved by train to Chattanooga, Tennessee. Near Dalton, Georgia, the train jerked violently and Joseph lost his balance. He fell out of the train car door and his rifle discharged. The Minie ball went through his hand, through the left forearm, and right leg, lodging in the calf. In his diary he wrote, "I fear for my very life for I am nearly destroyed."

His left arm was amputated and he was sent to a hospital in Chicago. In December of 1864, Burger was promoted to Captaincy and assigned to Hancock's Invalid Reserve Corps at Fort Douglas Camp in Illinois. In June of 1865, at the young age of 17, Joseph Burger was discharged and returned to Minnesota.

Post War Years
Even with his disabilities, Joseph Burger did not give up. After being discharged, he moved to Missouri to study law at Warrenton College. He met and later married 19-year-old Caroline Nolton on April 7, 1869 in Warrenton. Burger practiced law in Missouri for a time and even served in the state legislature in 1872, representing Franklin, 2nd district.

In 1877, he and Caroline moved back to Mankato, Minnesota. He served in the Minnesota House of Representatives in 1881

Caroline & Joseph Burger.

through 1882, representing District 14. He later moved to St. Paul and served as a military storekeeper on Governor Hubbard's staff.

He was awarded his Medal of Honor on September 11, 1897. The citation reads: "Was one of a detachment of 16 men who heroically defended a wagon train against the attack of 125 cavalry, repulsed the attack and saved the train."

His disability was nearly total, needing constant help in dressing, washing, and nearly everything else. The bullet still remained in his leg. However, he and Caroline raised seven children. In 1870, Charles Joseph (father of U.S. Supreme Court Chief Justice  Warren Burger) was born while they were still in Missouri. Also born in Missouri were Elizabeth (1872), Pauline (1874), Amelia (1876), and Minnie (1878). Both Julia (1880) and George Alexander (1887) were born in Minnesota.

Caroline died of bronchitis on November 6, 1920 in St. Paul, Minnesota. Joseph followed a few months later on January 3, 1921 at the age of 72. Both were buried together in Oakland Cemetery in St. Paul, Minnesota.

Compiled by Cynthia Jorgenrud
Anoka Chapter NSDAR

James A. Campbell 1844-1904

Medal of Honor
Action: Woodstock, Virginia
Date: January 22, 1865
Action: Amelia Courthouse, Virginia
Date: April 5, 1865

Early Years

James Alexander Campbell was born on December 20, 1844 in Brooklyn New York.

Civil War Years

At the age of 21 James Alexander Campbell entered the army for a three year term beginning in the fall of 1862 and lasting until mid-1865. Records show that he enlisted for the first time at age 20 on April 23 1861 at Kings County NY in Company F New York 13th Infantry Regiment on April 23 1861; and mustered out on August 6th 1861 at Brooklyn NY; and then re-enlisted at age 21 in Company A New York 2nd Cavalry Regiment on September 8th 1862; then mustered out on June 5th 1865 at Alexandria Virginia.

He served valiantly until the end of the Civil War receiving two medals for bravery. On January 22nd 1865 while James was a private, he rescued his commanding officer at Woodstock Virginia and on April 5th 1865 he captured two battle flags at Amelia Courthouse in Virginia.

He was honored on October 30 1897 for his two acts of bravery when he received the Medal of Honor. His inscription reads, "Voluntarily rushed example Confederate War Flag back with one companion while his command was retreating before superior numbers and rescued his commanding officer who had been unhorsed and left behind at Woodstock, Virginia."

Post War Years

James married Martha Spence, who was born on February 25, 1857. They moved to Montana about 1880 and had five children there, Philip (July 1882), Helen S (July 1884), Minnie R. (February 1886), Alma W (August 31 1890-March 19 1980), and Blanche I (October 31 1892-Nov 19 1987).

The 1900 census shows they moved to Minnesota and lived at Fort Snelling until James' death on May 6, 1904. He was buried at Arlington National Cemetery in Virginia. When Martha died in 1943 she was buried beside him.

Compiled by Diana Myers, Keewaydin Chapter NSDAR

Stephen E. Chandler 1841-1919

Medal of Honor
Action: Amelia Springs, Virginia
Date: April 5, 1865

Early Years

Born in late 1841 in Convis Township in Calhoun County, Michigan, Stephen Edwin Chandler was the son of Clark Chandler, a carpenter and farmer, and his wife, Hermona Slafter. He descended from Josiah Chandler of Barre, Massachusetts, a Revolutionary War veteran. He entered the service at the start of the Civil War, on May 4, 1861, one of many men from Oswego County, New York to answer in response to President Lincoln's call for 75,000 soldiers.

Civil War Years

Chandler was mustered into Company E, New York 24th Infantry in 1861; into Company A of the 24th New York Cavalry in 1863; was promoted to Quartermaster Sergeant; and then transferred to Company A of the New York First Provisional Cavalry in 1865. He mustered out of the military on July 19, 1865 at Cloud's Mills, Virginia. Chandler was awarded the Congressional Medal of Honor for his heroic efforts at Amelia Springs, Virginia.

According to author Bert Dunkerly, the little known engagement on April 5, 1865 illustrates well the chaos and confusion of the Civil War's Appomattox Campaign. A complex six-day campaign, it had many moving parts, as columns from each army used various roads, and at different points, encountered each other. Battles and skirmishes occurred every day. At different times each side had momentary numerical superiority over the other. Seven Union troopers earned the Medal of Honor in the action of this campaign. "As with most Medals of Honor awarded to Union troops, the citations were for the capture of flags. Yet Quartermaster Sergeant Chandler of the 24th New York Cavalry earned it for something else." His citation states that under severe fire of the enemy and of the troops in retreat, Chandler went between the lines to the assistance of a wounded and helpless comrade, and rescued him from death or capture.

The fellow soldier, Corporal Eugene Van Buren, claimed he owed his life to Sergeant Chandler: This is his account of his rescue and his rescuer."On the afternoon of April 5, 1865, General Sheridan, wishing to ascertain the whereabouts of the enemy, ordered a reconnaissance in the direction of Paines Cross Roads. Our brigade was selected for this duty. The route we took led us through a wooded country which was considerably cut up by hills and valleys, and near Amelia Springs, the fashionable summer resort of the south, we saw from the summit of a hill Lee's wagon-train in the distance. We soon found a cross-road not much wider than a bridle path, which we followed down through a valley, then across a stream and up the hill on the opposite side. Just as we neared the top of the hill we ran into a battery of five new Armstrong guns which we captured before they could fire a shot; and at the summit we found the wagon-train. Flankers were sent out in different directions, while the main body of the brigade 'went through' a couple of miles of the train. Judging from appearances the train was at a standstill at the time we struck it, as fires were burning all along the line with skillets and frying pans on them, in which 'hoe-cake' and other kinds of food were being cooked by the drivers and train escort.; but all was abandoned in their hurry to escape. Everything in sight was captured. Orders were given to fall back to the point where we captured the battery and we started on the return march, but we were somewhat hampered by our prisoners. Our progress was retarded to such an extent that the enemies began to crowd us, and it was found necessary to form a line of battle in an open field near Amelia Springs.

"No sooner was the line of battle formed than a rebel cavalry division made its appearance, and when at a distance of forty rods opened fire. In the subsequent fighting quite a number were wounded, among them Lieutenant-Colonel Richards, who commanded our regiment, and me. Sergeant Chandler's horse was struck in the forehead by a ball, the sergeant himself narrowly escaping death. He removed his personal effects from the saddle and hastened to the assistance of the wounded colonel. I saw him and said, 'For God's sake, Chan, help me off the field. I'm wounded and can't walk.' He at once came to my aid, and after examining my wound said: 'Let's get out of this as quickly as we can and go to some place where we can get help, or you'll bleed to death.' He helped me to my feet and we started for the rear. About this time the regiment was ordered to fall back to a new position, leaving Chandler and me between the fires. The bullets flew like hail around us. 'Chan,' I said, 'you will be shot or taken prisoner. I've got my death wound anyway. You'd better lay me down and save yourself.' 'I'll never do that,' his reply was. 'No, my boy, I'll stay with you till you are safe or we both go down.'

"A cavalry regiment of the enemy attempted to charge our men and was driven to the cover of the woods. Bullets were whistling over our heads and around us from both directions. How we ever escaped being riddled is more than I can tell. However, we struggled along slowly, I being too weak to go any faster. After much difficulty we finally reached the rear, where the regimental surgeon bandaged my wound, which stopped the flow of blood to some extent. Just then our men were compelled to fall back once more. Chandler took me by the arm and helped me along for a short distance, when I became so greatly exhausted that I could walk no farther. I despaired completely. 'Chan,' I said again, 'go on now; save yourself. I can't hold out any longer.' I lay down, but Chandler remained and sat down at my side. I pleaded with him to give up all further attempts to save me and think of his own safety. 'You've done enough for me. See how those bullets are flying again. Protect your own life; I can't live anyway.'

"Just then a cavalryman whose horse was played out came along. Chandler asked him to let him have the animal and he complied cheerfully; 'You can have her, certainly. She's played out. I can go faster on foot.' Chandler now helped me on that horse. I laid down over the pommel of the saddle, and thus we started along at a slow gait, Chandler constantly urging the horse forward. Soon after we were joined by Privates John Smith and George Back, of our company, who walked at the horse's side and held on to me, while Chandler led the horse. The enemy, outnumbering our forces, had by this time gotten on our flank and tried to cut us off, keeping up a terrific fire. Chandler found a stretcher, I can't remember where, and I, being then too weak to ride any farther, was placed on it and carried, Chandler keeping up the courage of his comrades by joking about the poor marksmanship of the Johnnies. Passing a farm barn they found an old buggy. Again I was removed and placed in the vehicle, so that I lay flat on my back with my feet dangling down at the rear. They were about to start off with me, hauling the buggy by hand, when Chandler, who was untiring in his efforts for my comfort, obtained a horse from a wounded cavalryman. Securing a collar and a pair of hames from the barn he hitched the animal to the wagon by means of pieces of rope used for traces. By this time the rebels were close upon us. They shouted, 'Halt!' and fired at us, but Chandler set the improvised though none too comfortable ambulance in motion and off we started, over ditches and across fields as fast as the horse could travel, the boys at some places where we were going downhill hanging to the buggy to keep it off the horse's heels. In this manner we soon reached a place of safety, where I found proper medical care and treatment. I certainly owe my life to the courage and persistency of my brave sergeant."

Chandler himself was wounded in 1864 by a Minie ball piercing his left side near his heart. Back in action, he was with the Army of the Potomac at Lee's surrender, April 9, 1865. He carried the colors of the 24th NY, being the last to exchange shots with the enemy. In later years, Chandler wrote newspaper articles about the extraordinary experiences of the 24th New York.

Post War Years
Chandler and wife Mary Amelia Valentine Gill were married 16 January 1868 and had five children (his first son Edbert dying in infancy in Ohio). They later homesteaded 160 acres near Worthington, Minnesota in the 1870s. He married Harriet M. (surname unknown) as his second wife and lived in Minneapolis, Minnesota. He spent his later life working as a carpenter and construction foreman. Chandler died in 1919 in Minneapolis, Minnesota and is buried in Lakewood Cemetery.

Compiled by Kathleen M. Barrett Huston, Lake Minnetonka Chapter NSDAR

Clinton A. Cilley 1837-1900

Medal of Honor
Action: Chickamauga
Date: September 19-20, 1863

Early Years

Clinton Albert Cilley was born in Rockingham County, New Hampshire in 1837 to Reverend Daniel Plummer Cilley and Adelaide Ayres Haines. His paternal grandmother was the sister of a governor of New Hampshire. He was raised in southeastern New Hampshire and well-educated. He attended the Boston Latin School in 1852 (the oldest school in the United States, founded in 1635 and still open today) where he was awarded the Franklin Medal for exceptional scholarship. He attended Harvard and upon graduating in 1859 he went to Minnesota to teach.

Cilley came from a long line of military heroes. His Revolutionary ancestor, Joseph Cilley served in the Second New Hampshire Regiment, formed in May 1775, as the second of three Continental Army regiments raised by the state of New Hampshire. He was later appointed Colonel of the First New Hampshire Continental Regiment. He fought in both battles of the American campaign in Canada, and the battles of Trenton Princeton, Saratoga, Monmouth and Stony Point.

Civil War Years

According to the *St. Paul Pioneer Press,* Professor Clinton A. Cilley, as President of the new Free Will Baptist Seminary in Wasioja, Minnesota in 1861, spoke to his students the day after the firing on Ft. Sumter, and said, "Would it were God's will that peace prevailed, but now we can do no other than serve our Union cause. Are you with me?" With the help of Wasioja attorney James George, Cilley and a large number of his students and faculty volunteered to form Company C of the Second Minnesota. They enlisted at the tiny stone building in Wasioja in Dodge County that then served as a Civil War recruitment office; it still stands and now houses a museum. Built as a law office by Mr. George in 1855, it is the only Civil War recruiting station to be preserved as a historic site in Minnesota and the only one west of the Mississippi. The seminary, just a short distance away, which had enrollment of over 300 students prior to the Civil War, burned down in 1905. The ruins, and the nearby historic buildings, are listed on the National Registry of Historic Places.

Just over a year after organizing, Company C stopped the Confederates at Chickamauga, Georgia, but at a high cost; of the 80 who enlisted, only 25 returned, which devastated the fledgling town.

According to the Minnesota Historical Society: "By the late summer of 1863, the campaign to control Chattanooga and eastern Tennessee resulted in some of the war's heaviest fighting. On September 19-20 the Second Minnesota clashed with Gen. Braxton Bragg's Army of Tennessee at the Battle of Chickamauga in northern Georgia. On the second day of the battle, a federal tactical error led to a Confederate breakthrough which swept half the Union army from the field. The Second Minnesota and their comrades took up a defensive position to delay the Confederates. From mid-afternoon until dusk they held their position in the face of repeated attacks. This brave defense earned their corps commander, Maj. Gen. George H. Thomas, the nickname "Rock of Chickamauga." The battle was a Confederate victory."

Cilley earned his Medal of Honor serving as Captain in Company C of the Second Minnesota Infantry at Chickamauga. His citation, awarded on 12 June 1895, reads, "Seized the colors of a retreating regiment and led it into the thick of the attack." He was subsequently promoted to Brevet Colonel. In his arguments for a disability pension due to post-war locomotary ataxia (partial paralysis) and nervous dyspepsia years later, he stated his service as:

- Enrolled 29 May 1861 in Company C of the Second Regiment of MN Volunteers
- Promoted to Second Lieutenant in said company and regiment 4 December 1861
- Promoted to First Lieutenant in said company and regiment 16 April 1862
- Promoted to captain in said company and regiment 10 July 1864
- Made assistant adjutant-general with rank of Captain 14 July 1864
- Promoted to Major and assistant adjutant-general 21 March 1865
- Brevet Lieutenant-colonel 13 March 1865
- Brevet Colonel 18 March 1865
- Honorably mustered out 1 September 1866

Because of his ability and bravery, Cilley advanced in rank and continued to receive promotions after the final Union victories. His assignment to General Schofield's headquarters brought him to North Carolina at the end of the war. This move, and his involvement in administrative matters related to the freedmen, represented a significant turning point in his later career. As commander of part of the defeated South, General Schofield had responsibility for public order and the administration of justice.

Post War Years

Cilley married Emma Harper, the daughter of James Harper, a former member of the North Carolina House of Representatives and the U.S. House of Representatives, 42nd U.S. Congress. He and Emma were the parents of four sons and one daughter: Albert Harper Cilley (1870-1873), John Harper Plummer Cilley (1871-1947), Gordon Harper Cilley (1874-1938), James Lenoir Cilley (1876-1965), and Katharine Adelaide Cilley, who died as an infant at seven months.

Being a Yankee army hero in the post-Civil War South made him a bit of an oddity. In the book *Bluecoats and Tar Heels*, he is described as a Harvard-educated, Union war hero who served in postwar North Carolina as a headquarters staff officer and Freedman's Bureau official before returning to civilian life, remaining in the state, establishing a law firm with a former Confederate officer, marrying the daughter of a prominent citizen, and settling in Lenoir, a small town in Western North Carolina, eventually emerging as a civic leader, appointed as a judge and becoming mayor. According to the author, "Unlike more notorious Union army veterans who settled in the Tar Heel State, Cilley managed to avoid controversy and thus faded into obscurity after his death in 1900."

In *Clinton A. Cilley, Yankee War Hero in the Postwar South: A Study in the Compatibility of Regional Values*, he is described as native of New England, from a family noted for its early political opposition to slavery. After working for the Freedman's Bureau, he continued to champion first education for blacks and publicly supported education. Yet he quickly became a prominent attorney and citizen, a leader of efforts to promote economic development and cultural progress. Even in his later years as a crippled war veteran, he gained widespread popularity as a public speaker and guest columnist for the *Charlotte Observer*. His success was attributed to his willingness to get along with the white majority in the South and ability to find or create common ground, but also the existence of common values between the New England values he was raised with and those of the leading citizens in the North Carolina Mountains, hidden beneath the sectional bitterness of postwar decades.

Cilley's personal papers may be found in the library of the University of North Carolina at Chapel Hill, and the Catawba County Museum of History, which contains a major repository of Civil War objects and displays the Clinton A. Cilley Collection, including this distinguished colonel's field desk.

Clinton A. Cilley died at the age of 63 on May 9, 1900 and is buried in Oakwood Cemetery, Hickory, Catawba County, North Carolina.

Compiled by Kathleen M. Barrett Huston, Lake Minnetonka Chapter NSDAR

William Andrews Clark 1828-1916

Medal of Honor
Action: Nolensville, Tennessee,
Date: February 15, 1863

Early Years:

William Andrews Clark was born in Pennsylvania on July 24, 1828. By time the Civil War started, William had moved to Shelbyville, Minnesota. When William Clark enlisted in 1861, Shelbyville was at the height of its days as a town. As the railroad moved through Shelby Township (named after Shelbyville, Indiana) the townsfolk moved two miles north to form the town of Amboy. By 1881 Shelbyville was completely deserted.

Civil War Years

William enlisted with Company H, Second Minnesota Volunteer Infantry Regiment, on July 15, 1861 at Shelbyville. On December 17, 1863, he re-enlisted and continued to fight with the Minnesota Second until he was discharged as a Sergeant on July 1, 1865, with the rest of his company.

William's recommendation for The Medal of Honor was for his part in the defense of a wagon train near Nolensville, Tennessee, on February 15, 1863. He was one of 16 men who repelled the attack of the 125th Calvary (Confederate), and saved the wagon train.

The following excerpt is from the book *The Heritage of Blue Earth County* by Julie Hiller Schrader. "On Sunday morning, February 15, 1863, fifteen men of Company H, Second Minnesota Infantry were detailed as guards on twenty-one supply wagons sent out to obtain forage, First Sergeant Livolo Holmes, Corporal William A. Clark, Privates Joseph Burger and Milton Hanna were among the Blue Earth County soldiers who went along on the relatively normal assignment. The main mission was to fill the wagons with corn and return to camp. They were near Nolensville, Tennessee and about nine miles from Triune. While on the road to their destination, they met a Negro who warned them that they had better go back at once, as a large detachment of Rebel cavalry had sized them up through field glasses from a neighboring hill and would attack them.

The orders were to get the forage and so they proceeded, but by a different route. This took them about a half mile to the left of a large plantation, where they commenced to load the wagons with corn and other supplies. In the meantime, two companies of the 1st. Alabama Cavalry had followed them to the plantation. The cavalry had come down the main entrance road into the plantation, which had a high split rail fence on both sides;

this lane was only sixteen feet wide. The Rebels charged down upon them firing their carbines and yelling, "Surrender, you damned yank!"

The men of the Second Minnesota stood at the end of the lane and fired into the horses and due to the narrowness of the lane, succeeded in stampeding them. Each soldier only had forty cartridges with him. They loaded, aimed and fired repeatedly until the Rebels withdrew. When the Minnesota boys counted their ammunition up afterwards they found that they had averaged thirty-two shots per soldier. A Confederate Captain, two Lieutenants and twelve enlisted men were killed; fifteen prisoners and forty horses were taken back to camp. The only casualties suffered by the Yanks were three slight wounds, including sixteen year old Joseph Burger. All of the men who participated in this brave defense were awarded Medals of Honor; President Lincoln even heard the news of this small, but glorious victory which was printed in many northern newspapers. All the soldiers received letters from the War Department similar to this one which was sent to Lovilo Holmes, dated July 30, 1863. "Lovilo N. Holmes, Esq., Sir-you are hereby notified that by direction of the President and under the provisions of the Act of Congress approved March 3, 1863 providing for the presentation of Medals of Honor to such officers, non-commissioned officers and privates as have most distinguished themselves in action, a Congressional Medal of Honor has this day been presented to you for most distinguished gallantry in action....Respectfully, R.A. Alger, Secretary of War"

William was awarded the Medal of Honor on September 11, 1887, over 24 years after he bravely faced the 125th Calvary.

Post War Years:
After being discharged from the army, William married Lorana Keene (1826-1908) in 1866. They had 2 children: a son William G. Clark (1867-1937) and a daughter Minnie Clarrie (Clark)  Dalh (1877-1947). While William G. never married, Minnie married Albin Dahl and had 11 children. William and his family lived in the Nicollet County area of Minnesota near Kerns.

William Clark died January 9, 1916, and was buried in Hebron Cemetery, Nicollet County, Minnesota.

The following excerpt is his obituary:"W.A. Clark one of the early settlers of Nicollet County, and a veteran of the Civil War, passed away at his home near Kerns yesterday afternoon at 5:30 from the effects of complications brought on by advancing years. He was born in Pennsylvania July 24, 1828, and moved to Indiana in 1855, and thence to Minnesota. Later in 1855, taking up the second claim pre-emptied in Shelby Township, this country.

At the outbreak of the Civil War he enlisted in Company H, second Minnesota volunteers, and served throughout the war with distinction. At the battle of Nashville, Tennessee, he received a medal for bravery on the field of battle. Nicollet County in 1866, when he was united in marriage to Miss Lorana Kand in 1869 he moved to Nicollet County, where he made his home near Kerns up to the time of his death. The deceased is survived by his son William Clark, who lives on the farm at Kerns, and two brothers living in Indiana. The funeral will be held from the Kerns church Wednesday afternoon a 2 0" clock and burial will take place in the Hebron cemetery."

Compiled by Ruth Carlson
Anthony Wayne Chapter NSDAR

James Flannigan 1833-1905

Medal of Honor
Action: Nolansville, Tennessee
Date: April 5, 1863

Early Years:

James Flannigan was born in Canada in 1833. His parents, James and Catherine (Fury) Flanagan, had emigrated from County Queens, Ireland, to Montreal, Canada. After James birth, the family moved to St. Lawrence County, New York, and purchased an 80 acre dairy farm. His siblings included Bridget, John, Peter, Thomas, Catherine, Maria, Mary, and four who died young. James was educated in Louisville's country schools, and then left his family and moved west to seek his fortune. He was engaged in the lumber business.

Civil War Years:

At age 28, in 1861, Flannigan enlisted as a Canadian soldier in the Second Minnesota Volunteer Infantry regiment. (Company H. 2d Minnesota Infantry) at Shelbyville. He resided in Louisville, Scott County, Minnesota and entered service at Ft. Snelling. Flannigan was one of 1,176 Canadians fighting with Minnesota units during the war. He served as private about three years in the Civil War with the Minnesota regiment. He was with the western army under General Thomas and fought at the battles of Mill Springs, Shilo, Perryville, Mission Ridge, Chattanooga, and Chickamauga, and was in Sherman's March to the Sea. During his service, he was promoted to corporal and later to sergeant.

Flannigan received the United States' highest award for bravery during combat, the Medal of Honor, for his action at Nolensville, Tennessee on 15 February 1863. He was honored with the award on 11 September 1897. He is the only Scott County, Minnesota resident to be awarded the Congressional Medal of Honor. The Citation reads: "Was one of a detachment of 16 men who heroically defended a wagon train against the attack of 125 cavalry, repulsed the attack and saved the train."

There are many references online about Flannigan, his regiment, and his Medal of Honor award. They all highlight Flannigan's special service and gallantry. The Canadian Medal of Honor website has an interesting article about James Flannigan:"During the war there were often times when troops on either side in the conflict had to scourge the area they were in for supplies. This was the case in mid-February of 1863 when Vale, Flannigan and 14 others were involved in the obtaining of supplies within a little wagon train of 10 carriages. Four of these had broken off and gone a distance when they came under very heavy fire from about 150 Confederate Cavalry. A skirmish broke out that saw the men being rallied by their Sergeant and moved into a cabin, returning fire and ultimately rebuffing the enemy who turned away. Five of the Confederate soldiers were wounded and three of these ultimately became Prisoners of War. Four enemy horses were also killed and three were captured, as were seven saddles and three guns. Two of the Union men were wounded in the battle."

In *The Story of a Regiment: Being a Narrative of the Service of the Second Regiment, Minnesota Veteran Volunteer Infantry, in the Civil War of 1861-1865* by Judson Wade Bishop (1890), the Report of Brigadier General James B. Stedman is as follows: "The Colonel commanding the brigade, takes pleasure in commending the conduct and sturdy valor of Lovilo N. Holmes and fourteen non-commissioned officers and privates of Company H, 2nd Regiment Minnesota Volunteers, for the heroic defense made by them near Nolensville on the 15th inst., against the attack of two companies of rebel cavalry numbering one hundred and twenty-five men, and repulsing them with loss. This little affair is one of the most creditable of the campaign and deserves to be remembered and cited as worthy the emulation of all.

"The Colonel desires that the names of these worthy men and brave soldiers may be preserved. First Sergeant Lovilo N. Holmes. Corporals Samuel Wright and William A. Clark, Privates Nelson Crandall, James Flannigan, Samuel Leslie, Louis Londrash, Charles Liscomb, Joseph Burger, Byron E. Pay, Charles Krause, John Vale, Samuel Loudon, Milton Hanna, and Homer Barnard, have his thanks. By order of F. Van Derveer, Colonel commanding 3rd Brigade. John R. Beatty, A. A. Adjutant General."

Report of Brig. Gen'l James B. Steedman War of Rebellion, Official Records, Vol. 22, Part 1, page 49, Series 1.) "Concord Church, February 15th, 1863. A forage train of ten wagons from my command, with escort of two companies of infantry; and while four of the wagons guarded by 13 privates under the command of a Sergeant, were being loaded one and a half miles from Nolensville, were attacked by one hundred and fifty rebel cavalry. The Sergeant immediately formed his men, took shelter in a cabin near the wagons and repulsed them, wounding five, three of whom I have prisoners, killing four horses, capturing three horses, seven saddles and three guns."

Flannigan continued to serve with his unit at major battles. There are several monuments in Tennessee, Georgia, and Minnesota, honoring the 2d Minnesota Infantry regiment. He reenlisted in 1864 and served until the end of the war.

Post War Years

After the war in 1865, Flanagan returned to his family's 80-acre dairy farm in Louisville, New York. He married Kate Mallen of Waddington, NY, in Sept 1868. They were the parents of four children: Frederick James, Agnes, Thomas and John. When Flannigan died on October 4, 1905, at age 72. He was buried at Saint Lawrence Cemetery, Louisville, St. Lawrence County, NY.

Compiled by Tracy Moore MacAllister
Maria Sanford Chapter NSDAR

Aloysius Joseph Frantz 1837-1913

Medal of Honor
Action: Vicksburg, Mississippi
Date: May 22, 1863

Early Years

Aloysius Joseph Frantz was born March 9, 1837 in France. According to the 1900 US Federal census, he immigrated in 1845 at age eight. A record was found as a possible match, with Alois Freutz, age 22, emigrating from Le Havre, France with Joseph (age 55) and Christine Freutz (age 50) on August 18, 1856 aboard the ship RL Gillchrest. More research would need to be done to confirm that this is a correct record of arrival and family.

Civil War Years

Aloysius was mustered into service in Company E, 83rd Indiana Infantry from Versailles, Ripley County, Indiana on August 20, 1862. The "Company Descriptive Book" lists him as age 26, 5-foot-10, blue eyes, light hair and complexion and a blacksmith by trade. He is listed as Pvt. Joseph Frantz, apparently foregoing his first name of Aloysius.

According to the U.S. Citizenship and Immigration Services website:
"His unit was at Vicksburg, Mississippi, on May 22, 1863, when Union General Ulysses S. Grant ordered an assault on a Confederate position. Private Frantz was among 150 volunteers for a storming party of 'forlorn hope' – in other words, an extremely dangerous mission." When the attack failed, Grant ordered a withdrawal. "Of the storming party eighty-five percent were either killed or dangerously wounded, and few of them escaped without a wound of some kind," Grant later wrote in his memoirs. Frantz survived and received the Medal of Honor more than 30 years later, on August 13, 1894.

The Northfield News in Minnesota published an article on Private Frantz in its September 22, 1894, edition: "Joseph Frantz, for several years a resident of Northfield, now living in Bridgewater, has just received a Medal of Honor from the U.S. government. He is a loyal member of the J. L. Heywood Post and during the late war was a member of Company E, 83rd Ind. Vols. One morning, just as he returned from duty on the picket line, his captain called for two men from the company to volunteer to join a forlorn hope storming party in front of Vicksburg. Only one man stepped forward. Comrade Frantz volunteered to fill the quota. The gallant storming party carried two lines of entrenchments but after suffering terrible loss failed to carry the third. The survivors, after exposure to the deadly fire of the enemy for many hours, found their way to our lines as soon as darkness came on. He was in all the battles around Vicksburg, in Gen. Sherman's Atlanta campaign and severely wounded at the battle of Atlanta. Mr. James Otis, of Portland, Maine, is writing, for publication in book form, a biography of all soldiers who have earned Medals of Honor during the war, and sent a request for Frantz to send his photograph. All honor to the heroes who risked their lives during these supreme moments of destiny to our Republic."

The Medal of Honor Citation reads: "For gallantry in the charge of the volunteer storming party on 22 May 1863." Private Frantz served August 20, 1862 to July 1865.

Post War Years
Aloysius married Theresa F. Roth on October 10, 1865, in Franklin, Indiana. Most, if not all, of their children were born in Indiana. Among the children whose records have been found: John Frantz, born April 7, 1873, Grace Matilda France, born in St. Leon, Dearborn, Indiana, and Josephine Evalyn Frantz, on April 26, 1874 in St. Leon, Dearborn, Indiana. The family moved from Indiana to Northfield, Minnesota in 1878.

According to an article in the Northfield News, *War Hero Recognized 140 Years Later*, "they may have also lived for a while in South Dakota. In 1884, Frantz was a charter member of the J.L. Heywood Post No. 83, Grand Army of the Republic, which was to Civil War veterans what the American Legion is to modern veterans. In 1894, probably through efforts of the GAR, Frantz was awarded the Medal of Honor for his heroism on May 22, 1863, at Vicksburg, Mississippi."

He and his wife lived in Minneapolis the last years of their lives. Aloysius Joseph Frantz died on October 4, 1913 in Minneapolis at the age of 76, and his wife Theresa died in 1915 at age 72. His obituary appeared in the Northfield News: "Friday, Oct. 17, occurred the burial of Aloysius J. Frantz, for many years a resident of Northfield. For the past seven years he has lived in Minneapolis. He was 76 years old. He is survived by his wife, five daughters and two sons: Mrs. Mary Frank of St. Paul; Mrs. Kate Knauer of Niagara Falls, N.Y.; Mrs. Anna Yates and Miss Josephine Frantz of Minneapolis; and Mrs. Flora Lynch of Dakota; Aloysius of Lily, S.D., and John of Humbolt, Canada.

Frantz has also had a Facility dedicated to his memory. U.S. Citizenship and Immigration Services (USCIS) is the government agency that oversees lawful immigration to the United States. They dedicated space in 18 of their facilities to recognize gallantry and tremendous courage of select immigrant Medal of Honor recipients. Seven hundred recipients of the Medal of Honor have been immigrants. "Their bravery serves as an enduring reminder that immigrant recipients of the Medal of Honor embody the best of American values and continues to inspire" today. The USCIS Indianapolis Field Office is named after Pvt. Joseph Frantz, Civil War.

On May 22, 2003, 140 years after Frantz was awarded the Medal of Honor, a Medal of Honor grave marker was placed at the Northfield cemetery through efforts by Northfield and Rice County Genealogy society's member Norma Gilbertson, Ray Ozmun of the American Legion Post No. 84, Calvary Cemetery caretaker Ray Johnson, and others.

Photos of grave markers courtesy of Don Morfe, "Find A Grave" contributor who researches and photographs Medal Of Honor Recipient gravesites.

Compiled by Tracy Moore MacAllister
Maria Sanford Chapter NSDAR

Thomas Parke Gere 1842-1912

Medal of Honor
Action: Nashville, Tennessee
Date: December 16, 1864

Early Years

Thomas Parke Gere was born on June 8, 1842 in Wellsburg, Chemung County, New York. He was the youngest of eight children of George and Sarah Gere. He moved with his family to Minnesota in 1852 and to Chatfield in Fillmore County in 1862. He was a student in 1858-1859 at the Chatfield Academy and assisted his principal, General J. W. Bishop, in the survey of government lands in southwestern Minnesota.

Civil War Years

Lt. Gere was mustered as a private in Company B, 5th Minnesota Volunteer Infantry, January 17, 1862 at the age of 19. In March of 1862 instead of heading off to the glory and honor of the Civil War, Company B was assigned to relieve two companies of men of the 4th Minnesota Regiment who were garrisoned at Fort Ridgely, Minnesota. Gere enlisted as a private but rose rapidly in the ranks to acting company first sergeant, then second lieutenant. He commanded a force of about 30 soldiers who repelled attacks of Santee Sioux while he was seriously ill with the mumps. The conflict with the Dakota was the result of starving Indians not receiving their treaty annuity. Gere saw his first action as an officer and was considered as one of the heroic defenders of Fort Ridgley in August 1862.

His company rejoined the Fifth Regiment, December 1, 1862 at Oxford, Mississippi, and Lt. Gere therefore participated with it in the following campaigns, battles and actions: Campaign through West Tennessee, January and February 1862; Campaign against Vicksburg, March, April and May, 1863; Action at Mississippi Springs, Mississippi, May 13, 1863; Assault on Jackson, Mississippi, May 14, 1863; Assault on Vicksburg, May 22, 1863; Action at Satartia, Mississippi, June 4th, Mechanicsburg, Mississippi, June 7th, Richmond, Louisiana, June 14, 1863; Siege and Surrender of Vicksburg, July 4, 1863; Campaign through Central Mississippi, December, 1863; Red River Expedition, Louisiana, March. April and May. 1864; Assault on Fort De Russy, Louisiana, March 14, 1864; Actions at

Henderson Hill, Louisiana, March 21; Grand Ecore, Louisiana, April 2nd,Compte, Louisiana, April 3rd, 1864; Battle of Pleasant Hill, Louisiana, April 9, 1864; Action at Cloutierville, Louisiana, April 24th; Bayou Rapids, April 26th; Moore's Plantation, Louisiana May 3rd, Bayon La Monre, Louisiana, May 6; Markersville, Louisiana, May 16th; Bayon de Glaise, Louisiana, May 18th and 19th; Lake Chicot Arkansas, June 6, 1864; Campaign through Northern Mississippi, August, 1864; Action at Oxford, Mississippi, August 21; Abbeyville Mississippi, August 25, 1864; Campaign through Arkansas and Missouri, September and October, 1864; Battles of Nashville, Tennessee, December 15 and 16, 1864; Campaign through Tennessee and Mississippi, December 1864, and January, 1865; Campaign against Mobile, Alabama, March and April 1865.

On December 16, 1864 the Minnesotans charged the enemy lines at Nashville and Gere, taking the colors of the 4th Mississippi Infantry, earned his the Medal of Honor. His citation reads "Capture of flag of the 4th Mississippi." His Medal of Honor was issued on February 24, 1865. Lieut. Gere mustered out of the army April 5, 1865.

Post War Years

Subsequent to the war, Lt. Gere followed the profession of Civil Engineer. For ten years he was the superintendent of the Sioux City division of the Saint Paul and Sioux City Railroad. Later he acquired large property interests in manufacturing lines located in Sioux City, Iowa. Lt. Gere married Florence Irene Howard January 1, 1869. They had a daughter, Florence Bertha Gere who lived less than a month. After Florence's death in 1871, Lt. Gere married Mary Emma Shepard on September 16, 1874. They had four children: Madge Shephard Gere Swan (1877-1949), Thomas P. Jr (1886-?), Frances Shepard Gere Carter (1887-1972) and Champlin Hedges Gere (1889-1969). Lt. Gere lived in St. Paul. MN in 1880, Fourth Ward Iowa in 1895, Sioux City, Iowa in 1900 and died in Chicago, IL on January 8, 1912. He was survived by his wife, daughters, Madge Swan and Frances Carter and sons Thomas, Jr. and Champlin. Lt. Gere was buried at Arlington National Cemetery.

Compiled by Linda Sugerman, Maria Sanford NSDAR Chapter

Lewis Addison Grant 1828-1918

Medal of Honor
Action: Chancellorsville Campaign
Date: August 15, 1861

Early Years

Born on January 17, 1828 in Winhall Hollow, Bennington County, Vermont, Lewis Addison Grant was the youngest of ten children born to James and Elizabeth Wyman Grant Lewis' boyhood was spent in the usual strict ways of the old New Englanders. He attended the district school of Townsend, Vermont until he was sixteen years old. The following year he taught in the same school. Later he attended the academy at Chester, Vermont. After academy days he taught school for five years meanwhile reading law. He was admitted to the bar in 1855 and began the practice of law in Bellows Falls, Vermont.

Civil War

Lewis Addison Grant was commissioned Major of the 5th Vermont on August 15, 1861 which was mustered into service on September 16, 1861 at St. Albans, Vermont. Promoted to Lieutenant Colonel, he participated in the 1862 campaigns in the East. At Savage's Station in June the 5th Vermont suffered grievous causalities. He was promoted to Colonel on September 15, assumed command of the famed Old Vermont Brigade, and led it at Fredericksburg, where he fell wounded. Given permanent command of the brigade, he gallantly performed during the battles of 1863 to 1864.

In the Chancellorsville Campaign in May 1863, the Vermonters captured three Confederate flags in the action at Salem Church, earning the Medal of Honor for "personal gallantry and intrepidity displayed in the management of his brigade and in leading it in the assault in which he was wounded."

Lewis Grant participated in the Gettysburg Campaign and, with the rank of Brigadier General, fought at the Wilderness, Spotsylvania and Cold Harbor. At the Wilderness his brigade lost nearly half its members. During the Shenandoah Valley Campaign of 1864, he commanded his division at Cedar Creek, on October 19. In this battle the Confederates launched a surprise attack at dawn, crushing the Union lines. The routed Federals reformed on his line, from which they counterattacked in the afternoon, defeating the Southern troops. For his distinguished conduct, Grant received the rank of brevet Major

General. Wounded during the war's final week, he mustered out in August 1865. Declining a commission in the Regular Army, he journeyed westward after the war.

Post War Years
Lewis married Agasta Hartwell March 11, 1857. They had one daughter, Grant Stone. Agasta Grant died January 27, 1859. Four years later Lewis Grant married Mary Helen Pierce. They had two sons: Captain James Colfax Grant and Dr. Ulysses Sherman Grant. General Grant lived in Illinois and Iowa before permanently moving to Minneapolis, Minnesota. From 1890 to 1893 he served as assistant Secretary of War.

Compiled by Linda Sugerman, Maria Sanford NSDAR Chapter

Milton Hanna 1842-1913

Medal of Honor
Action: Nolansville, Tennessee
Date: February 15, 1863

Early Years

Milton Hanna was born to James and Nancy (Bowden) Hanna on January 12, 1842 in Etna Township, Licking County, Ohio. In those days' large families were common in farming families and the Hanna family was no exception. Milton was the 9th child born to his Scotch-Irish father and his Pennsylvania-Dutch mother. The family eventually grew to include four boys and nine girls.

The James Hanna family arrived in the Mankato area on the 16th of April 1853, five years before statehood was granted to Minnesota. To provide living quarters for his family, James Hanna purchased a warehouse that was being built by a local flour company and finished it for their use. Hanna continued to farm in Minnesota and he was also active in community affairs. He organized the first Sunday school in the area in June 1853 in his home, taught by one of his older daughters, Sarah. This is considered the precursor of the present Presbyterian Church in Mankato. By July 1853, James Hanna had added a room onto his home to serve as a school which was also taught by daughter, Sarah. There were twenty-four scholars in this first classroom in Mankato which probably included eleven-year-old Milton. Unfortunately, James Hanna died on 15 May 1855 at the age of 53 in Mankato. Shortly after her husband's death, Nancy (Bowden) Hanna had pre-empted a tract government land and become an owner of a 132 acre farm. She continued to live in Mankato until her death in 1875.

Milton Hanna's education was begun in Ohio and continued in the schools of Blue Earth County until his father died when he was almost 13 years of age. After James Hanna's' death, Milton's formal education came to an end as it was necessary for him to earn his own livelihood which he did by following farming pursuits. He was 19 when the Civil War began and he was among the first to offer his services to his country.

Civil War Years

Milton Hanna enlisted as a private in Company H, 2nd Minnesota Infantry on June 22, 1861 in Henderson, Sibley County, Minnesota. He soon marched south where his regiment was engaged at Mills Springs, Kentucky and Shiloh, Tennessee. He took part in the Siege of Corinth, Mississippi and fought at Perryville, Kentucky. His regiment chased General Bragg through Tennessee, engaging in battles at Stone River, Shelbyville, Tullahoma, and in Chickamauga, Georgia.

It was right after the battle of Stone River that Milton Hanna and 14 other men from the 2nd Minnesota Infantry demonstrated outstanding bravery for which eight received the Medal of Honor. According to historian Roger Norland as reported in the *Mankato Free Press*, "It was February 15, 1863 in Tennessee. A group of men went to forage for food for their mules. They stumbled upon a corncrib and began to load up its contents when Confederate soldiers surprised them. Greatly outnumbered and essentially surrounded, the men hid in the crib and opened fire. By the time the rest of the Union group appeared to help, over 100 Confederate soldiers were firing at the men. The men crawled out of the crib and continued to fight. They captured three Confederate soldiers, rounded up seven of their horses and confiscated many weapons. The Confederates retreated, leaving three wounded Union soldiers and a dead mule."

Hanna was seriously wounded at the battle of Chickamauga which took place on September 19 & 20th, 1863, but he re-enlisted on the 15th of Dec 1863. He was in Atlanta during the one hundred days' fighting and then accompanied Sherman on his march to the sea. Milton Hanna was also there when Sherman marched his 65,000 troops down Pennsylvania Avenue during the Grand Review organized by President Johnson for May 23 and 24, 1865 which was an unofficial close to the Civil War. There was quite a contrast between the polished troops of General Meade on the first day of the Review with their precision marching and Sherman's on the second day. Sherman's troops were returning from their march through Georgia and the Carolinas and were sunburned, tattered and lean but even though they marched with less precision, it was with a bravado that thrilled the crowd. Sherman later spoke of the experience as "the happiest and most satisfactory moment of my life."

Hanna was a Sergeant when he was mustered out on the 11th of July 1865 at Louisville, Kentucky having served the duration of the whole war. He received an honorable discharge on July 21, 1865 at Fort Snelling, Minnesota. Due to an oversight, Milton Hanna did not receive his Medal of Honor until 1897.

Post War Years
After the war, Mr. Hanna returned to Mankato where on November 1, 1869 he married Miss Louise N. Purrier. The couple had two children, but unfortunately both predeceased them. Kitty was only five when she died and James L. died at the age of thirty-one. James had married Gertrude Corp and they had three daughters; Gladys, Doris and Louise.

Evidently Mr. Hanna was a gregarious man with many friends. "He was a man who devoted his life to make others happy." For awhile he ran a grocery store on South Front Street that was a mecca for chess and checker players with Mr. Hanna himself being a worthy opponent of all challengers. Later he had a bakery and grocery store that was a favorite for his fellow G. A. R. members of the Wilkin Post No 19 G. A. R. In an article appearing in the *Mankato Free Press* in 1936, Mr. Hanna related to the reporter that he had three gold awards of which he was proud. The first was a gold ring that was presented to him by the members of Excelsior Hose Company No. 1 of Mankato fire Department for his long and efficient services of twenty-seven years. The second was a medal he received by unanimous vote of Wilkin Post G.A.R. for being one of their most active members. The third was his Medal of Honor.

Louise Purrier Hanna outlived her husband by over three years, but she was not in the good health required to care for him during his last years. He died on January 21, 1913 in the Minnehaha Soldiers Home in Minneapolis. He had remained in Mankato until a week or so before his death when his friends moved him to the home hoping that he would receive the care he needed to improve his health.

Milton Hanna was buried in Glenwood Cemetery in Mankato. It was not until 1999 that his grave was marked to identify the fact that he had received the Medal of Honor. Marlin Peterson, a local member of the Army Reserve who served in the Gulf War, is a history buff. He had read of the surprise battle that Milton Hanna participated and for which he received the Medal of Honor. Visiting the cemetery, Peterson found the grave marker of Milton Hanna to be faded, chipped and spotted with mildew. There was no mention of his receiving the Medal of Honor. Mr. Peterson tried to contact living relatives, but finding no one, he took it upon himself to obtain from the Veteran's Services a marker that denotes Milton Hanna's Company, year of birth and death and the fact that he was a Medal of Honor recipient. This marker now stands beside his original one.

Compiled by Beth Cooper Zimmer, Anthony Wayne Chapter NSDAR

Lovilo N. Holmes 1830-1914

Medal of Honor
Action: Nolansville, Tennessee
Date: February 15, 1863

Early Years
Lovilo N. Holmes, son of Rachel Stowell (33) and Peter Holmes (36) was born on October 10, 1830, in Farmersville, Cattaraugus County New York. He had two sisters and four brothers. Lovilo learned the sawyer's trade in New York. He married Amanda Gail of Erie, New York. and they moved to Mankato, Minnesota in 1858 where he became employed as head sawyer in a combined grist and sawmill. Lovilo and Amanda had two children, Leora Holmes (1878-1879) and Myrtle E. Holmes (Campbell) in 1880.

Civil War Years
Lovilo Holmes entered the 2nd Minnesota Volunteer Infantry, Company H on June 22, 1861at age 31 in Mankato, Blue Earth County Minnesota. On January 30, 1863 Sergeant Holmes was transferred through Fort Snelling, Minnesota to Triune, Tennessee and mustered into service in February 1863.

On February 15, 1863 Sergeant Holmes joined a small detachment of men who heroically defended their wagon train against the attack of a Confederate Calvary of 125 men, repulsed the attack and saved the train. During the attack Sergeant Holmes told his comrades "We can die, but we'll never surrender." On that day Lovilo was party in a small squad of 14 men of which 8 received the Medal of Honor after the war. The day of the attack Sergeant Holmes was told to take four wagons and head in the direction where the Confederates were last seen. They came upon a small farmhouse without buildings and were soon hailed by a local that the enemy was spotted and coming. Sergeant Holmes took charge and ordered the group to prepare for defense. The enemy was quick, numbering 125 and fanned out around the small Holmes squad. Holmes gave his men orders to take refuge in the barn, hay mow, cribs, hog pens and additional buildings. They sighted their rifles and waited for the advance. The shots began from the Holmes squad wounding several Confederates and spawning confusion in those ranks. That gave Holmes and his men time to reload and keep up continuous fire on the rebels until the Calvary withdrew and were driven away.

Sergeant Holmes and two others were wounded and one mule killed. However, they took three prisoners, seven horses and several weapons. The Confederates lost two men, ten horses and many were wounded.

Post War Years

Sergeant Lovilo Holmes was promoted to 2nd lieutenant following the February 15, 1863 event for his leadership and astute action. He was later promoted to captain. Following the war Lovilo returned to Mankato, Minnesota and settled back into local life with his wife and daughter Myrtle. He spent his years as a carpenter and contractor and lived at 107 Broad Street, Mankato, Minnesota Lovilo and Amanda were married 42 years.

Lovilo passed away on May 7, 1914 at the age of 83 and Amanda died in 1922. Their only living daughter, Myrtle, married John D. Campbell on October 1, 1913 in Blue Earth County. They then moved to Spokane, Washington where her husband worked as an Attorney. At the age of 39 Myrtle had a daughter, Jean G. Campbell 1915-1991.

Jean G. Campbell married an Engineer, Robert E. Nordmark (23rd Avenue/Spokane, WA). They had a son Daniel Nordmark in 1939 and a daughter Linnea Nordmark (Feigenbutz). Daniel Nordmark relayed information that the family knows of Lovilo's history, has a portfolio of his life, years in the war as well as artifacts and mementos in their family's keeping.

In 1999, Gulf War Veteran, Marlin Peterson of Mankato, Minnesota took an interest in Civil War Veterans and found Lovilo N. Holmes' grave in Glenwood Cemetery in Mankato. He noticed Lovilo's grave did not have a commemorative marker for his Medal of Honor and worked hard to secure that plaque as well as one for Milton Hanna. As of 1999 both men have their Medal of Honor markers  placed with their grave stones in Glenwood Cemetery. In 1999, Mr. Peterson could find no family members of Lovilo Holmes. This information will now be passed on to link Mr. Peterson's work to commemorate Lovilo Holmes and Mr. Holmes living ancestors.

Compiled by Elizabeth A. Beck, Anthony Wayne Chapter NSDAR

Andrew John Kelley 1845-1918

Medal of Honor
Action: Knoxville, Tennessee
Date: October, 1863

Early Years

Andrew John Kelley was born September 2, 1845 in Lima, Lagrange County, Indiana, the youngest child of John Andrew and Maria (Baker) Kelley. The 1850 census shows Maria and four of her children living next door to Andrew Baker in Adrian, Lenawee County, Michigan without John Kelley. On August 12, 1862, a month before his seventeenth birthday, Andrew enlisted as a Private in Company E, 17th Michigan Infantry at Ypsilanti, Michigan.

Civil War Years

"During the summer of 1862, the State of Michigan began recruiting men to fill the ranks of the newly established Seventeenth Michigan Volunteer Infantry. On August 11, 1862, Company "E," of the 17th Michigan was mustered into service in Ypsilanti, Michigan. A majority of men that joined the ranks of Company E were students at Michigan State Normal School, now known as Eastern Michigan University. Due to the large number of students in the ranks, Company "E" acquired the nickname the "Normal Company."

Not even a week after Andrew enlisted, the Regiment departed Michigan for Washington, DC, taking steamboats from Detroit to Cleveland, and then boarding a train to Washington. Once there, they were assigned to the 1st Brigade, 1st Division, of the 9th Corp under the command of General Ambrose Burnside. They joined the Maryland Campaign under the command of General George McClellan.

"Less than two weeks after leaving the State of Michigan, the Regiment was hotly contested at the battle of South Mountain on September 14th, 1862. During this battle, the 17th Michigan gallantly charged Confederate forces that had taken up a defensive position along a stone wall. The charge by the 17th routed the Confederate and the Regiment acquired the nickname the "Stonewall Regiment." The aftermath of the battle resulted in twenty-seven men killed and one hundred and fourteen wounded. On September 17th, 1862, the Regiment was engaged at Antietam, sustaining a further loss of 18 killed and 87 wounded. After this battle which is still known as the single bloodiest day in American warfare with a combined loss on both sides of 23,000 men killed, wounded or missing, the Regiment left with its command and returned to Virginia."

The 17th Michigan fought in the siege of Vicksburg, Mississippi in June, 1863, and in the assault on Jackson, Mississippi in July 1863.

"In October 1863, the Regiment was assigned to the Army of Tennessee. On October 14th, 1863, the Regiment, then attached to the 3rd Brigade, of the 1st Division, or [sic] the 9th Corp, marched from Knoxville to Louden, Tennessee, to oppose the advance of Confederate General James Longstreet, then moving on to Knoxville. It lay under its arms during the night, and on the following morning commenced falling back, closely followed by the Confederates. It continued to retreat, acting as a rear guard for the rest of the Corp. While crossing Turkey Creek, Longstreet's men attacked in force, causing a severe engagement to occur. In this action, the Regiment lost 7 men killed, 19 wounded, and 10 missing. During the retreat to Knoxville, and during the Siege of Fort Saunders, the men suffered greatly, especially while being besieged from the want of proper and sufficient rations."

The regiment fought in many more battles, including at the Battle of the Wilderness and the battle of Spotsylvania Court House. In May of 1864 they were designated as an engineer troop and spent the remainder of the war building and reconstructing fortifications. Andrew Kelley was promoted to Full Sergeant on 1 May 1865, and was mustered out of service with the rest of the Michigan 17th on 3 Jun 1865.

Post War Years
Upon his return to Michigan, Andrew took up farming. On March 23, 1869 in Burr Oak, he married Ella A. Fleming, and for a short time worked as a guard at the prison in Jackson before returning to farming. The couple moved to a homestead in Crookston, Polk County, Minnesota in 1873. They had seven children: Herbert, Edwin, Clara, Mabel, Maude, Lulu, and Leonard. "Kelley eventually built a nice house, which was the only one on the prairie between Crookston and the Red Lake agency. Indians would often visit his place for food, and they were always civil. One time, the Native Americans 'borrowed' Kelley's ax, but he went after them to retrieve his much-needed possession."

"Kelley served as city clerk since the town of Crookston was organized. Kelley was the first Sunday school superintendent in Crookston, presiding over a Union Church Sunday school, which he started in 1874."

On April 17, 1900, Andrew J. Kelley was awarded the Medal of Honor for his heroic actions at Knoxville, Tennessee on November 20, 1863. The citation reads: "Having voluntarily accompanied a small party to destroy buildings within the enemy's lines whence sharpshooters had been firing, disregarded an order to retire, remained and completed the firing of the buildings, thus insuring their total destruction; this at the imminent risk of his life from the fire of the advancing enemy."

Andrew John Kelley died on June 4, 1918 in Crookston. His wife Ella died in 1925. They are buried in Oakdale Cemetery.

Compiled by Leslie Hartz Sprott
Anthony Wayne Chapter NSDAR

William C. May 1826-1894

Medal of Honor
Action: Battle of Nashville
Date: December 16, 1864

Early Years

William C. May was born on January 16, 1826, in Fayette County, Pennsylvania. He married Louisa Jane Dodd on July 22, 1852, in Huntington County, Indiana. Over the course of twenty-two years they had eight children. A resident of Franklin County, Iowa and a Mexican War veteran when the Civil War started, he enlisted in the Union Army at age 33, and was mustered in as a Private in Company H, 32nd Iowa Volunteer Infantry on September 13, 1862.

Civil War Years

Mays was awarded the Congressional Medal of Honor for his bravery in action on December 16, 1864 during second day of the Battle of Nashville, Tennessee, with his citation reading "Ran ahead of his regiment over the enemy's works and captured from its bearer the flag of Bonanchad's Confederate battery (C.S.A.)." The flag he captured was actually from Louisiana's Pointe Coupee Artillery battery, under command of Captain Joseph Alcide Bouanchaud. Private May was one of the first of his regiment to overrun the battery after attacking through terrible artillery and gunfire over an open field. Both sides had scores killed and eventually the guns of the Louisianans were captured by the Union troops. His regimental commander, Lieutenant Colonel Gustavus A Eberhart, mentioned his bravery in his official report of the battle.

Private May's Medal of Honor was awarded to him on February 24, 1865 in Washington, DC, where he had traveled with other soldiers from Major General George H. Thomas's Army of the Cumberland to present Confederate Battle Flags that they had captured Secretary of War Edwin M. Stanton. In addition to their Medals, each man received a one- month furlough.

Post War Years

After May returned to his unit he served through the end of the war and was honorably mustered out at Clinton, Iowa on August 24, 1865. After the war May resided first in Winsted, McLeod County, then in Howard Lake, Wright County, Minnesota before passing away on October 21, 1894. He is buried in Winsted Public Cemetery, Winsted, McLeod County, Minnesota.

Compiled by DeAnn Caddy, Captain Robert Orr Chapter DAR

Andrew McCornack 1844-1920

Medal of Honor
Action: Vicksburg Campaign
Date: March 29-July 4, 1863

Early Years
Andrew McCornack, son of John McCornack and Martha Malinda McMillan, both of Scotch parentage, was born April 2, 1844 near Elgin, Kane County, Illinois. Andrew grew to manhood on his father's farm, where he lived until he enlisted in the Union Army.

Civil War Years
McCornack enlisted August 22, 1862 at Elgin, Illinois at the age of 18. The Roll described him as 5 feet 5 inches in height, brown hair, and black eyes with a dark complexion. McCornack was listed as a single farmer at this time joining for a period of 3 years. He was mustered into service in Company I, 127th Illinois Infantry, September 5, 1862, in Chicago, Illinois, entering in at the rank of Private.

His regiment was soon sent to Memphis where it was assigned to Grant's army in the immediate command of General W. T. Sherman participating in all the maneuvers and battles. He helped to dig Grant's great ditch; was along with Sherman on the expedition to Young's Point; and was in the movement against Vicksburg from start to finish. He was on the skirmish line that drove in the rebel pickets as the army of Grant closed in on the doomed fortress.

It is recorded that Private Andrew McCornack fired the first shot over the walls of Vicksburg, aiming it at an officer who was riding along the works. At the first assault on the works of the city, young McCornack, along with a comrade, made himself conspicuous for noble courage and fearlessness by carrying from the field several wounded comrades in the midst of a perfect hail of shot and shell. On May 22, preceding the second great assault on the fortress, a number of volunteers were called to lead the assault, and McCornack was quick to respond. On the morning of May 22, General Grant launched what he hoped would be a crushing assault against Vicksburg. In the fighting that followed, the Union Infantry was repulsed and thrown back along a three-mile front. The Union Army suffered more than 3,000 casualties, and 97 Union soldiers earned Medals of Honor (the second largest single-day total in history.) Private Andrew McCornack was one of eighty soldiers cited simply for "Gallantry in the charge of the "volunteer storming party," Private McCornack was at the head of his attacking force where the enemy fire was hottest and the danger the greatest. Following the failed assault on May 22, a forty-seven day siege was laid against the city, which finally surrendered to Union forces on July 4.

The Vicksburg Campaign was waged from March 29 to July 4, 1863. It included battles in west-central Mississippi at Port Gibson, Raymond, Jackson, Champion Hill, Big Black River, and numerous smaller battle fields. Soon after Vicksburg surrendered McCornack was promoted to sergeant and given a furlough to visit home. Congress voted him the Medal of Honor for his conspicuous gallantry.

After the Vicksburg Campaign young McCornack joined Sherman on the campaign from Chattanooga to Atlanta, and for one hundred and ten consecutive days he was constantly within range of the enemies' bullets. He marched with Sherman from Atlanta to the sea and up through the Carolinas and Virginia to Washington. His regiment was detailed to forage for the Army of the Tennessee and on that great march they reveled in horses and cattle and turkeys and sweet potatoes.

Post War Years

Andrew McCornack mustered out June 5, 1865 in Washington, DC and he returned to his home and parents in Elgin, Ill. Shortly thereafter, Andrew, following Horace Greeley's advice, "went west." He settled in Monticello, Minnesota where he married Elsietta Hanaford on May 3,
1869. They had ten children in 18 years. Although a modest man, Andrew delighted in talking about the exciting days of his youth, and rejoiced in the fact that he was a worthy member of "Sherman's Bummers."

Andrew McCornack, died on May 4, 1920, in Monticello, Minnesota, at the age of 76, and is buried in Monticello, Wright County, Minnesota.

Compiled by DeAnn Caddy
Captain Robert Orr Chapter NSDAR

Charles Wesley McKay 1847-1912

Medal of Honor
Action: Battle of Dug Gap, Georgia
Date: May 8, 1864

Early Years
Charles McKay was born: January 25, 1847 in Mansfield, Cattaraugus County, New York to Cyrus and Mary (Butterfield) McKay. His early years were spent in the Mansfield New York area. He was apprenticed as a saddler in a harness shop when the call to arms was issued.

Civil War Years
Lying about his age to join McKay was only 15 at the time of his enlistment on July 26, 1862 in Allegheny, New York. He was mustered in as a Private in Company C of the 154th New York Volunteer Infantry, Army of the Potomac 11th Corps on September 24, 1862. He was wounded in action on July 1, 1863 at the Battle of Gettysburg. He was promoted to Corporal on April 1, 1865 and to Sergeant on May 1, 1865. At age 17, then Private Charles Wesley acted with great courage. McKay and his company comrade, Stephen Welch, were both issued the Medal of Honor on April 13, 1894, for a deed they performed on May 8, 1864 at the Battle of Dug Gap on Rocky Face Ridge, Georgia.

Welch later described their actions for the book, *Deeds of Valor*, (which also included an illustration of the act): "On the 9th [sic] of May, 1864, the enemy was found in a strong position at a place called Rocky Face Ridge, near Dalton, Georgia. In the afternoon the brigade was got in readiness for inspection of said ridge. A few of my company were detailed to act as skirmishers. We advanced slowly and cautiously, covering ourselves as best we could till we got within four rods of a perpendicular palisade crowning the top of the ridge. I found protection behind a rock, from which point I could occasionally see three or four of the enemy on top of the hill, and had a chance to discharge my gun in that

direction. Meanwhile the brigade came up our regiment on the right. They all went up to the perpendicular palisade of rock, some going up the crevices and to death. After about half an hour the bugler sounded a recall, and the brigade went down that hill much faster than it had gone up, but soon we got into proper order again. About this time the major came along and told me that he had seen a wounded soldier of my company, between the lines, adding that I had better get someone to help me go up and get him. Taking a tent-mate, Sergeant Charles W. McKay, we started out under a heavy fire, not only from the enemy, but also from our own lines. We found George Greek, a corporal of the color-guard, badly wounded in both legs. The poor fellow had been trying to drag himself along with his hands, and had sunk down, overcome by faintness and exhaustion. McKay revived him with a drink from his canteen, after which the corporal, raising himself on his elbow, asked if the colors were safe. We assured him that they were, and he dropped down again, satisfied and happy. We rolled him on a blanked, picked him up, and with bullets whizzing about us, managed to get him off the field."

Sergeant McKay mustered out with his company on June 11, 1865 near Bladensburg, Maryland.

Post War Years
Following the war, Charles returned to the Mansfield, New York area. On February 19, 1869, in Olean, NY, he married Clara Onan, daughter of Col. Warren Onan who served as 1st lieutenant of Company C, 154th New York in which Charles served. The couple moved to Indiana where children Grace, Blanche, and Georgia were born. They later moved to Fergus Falls, Minnesota where Charles served as rail agent for the Northern Pacific railroad

Clara McKay passed away in Moorhead, Minnesota on February 4, 1888 and is buried in the Prairie Home Cemetery there along with her parents. On July 23, 1890, Charles married Elizabeth Lockhart Thompson (born in Canada April 1856) in Otter Tail County, Minnesota. Their daughter Mildred was born in 1893 in Fergus Falls. In 1903, Charles and wife Elizabeth moved to Wahpeton, ND to accept a position as rail agent there. Elizabeth died on December 23, 1909.

In 1910 Charles was living in Staples, Todd County Minnesota with his daughter Mildred, while continuing to work for Northern Pacific. While working in Fergus Falls, Charles enlisted in the Minnesota National Guard, 2nd Regiment, Company F, and served as Lieutenant and Captain, finally resigning on May 23, 1895.

Throughout his life, Charles continued to work with and for his military comrades. As a member of the Grand Army of the Republic (GAR) he held many posts including Senior Vice Commander and Aide to General Stewart, Commander in Chief of the Grand Army in 1902. In addition, he was a member of the New York Society, ran for Sheriff of Crow Wing County, and operated the Lyceum Theater in Fergus Falls.

Charles died in Staples, Todd County, Minnesota on August 25, 1912 and is buried in the Oak Grove Cemetery, Fergus Falls with his second wife, Elizabeth.

Compiled by Merrilee Carlson, Nathan Hale Chapter NSDAR

John G. Merritt 1837-1892

Medal of Honor
Action: First Battle of Bull Run, Virginia
Date: July 21, 1861

Early Years
Not much is known about John G. Merritt's early life other than he was born October 31, 1837 in New York City, New York County (Manhattan) in the State of New York.

Civil War Years
John Merritt entered service in the U.S. Army in St. Paul Minnesota at Fort Snelling. He served as a Sergeant in the Union Army in Company K, 1st Minnesota Infantry. He was awarded the Civil War Congressional Medal of Honor for action at Bull Run, Virginia on July 21, 1861.

 Prior to this First Battle of Bull Run in Virginia, only five soldiers and one sailor had earned Medals of Honor. In the Bull Run battle alone, eleven soldiers and Civilian Contract Surgeon Mary Walker earned Medals of Honor. In the engagement with Confederate Forces at Bull Run, Sergeant John Merritt became the first of several hundred Civil War heroes to earn the Medal of Honor as a Color Bearer. His citation reads: "Gallantry in action; was wounded while capturing flag in advance of his regiment."

John Merritt told the story of the battle and this is a small part, "I never shall forget the first sight of dead, wounded and dying. Pity and sympathy, mingled with a feeling of fear, made me realize in an instant we were approaching death. But the feeling passed away as soon as it came."

Post War Years
It was many years before John Merritt received the Medal of Honor. The issue date was April 1, 1880 accompanied by a letter from Alexander Ramsey, the Secretary of War, who had been the governor of Minnesota during the conflict of Bull Run. He stated, "In connection with this award I find occasion to remember with renewed pleasure and gratitude the patriotism of Minnesota's citizens, who in answer to my call as governor, at the first dawn of the war period, valiantly responded with cheers, the trumpets and the drums of the First Minnesota Regiment, of which you were a member.Alexander Ramsey, Secretary of War"

John married Mary A. Hoddinott and lived in Washington, DC. They had three children: Harriet, (b 1866), Leonora (b 1868) and William (b 1872). He was the Chief Doorkeeper of the U.S. Senate when he died, December 17, 1892. He is buried at the Congressional Cemetery, Washington D.C., Plot: Range 72 Site 359. His wife, Mary is buried there also, along with William and Leonora.

Compiled by Glynae Deschene
Maria Sanford Chapter NSDAR

Henry O'Brien 1842-1902

Medal of Honor
Action: Battle of Gettysburg
Date: July 3, 1863

Early Years

Henry D. O'Brien was born January 21, 1842 at Calais, Maine. In 1857, he moved with his family to St. Anthony Falls, Minnesota. He was the oldest of ten siblings some being half-brothers and sisters.

Civil War Years

With the opening salvo of the Civil War, Minnesota Governor, Alexander Ramsey, made his appeal for 1000 men. Within two weeks, on April 29, 1861, the 1st Minnesota mustered and Henry D. O'Brien answered the call on September 28. 1861. By the time of the Battle of Gettysburg Henry D. O'Brien was a corporal in Company E, 1st Minnesota Infantry. On the second day of that battle, July 2, 1863, the First Minnesota was ordered to make a suicide charge against a vastly superior in number regiment of Alabamans to buy time for the Union Army. The casualty count was the highest ever recorded in military history costing the 1st Minnesota 262 men. Fifteen percent of their number survived, among them Corporal O'Brien and Ernest Jefferson, his wounded comrade who he carried back to the Union lines.

O'Brien was among the remnant forty-seven survivors of the 1st Minnesota which found itself defending against "Pickett's Charge" the next day on July 3. As the Confederates' 28th Virginia Infantry neared the Union lines, O'Brien's regiment attacked their flank. The 1st Minnesota's color bearer, Corporal John Dehn, was shot down, and the flag staff broken in two by the gunfire. O'Brien responded, picked up the flag by its remaining staff and with characteristic bravery and impetuosity led his regiment into hand-to-hand combat. He was struck in the side of the head by a spent bullet which never-the-less knocked him momentarily senseless. Still he retained hold of the flag and advanced with his unit though wounded a second time, this time by a bullet to the hand.

After Gettysburg O'Brien was promoted to lieutenant. After the 1st Minnesota was mustered out on May 5, 1864 O'Brien was appointed Second Lieutenant in Company B on May 12, 1864, On Aug 14, 1864 he was shot in the right shoulder and lung and carried to safety by Alonzo Pickle and others. His wound forced his withdrawal from active service.

Corporal Henry O'Brien was one of 63 men who were awarded the Medal of Honor for heroism in the Battle of Gettysburg, Pennsylvania. For his bravery, many years later Henry O'Brien was awarded the Medal of Honor on April 9, 1890. His citation read: "taking up the colors where they had fallen, he rushed ahead of regiment, close to the muzzles of the enemy's guns, and engaged in the desperate struggle in which the enemy was defeated, and though severely wounded, he held the colors until wounded a second time."

Post War Years

After the war, Henry married Emma Sinclair. They had a son, Robert Sinclair O'Brien, born June 4, 1870 in Minneapolis, Minnesota. Later, he became a government pension agent in St. Louis, Missouri. Henry D. O'Brien died November 2, 1902 in St. Louis and is buried at the Bellefontaine Cemetery, in that city: Plot: Block 292, Lot 4482.

Photos of grave markers courtesy of Connie Nisinger, Bellefontaine Cemetery, St. Louis, Missouri.

Compiled by Glynae Deschene,
Maria Sanford Chapter NSDAR

Byron Edward Pay 1844-1906

Medal of Honor
Action: Nolensville, Tennessee
Date: February 15, 1865

Early Years

Byron E. Pay was the seventh child of nine born October 21, 1844 in Le Ray Township, Jefferson County, New York to William and Susanne Pay. His father, William Pay, a farmer, emigrated from London, arriving in the port of New York 13 June 1836 on the Ship St. Laurence. The following year Byron's mother, Susanne Pay and four children, Eleanor age 9, Benjamin age 5, Thomas age 3 and Robert age 1 immigrated to the United States from London, England arriving in New York City 28 March 1837 on the ship Montreal.

The 1855 New York State Census lists William Pay and his wife Susanne both age 49 as born in England. Their children living with them, all born in New York State were: Warren age 17 (1838); Anna E. age 13 (1842; Byron E. Pay age 11 (1844); Asher F. age 9 (1846) and Edward E. age 6 (1849),

One year later in 1856, the William Pay family moved to Woodstock, Illinois and in March 1857 moved to Washington County, Iowa. The following May 1858, at the age of 13, Byron entered the office of the Washington Press as an apprentice but left this job during the summer to move to Blue Earth County, Minnesota where his oldest brother, Benjamin Pay lived. Byron worked on a farm in Vernon Center Township, Blue Earth County, for the next three years.

In the 1860 U.S. Federal Census, Byron E. Pay, age 16 [sic] and brother, Warren Pay age 22 were living in Ceresco Township, Blue Earth County, Minnesota with their oldest brother, Benjamin Pay, age 26, his wife Mary, and their children.

Civil War Years

Byron E. Pay was 16 years, 8 months old at the time of his enlistment in Company H, 2nd Regiment Minnesota Volunteer Infantry. He was mustered into service on July 15, 1861 at Fort Snelling, Minnesota. Three of Byron's brothers also served in the Civil War: Robert P., Warren W., and Asher F. Pay. Robert P., born in England was mustered in on

September 4th 1862 in Rockford, Illinois at age 27. He was 5'4", light hair, blue eyes and light complexion. His brother, Byron E. was probably the same size or smaller when he enlisted.

The records of Company H, or even of the 2nd Minnesota, in 1861 are a little sketchy. The soldiers were trained at Fort Snelling in the summer of 1861 and then shipped south to Kentucky that fall. In 1862, the 2nd Minnesota saw their first action at the Battle of Mill Springs in January, then had their share of skirmishes and small battles throughout the year in Kentucky, Tennessee, Mississippi and Alabama but by year's end, they were back in Kentucky.

On Feb. 15, 1863, a Sunday morning, the men of Company H, including Byron E. Pay, were one of a detachment of 16 men scouting for supplies near Nolensville, Tennessee who heroically defended a wagon train against the attack by 125 mounted men from the 6th Alabama Cavalry. They repulsed the attack and saved the train. When the smoke cleared away, they found two dead Cavalrymen, several wounded, and 10 dead horses and one of their own mules. They took three prisoners and three horses and had three men slightly wounded.

On September 20, 1863 at Chickamauga, Georgia, a battle the Union forces lost, Byron E. Pay was seriously wounded. He was treated for his wound. Notes in his record state, "This man is elsewhere, therefore no discharge paper furnished. Descriptive Roll Sent. Wounded at Chickamauga on Sept. 20/63. Absent wounded. Prov. Made for the muster out of roll sent." One record had his discharge date as May, 1864 and another July 14, 1864 by order of the Secretary of War for disability resulting from a gunshot wound in left shoulder".

Post War Years
Nineteen year-old Byron was still owed $100 from the military when he returned to Mankato. By June 1864 he was hired by Mr. J. B. Hubbell of the Northwestern Fur Company, assigned to load 86 wagons with flour at Mankato, Minnesota and deliver them across western Minnesota and eastern Dakota Territory to what became Fort Thompson in September. He left Mankato on the 1st of July, arriving with his wagon train at the fort during the month of August.

Upon returning to Mankato, his next assignment was to take several teams and join up with Company L of the 2d Minnesota, which had become an Indian fighting group, to scout the upper reaches of the Minnesota River and gather up the remnants of the Sisseton Tribe and take them to the Ft. Thompson reservation, also known as the Crow Creek Agency.

After accomplishing this, he took a supply train to the fur company posts deep in "Indian country" at Ft. Berthold in western Dakota Territory (later North Dakota). This required passing through the skirmishing area which was still being disputed by the Sioux and Mandan tribes. Byron Pay, now 20 years old, left on February 20, 1865, and by mid-March the fur company's posts had been resupplied, taking just six weeks to lead the supply train almost 400 miles in mid-winter through hostile territory from Fort Thompson to Fort Berthold.

Byron continued buying furs and delivering supplies to the Sioux Indians in 1866. However, on September 14, 1866, Byron E. Pay was listed as an invalid per government pension records although he remained in the employ of the fur company until 1871.

On September 10, 1867, Byron E. Pay married Hattie E. Youngman in Blue Earth, Faribault County, Minnesota. In May 1872 he and Hattie located a preemption claim on the NW 1/4 of section 8, township 108-49, Dakota Territory. He, his wife and young son settled in a sod house on the Big Sioux River south of Medary and lived there through the winter. A year later, May 18, 1873, Byron E. Pay, wife and son moved into Brookings County, on the Northeast quarter of section 9, and made the first homestead filing in the township. On July 3rd his brother, Warren, and wife arrived. The following day, July 4, the first celebration of the national holiday took place with the entire population of the northwestern part of Brookings county participating – the five Pay family members. On this day the claim of B. E. Pay was christened Oakwood Farm by Mrs. Pay. Oakwood was either the 2nd or 3rd settlement in Brookings County during the early 1870s.

In 1872-73, Byron Pay served as sergeant-at-arms in the Dakota Territorial House of Representatives and in the fall of 1873, Byron and Warren Pay and three other men were the first United States jurors from Brookings County to attend court in Pembina, now in North Dakota. "The trip was made overland in a covered wagon, drawn by a span of mules . . . They did not see any settlers on the route after leaving Oakwood until they reached Fargo. Mrs. Hattie Pay, her young son, Charles and Mrs. Anna M. Pay, were the only white people around the lakes, and they remained alone taking care of the stock while their husbands were away."

In 1874 Byron Pay's home became the post office and he the postmaster at Oakwood. Postmaster total compensation for Byron E. Pay in 1875 was $5.49. In the fall of 1878, he built and ran a hotel, Oakwood House in Oakwood and also acted as a locating agent in the early days locating homesteads for early settlers. In 1874 at age 30, he became a U.S. Marshal serving from 1874-1885. He also served five years as a Brookings County Commissioner.

In May 1879, Mr. B. E. Pay returned from Yankton after an absence of several weeks on the grand jury and was soon back in the employ of the U.S. government, working for the Department of Justice as an Indian Agent, traveling between Yankton and the Black Hills in the winter of 1880-1881. He served in the territorial legislature and held various positions of trust. By 1883, the town of Oakwood was a casualty of the railroad when it extended a branch bypassing the town. Oakwood dwindled away while a new town of Bruce, on the railroad line several miles east of Oakwood, sprang up. Almost all of the buildings at Oakwood were moved either to Bruce or Volga. About all that remained was Byron Pay's hotel.

Byron, his wife Hattie and their two sons moved to Volga, South Dakota, when he was still in his early 40's and he worked for the Bank of Volga. He was a staunch Republican and an alternate to the National Convention in 1884. Byron was also a Vice-President of an Old Settlers' Association and was active in the GAR (Grand Army of the Republic – a precursor of the American Legion.) He was the commander of the Brookings GAR post in 1891 and 1892.

At age 53, thirty-four years after the Civil War battle near Nolensville, Tennessee he was awarded the Medal of Honor by President William McKinley on Sept. 11, 1897.

On November 20, 1902, Byron E. Pay wrote a deposition, which is now among J. B. Hubbell's papers of the Northwestern Fur Company at the Minnesota Historical Society, St. Paul, Minnesota. "Byron Pay was the man engaged by Hubbell to make the trip with the Indians. Pay not only describes his journey from Fort Ridgely to Pipestone, (Minnesota) where his train was joined by fifty of Hubbell's wagons loaded with supplies for the Indians, but he tells of the difficulties encountered in carrying out his task."

Less than four years later, at the age of 61, Byron E. Pay died suddenly at his home in Volga, probably of a stroke, on Monday, February 19, 1906. He left behind a wife, Hattie and two sons, Charles W. and Mell B. Pay. His obituary said, "Mr. Pay was one of the oldest and most universally respected residents of Volga, and was well-known throughout the state of South Dakota." "Few men have been through more varied scenes and vicissitudes in life than he, and few men have come to the end of their earthly journey with more warm friends and fewer enemies than Mr. Pay." Byron Pay is buried at Arlington Cemetery, Arlington, Brookings, South Dakota.

Compiled by Joyce Rohloff Gardner
Anthony Wayne Chapter NSDAR

Alonzo H. Pickle 1843-1925

Medal of Honor
Action: Deep Bottom, Virginia
Date: August 14, 1864

Early Years
Alonzo Huntingdon Pickle, son of Simon and Sarah (Taylor) Pickle, was born July 2, 1843 in Farnham, Quebec, Canada... He was baptized, along with his sister Alma on April 9, 1849 at the St. James Anglican Church in that town.

In 1855, the Pickle family came to the United States, settling first in Illinois and two years later, on a quarter section of land obtained by Alonzo's father midway between Dover and Eyota, Olmsted County, Minnesota. Alonzo worked on the family farm until he enlisted in the Union Army.

Civil War Years
Alonzo was mustered into service in Company K, First Minnesota Regiment on August 14, 1862, at St. Charles, Winona County. The tall blond 19-year-old was photographed in his neat grey uniform which was presented to members of Company K by the citizens of Winona. Of the First Minnesota, this company appears to have been the only one with proper uniforms. The state had issued black pantaloons, black felt caps, along with red flannel shirts, and this outfit comprised the uniform of the other companies.

Although Company K, First Minnesota, was engaged at Antietam in September, Alonzo may not have been present. He probably would have been on the march up Loudoun Valley and on to Falmouth, Virginia, October 30-November 17, 1862, and saw his first action at Fredericksburg in December 1862. He observed his twentieth birthday—if he had time to think about it—while he was engaged in action at the battle of Gettysburg on July 2, 1863.

He is quoted as saying of Gettysburg: "The Minnesota Monument represents the place we started down the slope and the figure atop faces the direction we went down into the woods with our 262 men. After we did what we were ordered to do, we rallied around our flag - 47 of us were left, the other 215 lay wounded and dead. Fifty years later he attended the famous "blue and gray" reunion on that field.

After being promoted to corporal on February 1, 1864, he was sent home with a recruiting squad. In the meantime the First Minnesota was ordered to Fort Snelling, Minnesota on February 5 and was on duty there until April 29 when they were mustered out at the expiration of their three year term. The men of the First Minnesota Regiment, whose term of enlistment had not expired, re-enlisted and became the First Minnesota Infantry Battalion. Alonzo, of Company B, was promoted to sergeant on July 22, 1864.

In August the unit fought on the 13th to 20th at a place called Deep Bottom, Virginia. It would be here that the unit was driven back after attempting an assault. But while most backed away Alonzo remained because he saw his officer, [Major H. D. O'Brien,] being knocked to the ground by bullets, he crawled out to save the man and brought him back to safety." Many years later, Alonzo was awarded one of the nation's highest awards, the Medal of Honor, for this act of bravery.

Although he did not mention Alonzo Pickle, H. D. O'Brien wrote "At Deep Bottom, Va., August 14, 1864, I took part in a charge after being excused from duty on account of sickness, and was shot through the right lung while in advance of my company."

Alonzo was present at Lee's surrender at Appomattox on April 9, 1865. "The battalion was on picket duty at the time and he watched, as many beaten rebel soldiers crossed their lines and surrendered their arms."

He was promoted to first sergeant on May 1, marched with his regiment to Washington, D.C., May 2-12 and participated in the Grand Review in Washington on May 23. He was discharged at Bailey's Cross Roads, Virginia, on June 7, 1865.

According to his biographical sketch in the *History of Brown County, Minnesota*, he saw action at Loudoun Valley (Oct 30-Nov 17, 1862), Fredericksburg (Dec 12-15, 1862), Hay Market (Jun 25, 1863), Gettysburg (July 1-3, 1863), Bristow Station (Oct. 14, 1863), Mine Run (Nov 27-Dec 2, 1863), Petersburg (series of campaigns), Jerusalem Plank Road (June 21–23, 1864), Deep Bottom (Aug. 14-20, 1864), Reams Station (Aug. 25, 1864), Hatchers Run (Feb. 5-7, 1865), Farmhill and High Bridge (April 6-7, 1865).

Post War Years
After the war Alonzo Pickle returned to his father's farm near Eyota, Minnesota. He may have met Rhoda Jane Smith in Rochester, Minnesota. In any event, they were married in Rochester on October 24, 1867. She was from Burlington, Iowa. Shortly after their marriage, the couple moved to Winona and Alonzo found a job working for W. S. Nevins, a horse dealer according to the 1870 census. He also hauled brick for the construction of the first normal school in that city.

Within a year or two, he moved back to Olmsted County and rented a farm where he made his home for the next fifteen years. The 1875, 1880 and 1885 censuses confirm that Alonzo and his family were living in Dover Township, Olmsted County. Alonzo worked for Nevins again from 1886 until the fall of 1888, presumably when "He was engaged as the overseer of the big Nevis ranch at Tracy, where he remained for two years and six months."

About the fall of 1888, he moved to land he had purchased earlier near Golden Gate, a town that took its name from the U. S. Post Office established in 1868. "Two general stores, blacksmith shop, a grist mill, the post office and a few dwellings scarcely merited the high-toned name 'Golden Gate' so the pioneers used the nickname 'Podunk'." The railroad by-passed the village in the early 1870s and the community slowly vanished. A Historic Marker indicates the site of the former village in Home Township, Brown County, Minnesota.

Alonzo retired from farming after four years at Golden Gate and moved to Sleepy Eye, a community with a population of 1513 in 1890, roughly fifteen miles from Golden Gate. The 1895 state census confirms that he and Rhoda were there although his biographical sketch claims that he moved to Sleepy Eye in 1906—probably a typographical error in Fritsche's History of Brown County.

Alonzo's next undertaking was in the real estate and insurance business, at first in partnership, then as the sole proprietor. "He was the local agent for a number of the leading insurance companies of the country and had a very well-established business in Sleepy Eye."

Over thirty years later, on June 12, 1895, Alonzo was awarded one of the nation's highest awards, the Medal of Honor. The commendation reads: "The President of the United States of America, in the name of Congress, takes pleasure in presenting the Medal of Honor to Sergeant Alonzo H. Pickle, United States Army, for extraordinary heroism on 14 August 1864, while serving with Company B, Minnesota Infantry, in action at Deep Bottom, Virginia. At the risk of his life, Sergeant Pickle voluntarily went to the assistance of a wounded officer lying close to the enemy's lines and, under fire carried him to a place of safety."

Alonzo died in Sleepy Eye on May 24, 1925, at the age of 81. He was buried in Home Cemetery, Sleepy Eye, Minnesota. His wife, Rhoda, died 31 Aug 1923.

His biographical sketch in the 1915 *History of Brown County*, listed his children: Frank A., born 1868, deceased; Burton O., born 1869, who married Milla Burkhardt and has three children; Anna, born 1871, who married George Dreher and has five children; Ella, born 1872, who married Ernest Tompkins and has one child; Roy B., born 1883, who married Josie Wisby and has four children; and Arthur T., born 1886, unmarried.

Compiled by Lorraine Hall Keith
Rochester Chapter NSDAR

Axel Hayford Reed 1835-1917

Medal of Honor
Action: Chickamauga, Georgia
            Missionary Ridge, Tennessee
Date: September 19, 1863

Early Years

Born March 13, 1835 at Hartford, Maine, Axel Hayford Reed was the son of Sampson Reed and Huldah Bisbee and the youngest of seven siblings, three brothers and three sisters. His mother passed away when he was only seven. An unappreciated step-mother came into the family three years later causing a scattering of all of the children from the home except young Axel. Due to his age, he was made to endure the monotony of farm life until he turned 19. During those years he accompanied his father on cattle drives to Brighton, Massachusetts, continually imploring his father to "let me go for myself." Finally at age 19, his father gave his consent and five dollars saying, "I predict you will always be poor."

From the maps he studied while in school Axel thought the west was the best place for a permanent home, so in April, 1854, he left the Maine homestead (originally settled by his grandfather in 1795) arriving in Minnesota in November, 1855, where there wasn't a single acquaintance to welcome him. The first winter he worked in the woods for $20 per month, and in the spring of 1856 he got a job working in a new town, Glencoe, making bricks. He farmed and trapped, invested all his earnings in the plant, and preempted 160 acres of land which made him a permanent settler until the start of the Civil War.

Civil War Years

Reed enlisted August 6, 1861, at the rank of Sergeant in Company K, Minnesota 2nd Infantry Regiment in Glencoe, McLeod County, Minnesota. He was promoted to Full 2nd Lieutenant on August 17, 1864, and Full 1st Lieutenant on February 18th, 1965. During his service, Reed participated in nearly every siege and skirmish that his regiment engaged including Sherman's March to the Sea, marching through Kentucky, Tennessee, Mississippi, Alabama, Georgia, Virginia, North and South Carolina.,

Reed's Medal of Honor was presented for heroism for two separate events, on September 19, 1863, at Chickamauga, Georgia, and November 15, 1863, at Missionary Ridge, Tennessee.

While encamped at Winchester, Tennessee in July, 1863, Sergeant Reed violated military discipline by indiscreetly criticizing the food. He was arrested, stripped of his weapons and sent to the rear of his company where he continued to accompany his regiment across the Cumberland Mountains.

He was still a prisoner when on September 19, 1863, the regiment engaged Bragg's Confederate forces at Chickamauga, Georgia. Once the placement of the enemy was identified, the regiment dropped their knapsacks and left them under guard along with the prisoners, including Reed, while they marched off to meet the enemy.

As the cannons began to boom, Reed begged his guard to let him help his fellow soldiers. It was his strong belief that the government had fed and trained him for just this occasion. He grabbed a rifle and went to the front of enemy lines. He found comrades pinned down; he fought with them for two solid days. When the regiment lieutenant was wounded and only one commissioned officer remained, Reed took command of the regiment. He was one of nine soldiers awarded the Medal of Honor at Chickamauga, Georgia.

After this skirmish, General Thomas issued a special order releasing Reed from arrest and restoring him to full duty, in recognition of his true devotion to service and recognition of his bravery.

At the front line of the battle at Missionary Ridge, on November 25th, 1863, Sergeant Reed was amongst the first to cross into enemy territory to capture their cannons. The cannons were then turned on the fleeing enemy, but they were out of ammunition. He found two rebel soldiers trying to hitch horses to a caisson in a get-away attempt and demanded their surrender in order to acquire the ammunition in the caisson. They refused, and Reed aimed his gun at one of them and fired. As he was reloading, he was hit with a minnie-ball which shattered his arm between the shoulder and elbow. He fell to the ground and laid there until the firing ceased. Another wounded soldier helped him put on a tourniquet to stop the bleeding. He walked to the foot of the ridge, and was taken to a hospital in Chattanooga, Tennessee. Some reports indicate that he lost that arm.

His generals recognized his bravery with this communication. "The purpose of placing on record the names of officers and men of my regiment, who by gallant and meritorious conduct under fire during the assault on Mission Ridge on the 25th, ultimo, have

67

entitled themselves to special mention. I respectfully submit the following report as supplementary to the General Report already on file in your office. 1st Sergeant A. H. Reed commanded his company (K) during the engagement, behaving with marked coolness and courage. He was severely wounded near the close of the fight on the Ridge. "He declined discharge and continued in active duty until the end of the war.

This communication was followed up some 35 years later on March 22, 1898 with this letter from the War Department: Subject Medal of Honor.

"Mr. Axel H. Reed: Sir, you are hereby notified that by direction of the President, and under the provisions of the act of Congress, approved March 3, 1863, providing for the presentation of medals of honor to such officers, non-commissioned officers and privates as have most distinguished themselves in action, a Congressional Medal of Honor has this day been presented to you for Most Distinguished Gallantry in Action, the following being a statement of the particular service, viz: At Chickamauga, Ga., September 19, 1863, this officer, then a sergeant in Company K, 2nd Minnesota Volunteers, was in arrest for a breach of discipline. When the action opened he left his place in rear voluntarily and went unarmed to the line of battle, secured a musket and equipment of a wounded soldier participated in the two days' battle, and in recognition of his distinguished gallantry was released from arrest and restored to duty by the special order of General Thomas. On November 25th he was wounded at Mission Ridge and as a result suffered amputation of an arm. After recovery from this wound he declined a discharge for disability which was offered him, and served during the remainder of the war, participating in the Savannah and Carolina campaigns.

This Medal will be forwarded to you by registered mail, as soon as it shall have been engraved." It was signed by R.A. Alger, Secretary of War."

Axel's commendation reads: "The President of the United States of America, in the name of Congress, takes pleasure in presenting the Medal of Honor to Sergeant Axel Hayford Reed, United States Army, for extraordinary heroism on 19 September 1863, while serving with Company K, 2d Minnesota Infantry. While in arrest at Chickamauga, Georgia, Sergeant Reed left his place in the rear and voluntarily went to the line of battle, secured a rifle, and fought gallantly during the two-day battle; was released from arrest in recognition of his bravery. At Missionary Ridge, Tennessee, on 15 November 1863, he commanded his company and gallantly led it, being among the first to enter the enemy's works; was severely wounded, losing an arm, but declined a discharge and remained in active service to the end of the war.
Axel mustered out at Fort Snelling, July 18, 1865.

Post War Years

After the war Reed returned to Glencoe with an Army comrade. On April 15, 1869, he married Hannah Antoinette Morrison of Bradford, New Hampshire who had moved to Minnesota with her parents. They had four children: Cora Lydia (b. 1872), Nelly Antoinette (b. 1873, d. 1875 scarlet fever), Axel Hayford Jr. (1876) and Frank Elisha (1880, graduate of the U of MN Law School 1904).

Reed bought a mercantile and traded grain and general merchandise for more than thirty years. He also contributed to buying land and helping to build the first railroad coming into McLeod County in 1873. He built two grain elevators, and established the First National Bank of Glencoe in 1881 (was President for ten years). He was the publisher of the *Glencoe Enterprise* (1878-1889). He was actively connected with the political affairs of McLeod County as a member of the board of county commissioners (1876-1878), sergeant at arms of the state legislature (1868-1869) and a representative from the 6th district (1870). However, he was mostly interested in farming and agriculture, being one of the first members of the Minnesota Horticulture Society. He had one of the largest apple orchards in McLeod County and was one of the largest producers of wheat. In 1915, Reed published his *Genealogical Record of the Reads, Reeds, the Bisbees, the Bradfords of the United States of America.*

Reed passed away on January 21, 1917, and is buried in Mount Auburn Cemetery (MH 3-158) Glencoe, Minnesota.

Axel Hayford Reed was a member of the following military organizations: Army of the Cumberland, Grand Army of the Republic, Military Order of the Loyal Legion of the United States, Medal of Honor Legion, and Union Veterans Legion. He was elected a life member of the Minnesota Historical Society and the Mayflower Society, as an eighth descendent of William Bradford (1590-1657), a founder and governor of Plymouth Colony who was a passenger on the Mayflower, and signed the Mayflower Compact upon arriving in Massachusetts in 1620.

Compiled by Jane Homme
St. Croix River Valley Chapter NSDAR

William Schmidt 1844-1905

Medal of Honor
Action: Missionary Ridge, Tennessee
Date: November 25, 1863

Ohio State Monument

Early Years

The background information on William Schmidt is very minimal. He was born on October 7, 1844 in Tiffin, Seneca County, Ohio. History pertaining to the Schmidt family via censes records or county records are not certain since ability to identify family members has not been determined. A photo or an illustration of William Schmidt has not been located. The photo of the Ohio State Monument located at the site of the Missionary Ridge is shown where William's photo would be displayed.

Civil War Years

It can be stated that based on William's birth year, this soon to be sixteen-year-old young man made the roughly fifty-mile trip from Tiffin, Ohio to the city of Maumee, Ohio to enter the service on September 12, 1861 at Maumee, Lucas County, Ohio where he became a member of Company 6, 37th Ohio Infantry Regiment..

Infantry regiments formed in Ohio became known as regiments of Ohio Volunteer Infantry. Soldiers of Ohio infantry regiments served the Union for varying lengths of time, ranging from one hundred days to three years. One of the three-year regiments was the 37th Regiment Ohio Volunteer Infantry. The regiment consisted primarily of Germans from Cleveland, Toledo, and Chillicothe, Ohio. The organization mustered into service at Camp Dennison, near Cincinnati, Ohio, on October 2, 1861. This is the regiment of which William Schmidt was a member.

The history of the 37th Regiment Ohio Infantry is quite extensive. During the three years that William Schmidt served, this military group covered much territory with various locations from Virginia (current day West Virginia), Arkansas, Alabama, Louisiana, Mississippi and Tennessee.

On November 21, 1863, the 37th arrived in the vicinity of Chattanooga, Tennessee, where the Confederate Army of Tennessee had besieged the Union Army of the

Cumberland since late September 1863. On November 24, 1863, the regiment was in position in front of Missionary Ridge. On the next day, Union forces stormed the Confederate lines on the ridge, driving the enemy from the heights and bringing the Chattanooga Campaign to a successful conclusion for the North. In the Battle of Missionary Ridge, the 37th had five men killed and thirty-six more wounded.

At the Battle of Missionary Ridge, November 25 1863, under heavy enemy fire, William Schmidt picked up fallen 37th Infantry drummer, John S. Kountz, and carried him to safety. "As the drummer had been ordered to the rear in preparatory of the charge, the little drummer-boy threw away his drum, and, falling in with his company, was wounded in the first assault, being shot in the left leg, and left on the field under enemy guns."

Battle of Mission Ridge

When the brigade got back to its old position, Captain Hamm, of Company A, told the boys of Company G, that Kountz was lying in the front severely wounded, and asked: "Who will go and get him out?" Private William Schmidt shouted: "I will," and made for the front, advancing as far as he could under cover of the hill. When he came to the point where cover was no longer available, he made a dash for the spot where Kountz was lying, the enemy pouring a heavy fire upon him. Kountz shouted: "Save yourself. I am a goner anyhow," but Schmidt picked him up on his back and in spite of all protests, carried him back to the Union lines. Kountz's leg was so badly shattered that it had to be amputated the same night. When he was picked up, he was nearer the rebel works than any other man of his regiment.

For his outstanding courage, William Schmidt received the Medal of Honor, with the citation stating: "Rescued a wounded comrade under terrific fire".

Post War Years
After serving three years, and the whereabouts of twenty-year old William was not known. Nor was there any knowledge of

Lakewood Cemetery, Minneapolis
Monument erected by G.A.R.

his occupation. Presentation of the Medal of Honor did not come until November 9, 1895, when he was forty-nine. At this time, he was living in Duluth, Minnesota. It is not known when William moved to Minneapolis, Minnesota. There is no knowledge if he was ever married and no information on parents or siblings, as stated earlier.

At the time of his death on June 3, 1905 in Minneapolis, Hennepin County, Minnesota, William Schmidt was living at the Old Soldiers Home and within three days he was buried at Lakewood Cemetery in Section 8, Tier E, Grave 74. Currently this grave site has no headstone that gives honor to this individual for his distinguished gallantry.

In addition to William Schmidt being recognized for the Medal of Honor, John S. Kountz, the drummer he saved, was also given the Medal of Honor for his heroic willingness to engage the oncoming forces. It is stated, "That was the first time one Medal of Honor recipient saved the life of another Medal of Honor recipient."

Compiled by Dianne Lawson
Josiah Edson Chapter NSDAR

Irwin Shepard 1843-1916

Medal of Honor:
Action: Fort Sanders
Knoxville, Tennessee
Date: November 20, 1863

Early Years

Irwin Shepard, born July 5, 1843 in Skaneateles, Onondaga County, New York, was the son of Luman Shepard, a farmer, and his wife, Betsy L Pangburn. His descent on his father's side is English, and his mother's ancestors came from Holland. Irwin attended rural schools in New York until he was 13 years old when the family moved to Chelsea, Washtenaw County, Michigan. He attended the village school until 1859 when he entered the State Normal School at Ypsilanti, Michigan.

Civil War Years

When the Civil War began in 1861, Irvin and some college friends joined Company E, 17th Michigan Volunteer Infantry. Initially, he was a Private but was soon promoted to Corporal. He was awarded the Medal of Honor as a Corporal for action on November 20, 1863 near Fort Sanders, Knoxville, Tennessee, when he voluntarily joined in a mission to destroy and burn buildings on the Judge Reese farm. The farmhouse was being used by Confederate sharpshooters to harass Union lines. During that mission a sharpshooter was firing at the group from above. Irwin's group was ordered to retreat, but he stayed behind and continued in that mission to burn those buildings, thus insuring their total destruction. This was accomplished at imminent risk of his life. He was awarded the Congressional Medal of Honor 34 years later.

Irwin was also engaged in the following battles: South Mountain, Antietam, Brandy Station, Fredericksburg, Virginia; Green River, Kentucky; Vicksburg and Jackson, Mississippi; Loudan, and The Wilderness. He was wounded at the Battle of the Wilderness.

Post War Years

After his recovery Irvin resumed his college studies at Olivet College, Olivet, Michigan, receiving his degrees of A.B., A.M, and Ph. D. at that institution. In 1871 he married Mary Bassett Elmer of Olivet, Michigan. Three children were born to them: a daughter who died in childhood, and two sons, Elmer I. Shepard and Ernest E.. Shepard.

He began his professional career at Charles City, Iowa, where he became Superintendent of Schools for four years. In 1875 he came to Winona, Minnesota, as principal of Winona High School. Three years later he was made Superintendent of the Winona public school system, and in 1879 he was appointed President of Winona State Normal School. At the Normal School Dr. Shepard established the first kindergarten west of the Mississippi. He also started a training course for prospective kindergarten teachers. One of Dr. Shepard's most important contributions to the Winona Normal School and the Normal School System in Minnesota was the establishment of a Normal School diploma as a certificate of qualification to teach.

In 1893 Dr. Shepard resigned his position at Winona Normal to become secretary of the National Educational Association, a position he held until he retired. He handled correspondence and convention planning from an office in his home.

Dr. Sheppard was a member of the John Ball Post No. 45, G.A.R., Department of Minnesota, and served as aide on the staff of the department commander.

Dr. Irwin Shepard died on April 17, 1916, in Winona, and was survived by his wife, Mary, who died in 1919. Other survivors included his two sons, Elmer who was an Assistant Professor of Mathematics at Williams College, Williamstown, Massachusetts, and Elmer, who was an assistant cashier at the Deposit Bank of Winona. He and his wife are buried in Woodlawn Cemetery in Winona. Through the combined effort of the Winona

County Veteran's Affairs office / a local Civil War re-enactor and the Disabled American Veterans an official bronze marker was placed on Shepard's grave in the summer of 2000.

Compiled by Marilyn Burbank, Rochester Chapter NSDAR

Marshall Sherman 1823-1896

Medal of Honor:
Action: Pickett's Charge, Gettysburg
Date: July 3, 1863

Early Years
Marshall Sherman's early years in Vermont are a mystery. While it is known that he was born in Burlington, Chittenden County, Vermont in 1823, documentation of parents and possible family members is unknown. The first indication of his arrival in Minnesota is the year of 1849 where he is employed as a house painter and in partnership with James McClellan Boal, a partnership that begin that year and into 1850.

Marshall was mustered into the First Minnesota Volunteer Infantry, on April 29, 1861, as a 37 year-old private. He is described as standing 5' 6" tall, with a fair complexion, black eyes and black hair.

Civil War Years
Marshall became one of the first to enlist in the Union Army from Minnesota, entering the service on April 29 1861 in Ramsey County, Minnesota, Company C 1st Minnesota Infantry. This would end up being a length of three years in which he fought at Bull Run, Ball's Bluff, The Seven Days, Antietam and Gettysburg

Private Marshall Sherman captured the Army of Northern Virginia Confederate battle flag of the 28th Virginia Volunteer Infantry Regiment while serving with the 1st Minnesota Volunteer Infantry Regiment, Company C, during Pickett's Charge at the Battle of Gettysburg on July 3, 1863. Private Sherman was awarded the Congressional Medal of Honor for his gallantry at Gettysburg.

After his three-year enlistment was up he was one of only a few veterans of the "Old First" to re-enlist and form the nucleus of the First Minnesota. Battalion. On August 14, 1864, at the battle of Deep Bottom, Virginia, he was shot in the left leg. The bullet broke two bones and was severe enough that it was necessary to amputate his leg below the knee. After this was done at Campbell Hospital he was sent to the Soldier's Rest General Hospital in Boston. He was fitted for and on July 8, 1865, furnished with an artificial leg, which was made by Jewitt of Salem, Massachusetts. Marshall was determined to be unfit for service in the Veteran Reserve Corps and was discharged for disability at Boston, Massachusetts, on July 25, 1865.

Post War Years
Like thousands of veterans Marshall Sherman returned to a different life in St Paul--the life of a civilian crippled from the war. He first returned to his previous work as a painter. Later, he went into the life insurance business earning his living as a representative for Fenton G. and Henry E. Warner in their business, Warner & Warner Fire Insurance and Loans, 30 East 4th, St. Paul, Minnesota. He then was living at 96 East 11th Street in the city. Later, from 1893-1896, Marshall lived at 656 Lincoln Avenue, St. Paul as a boarder.

Oakland Cemetery Association internment records indicate that he died of intestinal nephritis on April 19, 1896, in St. Paul, and is buried in the Soldiers Rest area of the cemetery, Block 41, Lot 17. Next of kin is listed as a friend, George Morton. When Marshall died he was a member of the William Acker G.A.R. Post #21, which he had joined on July 19, 1870.

According to a newspaper account, the flag of the Twenty-eighth Virginia Regiment, along with the regimental flag of the First Minnesota, was brought by surviving colleagues, to Sherman's funeral which was held at the Lincoln Avenue residence.

Many stories surround the various places that the flag had been stored. Currently the captured battle flag of the 28th Virginia Infantry remains in possession of the Minnesota Historical Society in St. Paul, Minnesota.

Oakland Cemetery, St. Paul, MN

Compiled by Dianne Lawson
Josiah Edson Chapter NSDAR

John Vale 1835-1909

Medal of Honor
Action: Battle at Nolensville, Tennessee,
Date: February 15, 1863

Few receive the Congressional Medal of Honor and even fewer live to receive it themselves. "Under the provisions of the Act of Congress approved 3 March 1863, the Medal of Honor is presented to officers and privates for their most distinguished gallantry in action." Following is the story of one such soldier, John Vale, who was inducted into the Civil War from Rochester, Minnesota, 22 June 1861.

Early Years

John Vale was born in the Borough of Lambeth, London, England, on August 9, 1835, the son of Thomas and Elizabeth Vale. He attended school until he was thirteen years old, and then spent three and one-half years as clerk in a grocery store in Kensington. His father, Thomas, died in 1840. In November 1851 John decided to join his uncle, William Russell, in Davenport, Iowa. He sailed aboard the Lenobia which arrived in New York on November 12, 1851, and then traveled on to Iowa. As government land became available in the Minnesota Territory, John went west and began farming in Blue Earth County, Minnesota.

Civil War Years

On July 15, 1861 John joined Company H, 2nd Regiment, Minnesota Veteran Volunteer Infantry as a private and was inducted from Rochester, Minnesota. He served four years reaching the rank of Sergeant and was discharged 11 July 1865 in Louisville, Kentucky. Remarkably he was never wounded although he fought in the siege of Corinth and the battles of Chickamauga, Chattanooga, and Missionary Ridge. He also was with Sherman in the Atlanta campaign and March to the Sea, and from Savannah to Raleigh and Richmond. He received the Medal of Honor for his bravery in the following battle as quoted from *The Story of a Regiment, Service of the 2nd Regiment, Minnesota Volunteer Infantry,1861-1865,* Judson W. Bishop, pages 1-6.

"When the men of Company H awoke in the cold and gray Sunday morning of February 15, 1863, they found themselves camped on the farm of Colonel Battle of the

20th Confederate Tennessee, the regime they had faced in the fight across the fence earlier at Mill Springs up in Kentucky. The closest town was Nolensville, about 12 miles from Nashville. As the 14 men from the Blue Earth County reported to regiment headquarters, they found that Lieutenant Harrison Couse of Company C would be in charge of men to guard a group of ten wagons.

As Corporal Milton Hanna, one of the members of this little squad reported, "We received orders to go to the front to forage for mules, and started with ten teams. We marched south along the turnpike about three miles from camp, on a crossroad known as Concord Church Road. Here a colored man informed us that just over the hill, about a half-mile away, near where the turnpike crossed over, the 6th Alabama Calvary, 600 strong, had camped the night before. After satisfying ourselves that this was true, we turned to the left on the mud road and went a mile east to a farmhouse.

"At this point, Sergeant Lovilo Holmes received orders from Lt. Couse to take 14 men and four wagons and go in a southwesterly direction to the foot near where the turnpike crossed over, and where the enemy was supposed to be, while he, with the rest of the company, should keep on east about three miles to another farmhouse to load the other six wagons. We could not understand why we were separated, as there was more forage at either place than the ten wagons could hold."

Corporal Hanna continued, "On reaching the farmhouse, located on a little hill with a small some eight or ten rods, we came to a lane leading from the house, running east and west, at the head of which were some barns, cribs, etc. arranged in the form of a letter V. The sergeant at once stationed sentinels at different points to prevent surprise, and John Vale" who stood at the foot of the hill, was soon hailed by a colored man coming on the run, and nearly out of breath, yelling 'See {em' see 'em! The enemy (was) west of the turnpike and had passed into the timber where we were unable to see them. They aimed to cut us off from our camp and the other foraging party. Sergeant Holmes ordered me to go to the crossroad and see what they were doing. While he returned to the cribs to prepare for defense, I placed myself in a cedar thicket a few rods from where the enemy crossed over the turnpike and could hear them talk and laugh as the horse's hoofs pattered over the road.

"I returned at once and reported, but the enemy had already arrived at the farm. They filed into the field following the same course we had taken, spreading out and making as large a showing as possible, giving us a chance to count them. They numbered 125, all mounted.

"Holmes saw they were coming to us first, and ordered us to get under cover as best as we could, and hold our fire until he shot first. 'We can die,' said he, 'but we'll never surrender.'

"With these orders we took refuge in the buildings. I took shelter in the lower part of the barn. Holmes with two men, in the hay mow, the others in cribs, hog pens, and other out-buildings between the house and barn. When the enemy reached the head of the lane, they put spurs to their horses, each trying to be the first to catch a Yankee. On they came, across the creek, yelling: 'Surrender, you damned yanks!' Moments seemed like hours as we sighted our rifles and waited for the signal gun.

"The advance was less than two rods from us, when three shots from the haymow took down the leading horse, which fell on the rider and held him down during the fight, after which he was taken prisoner. Other shots quickly followed, killing eight horses and wounding several men. The others quickly dismounted and, running back, took shelter behind the fences. During their confusion, we had time to reload our guns, and as some loaded quicker than others, we kept up a continuous fire until the enemy (was) driven away.

When the fight had continued for some time, I noticed a man sitting on his horse in a very dignified manner who, we afterwards learned, was the captain in charge of the command. He was out of my range but I took careful aim and fired. As he did not heed my salute, I gave him two more charges of powder and ball. Those familiar with the old musket know that this meant at the end of my gun. He had occasion to dismount and lead his horse further back. I yelled that I had to do something on account of my shoulder. This, of course, was done in jest, and the other boys began yelling and asking why they didn't come and take the 'damned Yanks,' if they wanted us.

"The Confederates finally withdrew, and when the smoke had cleared away, we found two dead rebels, several wounded, and two dead horses. We took three prisoners and three horses who broke from their riders and came to us. Jim Flannigan was mounted on one of the captured horses and sent to camp, and Charles Kraus, on another, was dispatched to the remainder of the company, which was nowhere to be seen at that time.

"We finished loading our wagons, and prepared to return to camp. Our loss was Sergeant Holmes, Charles Liscomb, and Sam Louden, slightly wounded, one mule killed and a wagon- tongue broken. We had three good horses to return to Uncle Sam for the dead mule."

One of the two men sent back on a captured horse brought up the balance of the Second Minnesota. The Confederates, seeing them displayed as skirmishers, retreated when concerned that their unit might be outflanked. Ironically, the other rider was able to warn three Union officers, including his own brigade commander, Colonel Van Derveer, who was riding into the path of the retreating rebels. Van Derveer expressed his gratitude in Complimentary Orders published in the St. Paul Pioneer, 28 February 1863. Sergeant Holmes was promoted to lieutenant and given an inscribed sword and officer's sash by the members of his company, and Brigadier General James B. Steedman presented him with an ivory-handled revolver. Even President Lincoln heard of the incident, and it was reported in the eastern newspapers. Out of this one incident, involving just one company, eight Congressional Medals of Honor were awarded to the known survivors, although all of the men in the action were entitled to them.

Not awarded the Congressional Medal of Honor because of death or unknown location were Homer Barnard, who died on February 28, 1864, Nelson Crandell, who died at Chattanooga on January 15, 1864, Charles Kraus, who was mortally wounded at Chattanooga; Louis Loudon, who died at St. Clair, Minnesota, after the war; Samuel

Louden, who was killed at Missionary Ridge in November 25, 1863; Charles Liscom and Samuel Leslie both unknown."

Post War Years

John returned to Minnesota but did not stay long. By 1870 he had moved to Scott County, Iowa, where he worked in the Davenport Post Office until his retirement. On 13 July 1881 he married Mary Middleton, daughter of J.N. and Mary Gilchrist Middleton. Following her death he married Margaret Peters in 1888. Two children were born to them, Annie Francis and William John. In September 1897 the U.S. War Department awarded long overdue the Medal of Honor to him. Mr. Vale died 4 February 1909 and is buried in Oakdale Cemetery in Davenport, Iowa.

Compiled by Marilyn Burbank, Rochester Chapter NSDAR

Samuel Wright 1828-1918

Medal of Honor
Action: Nolensville, Tennessee
Date: February 15, 1863

Early Years

Samuel Wright and his twin, Alexander, were born January 20, 1828 in Harrison County, Indiana, probably in Posey Township. According to the bio information found with Billion Graves, his parents were Joseph Wright and Catherine McRae. The 1850 census states that widowed Catherine Wright was the head of the household that included the twins, one additional son, Joseph, and one daughter, Nancy. All four of the children were born in Indiana while Catherine was born in South Carolina. Later census records state that Samuel's deceased father was born in Kentucky. His brothers, Alexander and Joseph, were identified as farmers, while Samuel is listed as a carpenter. It is not known what type or how much schooling Samuel had, but he could read and write.

Sometime after 1850, Samuel married Susan F. Armstrong. They began their married life in Webster Township of Harrison County, Indiana but she died sometime before 1857 in New Albany, Indiana. The cause of her death is unknown. They had no children.

Probably at loose ends after the death of his young wife, Samuel Wright was next found in Blue Earth County, Minnesota in September of 1857. Living in the same boarding house with Samuel, were a number of young, unmarried men with various occupations that would be useful in developing the area that was soon to become a state. The anticipated statehood promised a bright future for all, especially for Samuel, 29 years old and a carpenter.

In 1860 Samuel was the only boarder in the home of George W. Wolf in Nicollet Township of Nicollet County, Minnesota. Samuel was probably attracted to the family since, they too, came from Indiana. Nicollet County is an adjacent to Blue Earth County. Samuel Wright's enlistment papers state that his home was in the now extinct town of Swan Lake, Blue Earth County, Minnesota. The lake from which the town received its name is known for its attraction for ducks. It is wondered if Samuel enjoyed shooting them.

Civil War Years

According to the Muster-out rolls of Captain Beaty, Samuel Wright was enlisted for three years in the Union Army at Mankato on Jun 23, 1861 by Captain Dickinson. He was mustered into the 2nd Minnesota Volunteer Infantry on 15 July 1861 at Fort Snelling, Minnesota with other men from Blue Earth and Ramsey Counties making up Company H. (12). He was promoted to Corporal on 01 Jan 1862.

Company H, Minnesota 2nd Regiment took part in many battles but it is not known in which of these Samuel Wright participated. During the time that Corporal Wright was a part of Company H the Regiment is known to have been at the Battle of Mill Springs, Siege of Corinth, Battle of Perryville, Battle of Stone River, the Tullahoma Campaign, Battle of Chickamauga and the Siege of Chattanooga.

It was after the Battle of Stone River on the 15th of February 1863 while Company H was stationed outside of Murfreesboro in Nolensville, Tennessee that Corporal Samuel Wright participated in the action that was worthy of receiving the Medal of Honor.

According to historian Roger Norland as reported in the *Mankato Free Press*, "It was February 15, 1863 in Tennessee, a group of men went to forage for food for their mules. They stumbled upon a corncrib and began to load up the contents when Confederate soldiers surprised them. Greatly outnumbered and essentially surrounded, the men hid in the crib and opened fire. By the time the rest of the Union group appeared to help, over 100 Confederate soldiers were firing at the men. The men crawled out of the crib and continued to fight. They captured three Confederate soldiers, rounded up seven of their horses and confiscated many weapons. The Confederates retreated, leaving three wounded soldiers and a dead mule."

On the 14 March 1863, Samuel Wright was detailed for extra duty under Lt. Col. Bishop. His great granddaughter stated that he was a wheelwright and was detached from Company H apparently to serve as the Brigade wagon maker until he was mustered out of the service on the 14th of July 1864 when his three years enlistment was over.

It is known that Samuel Wright was in Chattanooga (Sep 24-Nov 23, 1863) since the only picture known to be of him was taken on Lookout Mountain with a group of his buddies. The buddies were seen sitting in the background while each man took his turn standing on a mountain ledge in the center to have their picture taken.

Post War Years

Corporal Wright did not return to Minnesota after his service was over, but instead went to his birthplace of Harrison County, Indiana where, on 25 April 1865, he married Permelia A. McRae. Permelia was "the girl next door" having been born on 16 Jun 1842 on a neighboring farm. The couple lived in Indiana for the first years of their marriage. They had four children: Lorah, who had a twin that died in infancy, Charles, and Nellie.

Nellie was the youngest child and she was born in June of 1882. Sometime after her birth, the family moved to a farm on the Sedgwick-Harvey County line in Kansas. According to the 1880 Federal Census record of Harrison Co, Indiana and the 1900 census of Sedgwick County, Kansas, Samuel now earned his living as a farmer. It was noted in Samuel's obituary that he was a member of the Garfield Post of the GAR.

After his wife died on 05 Oct 1899, Samuel lived with various children. In 1900 Charlie and Nellie were living with him, but by 1910 he was living with his daughter Lorah Wright Baird and her family in Wichita. By 1915 he had moved in with Nellie Wright Kohl and her family in Furley, Kansas. At the time of his death at the age of 90 on July 7, 1918, he was living once again with the Sydney family in Wichita, Kansas. He died at the home of his son C. F. "Charlie" Wright in Triune, Kansas while visiting.

He is buried next to his wife at Maple Grove Cemetery in Wichita, Kansas. Beside their twin marker, there is a second marker denoting that Corporal Wright was a recipient of the Medal of Honor.

In 2012 Christian Kramer, a Past Department (State) Commander for the Disabled American Veterans of Kansas contacted Lois Nixon to obtain information about Corporal Wright to be included in his presentations before schools and civic groups. He was investigating recipients of the Medal of Honor who were buried in Kansas with future intentions of writing a book.

Added by: Don Morfe

Compiled by Beth Cooper Zimmer
Anthony Wayne Chapter NSDAR

INDIAN CAMPAIGNS

After the Civil War the floodgates opened and people from the east and Europe headed west as land west of the Mississippi was becoming available for settlement. Driving forces behind that push was population pressure, opportunity, and the Manifest Destiny, which held that the United States was destined to expand from coast to coast on the North American continent. This entailed invading territory that had been the home to the indigenous peoples for centuries. Some land was obtained by the United States Government through treaties—most often broken—and some by force.

Sometimes white settlement in these areas was peaceful; often it was not as the native peoples disputed occupancy and ownership. The U.S. Army was called in to protect white settlers from "hostile Indians." The result was the Indian Campaigns. Many of the "Indian Fighters" were drawn from the ranks of the military after the Civil War. The first Medal of Honor awarded to a Minnesota man for his part in that campaign was for action seen in 1869; the last for action in 1898.

June Gossler Anderson

INDIAN CAMPAIGNS

1869-1898

George Emerson Albee 1845-1918

Medal of Honor
Conflict: Brazos River, Texas
Date: October. 28, 1869

Early Years
George Emerson Albee was the first child born to Maria S. (Gould) and Otis A. Albee, the 27th of January 1845 in Lisbon, Grafton County, New Hampshire. Eventually the family moved to Madison, Dane County, Wisconsin where they settled on a farm. By 1860 the family had grown to include an additional three children, Mary K., age 5, Francis, age 2 and Ellen G., age 2 months.

During his military service George married Mary Elizabeth (Hawes) on July 11, 1872 and to them were born two daughters, Mab Corbin Albee, in 1873 at Fort Brown, Cameron, Texas and Maria Hawes Albee, in 1883 at Baraboo, Sauk County, Wisconsin.

Civil War
At age 17 George Albee enlisted in Company G Berdan's Sharpshooters on June 25, 1862 in Owatonna, Steele County, Minnesota, serving from 1862, 1863-1878. After two months in the field he was wounded at the Second Battle of Bull Run on August 29. He was with a group that crossed an open field under a heavy fire, and took position in a small ditch, where they went to work as sharpshooters. This encounter took the life of two and wounded seven. Soon afterwards, Albee was discharged for disability. In 1863 he enlisted again as an artilleryman in the 3rd Wisconsin Light Artillery but was discharged to accept a commission as 2nd Lieutenant in the 36th Wisconsin Infantry; he was later promoted to 1st lieutenant.

Indian Campaign
After the Civil War, Albee served as 2nd Lieutenant in the 36th U.S. Colored Infantry (1866), 2nd Lieutenant 41st U.S. Infantry (1866–1869), 1st Lieutenant, 41st U.S. Infantry (1869-1878) in the Indian Campaign. In Texas on October 28, 1869 while serving with the 41st United States Infantry Regiment, he led a wild charge with only two men against a war party of eleven and drove them off a vital hill territory. Albee was awarded the Medal of Honor in January 18, 1894 for this action at Brazos River.

Post Military Life

George Albee retired from the US Army in 1878, and later became Captain of the "National Blues" Company D 2nd Regiment Connecticut National Guard in 1891. Shortly thereafter, Albee was promoted to Major and Brigade Inspector of Rifle Practice of the Connecticut National Guard.

After the war, he attained a national reputation as an expert marksman among American rifleman as the winner of the rapid and accuracy contests. He said, "Any success I have had in the profession of arms is due to the fact that I was properly started in Company G, 1st United States Sharpshooters."

With his lifelong interest and expertise, George pursued a career in firearms and their development. He was employed by Winchester Repeating Arms Co. of New Haven, Connecticut in developing the Hotchkiss rifle and became a company exhibition shooter. In addition, Mr. Albee is known to have received at least two patents pertaining to a magazine for a pump action rifle and the other for a sight of which accompanies the Volcanic Arms no.2 Navy lever action pistol.

By 1900, the family had moved to New Haven, Connecticut living on Harvard Avenue. The youngest daughter, Maria, remained at home. Daughter Mab was married and living in Killingly, Connecticut.

On January 6, 1907, George's wife, Mary, died. He then married Fredericka Strong on June 20, 1910 and they resided in Maryland.

George E. Albee died March 24, 1918 in Laurel, Prince George's County, Maryland and is buried at Arlington National Cemetery, Plot: Section 2, Site 850ES.

The Library of Virginia, Richmond, Virginia contains the 1864 diary of George E. Albee (1845–1918) that he kept while serving with the 3rd Wisconsin Light Artillery and the 36th Wisconsin Infantry, Company F. Topics include camp life, troop movements, a list of soldiers in his company, the Battle of Cold Harbor, the Siege of Petersburg, the Battle of Ream's Station, his imprisonment at Libby Prison in Richmond, and his exchange, and his return to Madison, Wisconsin, after visiting family members in New Hampshire. Also included is a pass dated 22 January 1864.

Compiled by Dianne Lawson
Josiah Edson Chapter NSDAR

Oscar Rudolph Burkard 1877-1950

Medal of Honor
Conflict: Bear Island Reservation of the Chippewa
Date: October, 1898

Early Years

Born in Achern, Germany, on December 21, 1877, Oscar immigrated to the United States in 1895 and in 1898 enlisted in the military at Hay Creek, Minnesota. He was assigned to the 3rd U.S. Infantry at Fort Snelling. He served as a private in the Hospital Corps and was present as an acting hospital steward at the Battle of Sugar Point/ Battle of Leach Lake on October 5, 1898. He married Emma P. (Bernhard) Burkard (1881-1951). His known children are Elsie, Katherine and Emma Burkard.

Indian Campaign

In October 1898 an Indian uprising occurred at the Bear Island Reservation of the Chippewa in Minnesota. It was to be the last major conflict of the Indian Campaigns, though in and of itself this action was little more than resistance of a few hundred Indians against the execution of an order from the U.S. Government. Even so, in the brief battle between 100 Army regulars that accompanied a United States Marshall in efforts to execute the order, seven soldiers were killed and sixteen wounded. Hospital Steward, Army Private Oscar Burkard, was cited for his own distinguished bravery in this action. During the battle, he rescued several soldiers while under heavy fire from the Pillagers and continued to do so throughout the day. He was later awarded the Medal of Honor "for distinguished bravery in action against hostile Indians" and officially received the award on August 21, 1899. Aside from being the only non-combatant to be decorated from that engagement, Burkard was also the last man to receive the medal during the Indian Wars.

Post Military Life

Seeing service during World War I, he retired at the rank of Major on October 31, 1930. He was a member of the Board of Education in Rome, NY. He died in Rome, New York on February 18, 1950 at the age of 72 and is buried in Rome Cemetery.

Compiled by Diana Dickinson Lynch, Monument Chapter NSDAR

Denis Byrne 1828-1905

Medal of Honor
Conflict: Battles against the Sioux
Date: October 1876 - January 1877

Early Years

Denis Byrne was born in Wexford, Ireland in May, 1828 and emigrated to America before 1860. He initially settled in New York City, and enlisted for five years in the U.S. Army on March 16, 1858, in New York stating his occupation at the time as shoemaker. He was sent to the frontier to serve with the 5th U.S. Infantry. A career soldier, he would spend the majority of his life in the military.

Indian Campaign

The 5th U.S. Infantry spent the Civil War in the territory of New Mexico. Byrne re-enlisted January 16, 1863 at Albuquerque, New Mexico. When the Civil War ended and the bulk of the Regular Army returned from war service in the east to frontier duty in the west, the 5th Infantry moved slightly in the other direction, transferring from New Mexico to Kansas. Byrne is listed on records at Ft. Bliss, Texas from 1866. By October, 1868 the 5th Infantry was strung out across seven different posts in western Kansas, with headquarters at Fort Riley. Congress expanded the Army to 41 infantry regiments in July, 1866; then reduced them to 25 in March, 1869. The 5th absorbed half of the 37th Infantry, including its commander, Colonel and Brevet Major General Nelson A. Miles. Under his command, the 5th, with some companies operating at times as mounted infantry, took part in many of the major Indian wars of the next twelve years.

From 1865 to 1889, Fort Hays was a key frontier post for the United States Army during the Indian Wars, serving as a base of operations for combat forces and a supply point for Fort Dodge and Camp Supply to the south. Major General Philip Sheridan, supported by Lt. Col. George Custer and the 7th Cavalry Regiment, used it as his headquarters during his 1868-1869 campaign against the Cheyenne and the Kiowa. Both Buffalo Bill Cody and Wild Bill Hickok served as Army scouts at Fort Hays during this period. Custer and the 7th Cavalry continued to operate from the fort when Col. Miles assumed command in April, 1869. Miles and the 5th Infantry Regiment were assigned to protect the railroad from Indian attacks as its construction extended west into Colorado Territory. In 1871, Custer and the 7th Cavalry were reassigned to the South, and Miles and the 5th Infantry headquarters relocated to Fort Leavenworth, Kansas.

Byrne's commanding officer, Lt. William Reed of the 5th Infantry, is mentioned by Buffalo Bill Cody as someone he hunted buffalo with near Ft. Hays. According to Byrne's military record, he re-enlisted in 1868 at Fort Hayes, was discharged Jan 16, 1871, a sergeant under Lt. Reed with exceptional service at Ft. Hays. He also re-enlisted on that date. And Byrne is shown on records at Ft. Leavenworth in 1873.

From July 1874 to February 1875, Miles led a mixed force of the 5th Infantry and 6th Cavalry in campaigns against the Southern Cheyenne, Comanche and Kiowa Indians along the Red and Washita Rivers in Indian Territory and Texas. The 5th Infantry also played a major role in the Red River War.

Byrne re-enlisted again in 1876. The Battle of Cedar Creek was part of the Great Sioux War of 1876; that summer the Battle of Little Bighorn and Custer's Last Stand had been a major victory for the Sioux and Cheyenne Indians.

In the aftermath of the Battle of the Little Bighorn, the U.S. Army sent reinforcements to Montana to scour the northern plains after Custer's defeat, forcing the Sioux in Montana Territory onto reservations. One of these units was the 5th Infantry Regiment led by Miles from Fort Leavenworth, Kansas to the Yellowstone River in Montana Territory, where he came under command of General Alfred Terry.

Byrne is found moving with the 5th under Miles into Montana Territory. He is shown on military documents from Fort Ellis, Montana. He is also listed as on the rolls of the Army Quartermaster's Department, Fort Custer, Montana as a Wagon and Forage Master, 1877-1880, and he is on the 1880 federal census for Fort Custer.

Terry's men moved to Glendive on the Yellowstone River where he established winter quarters. Under Terry, Miles' troops set up a temporary base at the mouth of the Tongue River. Supply trains attempting to reach Terry's men were ambushed by Sioux warriors several times in October, 1876. After a few engagements Indian messengers contacted the commander of one wagon train suggesting a meeting between Miles and Sitting Bull at Cedar Creek. The two men met on October 20th. Miles demanded the surrender of all the Sioux while Sitting Bull wanted to trade for ammunition so he could hunt buffalo. The two agreed to meet again the following day.

On the 21st Miles again demanded an Indian surrender while Sitting Bull demanded a halt to white encroachment on Sioux territory. The talks broke down and a gunfight erupted in which two soldiers and five Indians were killed. The Sioux withdrew and were chased for about eight miles by the army. Crucially the Indians abandoned food, horses and their shelters. With no means of surviving the winter, some 2,000 surrendered on October 27th. Sitting Bull and his more ardent warriors were not among them. They were headed for Canada and the army engaged in a winter campaign in pursuit of the renegades.

By the start of Miles' winter campaign of 1877, during which he drove his troops on a forced march across Montana and eventually intercepted the Nez Percé band led by Chief Joseph, Byrne had become a veteran Indian fighter and had reached the rank of Sergeant in Company G, 5th U.S. Infantry. Between October 1876 and January 1877, he participated in many battles against the Sioux, most notably, against Chief Sitting Bull at Cedar Creek, Montana. On the latter date Byrne and the 5th Infantry defeated a band of Sioux and Cheyenne at Wolf Mountain, Montana. Byrne was awarded the Congressional Medal of Honor for his fighting in these battles. In total, there were 31 men who received Medals of Honor for their efforts in this period, the Irish-born soldiers well represented with eleven awards. Byrne's citation, issued 27 April 1877, reads "Gallantry in engagements."

Post-Military Life
After finally leaving the military, Byrne homesteaded 160 acres in Minnesota on 31 Mar 1888. In 1890, he filed for a Civil War pension in Minnesota.

On the Minnesota State and Territorial Census for 1895 Denis Byrne was living in Melville, Renville County, Minnesota, a boarder with Joseph Haggitt (also of the 5th Infantry) and wife Cora. He was age 60, a farmer, and claimed he had been in the district and state for six years. On the 1900 Federal Census he was single, still boarding with Haggitt and his wife. He had been in the country for forty years, and had been naturalized in 1860.
This time he listed his occupation as "old soldier".

Byrne died in on the last day of 1905 at the age of 72 at Bird Island, Renville County, Minnesota, and is buried in Calvary Cemetery, St. Paul, Ramsey County, Minnesota.

Compiled by Kathleen M. Barrett Huston,
Lake Minnetonka Chapter NSDAR

Harry LeRoy Hawthorne 1859-1948

Medal of Honor
Conflict: Wounded Knee Creek, South Dakota
Date: December 29, 1890.

Early Years

Harry LeRoy Hawthorne was born in Minnesota to LeRoy Hawthorne from Morgantown Virginia (now West Virginia) and Louise Tate Smith of Boone County, Kentucky on November 27th, 1859. Although not stated, his probable birthplace was in or close to Winona as his father ran a hotel in that city during the 1850s, and his only sibling was a sister named Winona born in 1856. Due to hard times in the hotel business, LeRoy moved his family back to his previous home in Newport, Kentucky in 1861 where talk centered on the prospects of war.

Harry's inspiration for a career in the military may have come from his father who was an early Kentucky volunteer in the Union Army, serving in the 23rd Kentucky Volunteer Infantry Regiment which later became a part of the Army of the Cumberland which joined the troops of General William Tecumseh Sherman for his infamous "March to the Sea." In 1868 when Harry was nine years old his father, LeRoy Hawthorne, left the army as a brevet major.

Appointed from Kentucky to the U.S. Naval Academy, Harry LeRoy Hawthorne served as a Midshipman from 1878 until graduation in 1882; then as a Cadet Engineer until 1884 when he took a commission in the U.S. Army serving in the Second U.S. Artillery. According to the *Encyclopedia of Northern Kentucky,* "Minnesota born Col. Harry LeRoy Hawthorne was stationed for a time at the Newport Barracks and his parents lived nearby in the City of Newport...."

Indian Campaign

The year after LeRoy Hawthorne left Minnesota for Kentucky, trouble was brewing back up in the North Country. The Sioux, as their enemies called them, or Lakota, their preferred name, after losing their lands to coerced treaties and facing starvation from non-forthcoming annuities promised by the U.S. government, staged a bloody but short-lived uprising in August of 1862. The defeated Lakota were banished from Minnesota and pursued by the U.S. military for the next thirty years. The *Military Times* sets the scene for the final event: "On the morning of December 29, 1890, the Sioux chief, Big

Foot, and some 350 of his followers camped on the banks of Wounded Knee Creek, a tributary of the White River. Surrounding their camp was a force of U.S. troops charged with the responsibility of arresting Big Foot and disarming his warriors. In a frantic attempt to return to their glory days, many Sioux sought deliverance in a new mysticism preached by a Paiute shaman called Wovoka, and fought fiercely believing that their "Ghost Shirts" would protect them from the bluecoats' bullets. In the savage battle twenty soldiers distinguished themselves to the degree that they were awarded the Medal of Honor...." (Official reports listed 25 U.S. soldiers killed, 34 wounded.)

Thirty-one year old Harry was there, fighting in the Indian Wars at Wounded Knee, South Dakota as the Second Lieutenant of A Battery, Second U.S. Artillery. Attached to Captain Capron's Light Battery E, First Artillery Harry was commanding a platoon of two Hotchkiss steel mountain rifles when he was severely wounded. He was awarded the Medal of Honor on the 11th of October, 1892 for "gallantry, coolness, discretion and effect in handling and serving the guns of his command in action against hostile Sioux Indians on Wounded Knee Creek, South Dakota on the 29th of December, 1890." Harry's Medal of Honor citation reads "for distinguished conduct in battle with hostile Indians."

Three hundred Sioux--men, women, and children--caught by surprise in the crossfire, were killed in this battle which has later been deemed a massacre. The Lakota, in an effort to correct this tragic history, have embarked on a campaign to rescind the medals of the twenty U.S. soldiers who were awarded the Medal of Honor for their actions in the Wounded Knee Massacre.

Post Campaign
Harry LeRoy Hawthorne was a career military officer and was promoted through the ranks to Colonel. After the Battle of Wounded Knee he attended the War College and served during the Spanish American War, as a military attaché to Japan from 1909-1911. Retiring as a Colonel in 1914 he was recalled to serve during WWI as Inspector General in the Panama Canal Zone and was awarded the Purple Heart and a Silver Star. An expert in military weaponry, there is some evidence to suggest that he lectured and possibly taught classes on this subject.

Little note has been made of Harry's personal life other than he had a daughter, Marion M. Abbate, born in 1906, and his wife's name was Elizabeth.

Harry died on April 10th, 1948 and is buried at Arlington National Cemetery. Nearby are the graves of his father, LeRoy R. Hawthorne, Brevet Major U.S. Army, his mother Louise Hawthorne, his sister Winona Hawthorne Buck and her husband William Langdon Buck, Colonel, U.S. Army.

In addition to his military career, Harry LeRoy Hawthorne had the soul of a poet. His poem, *Song of the Bullet*, was among the second place prize winners published in *Munsey's Magazine*, Vol. 15, p. 254.

Song of the Bullet

In the crystal crevice deep
  When the plastic world was cold
  While the peopled cycles rolled
Formless lay I, dulled in sleep
  Chaos born and old.

Then the battle's trumpet blare
  Echoing through the woody glen
  Woke me in my rock clad den
Strode I forth in upper air---
  Arbiter of men.

In the fierce tumultuous fray
  Never a recreant I, nor slow;
  Eager I rush to meet the foe,
Swift along my pathless way,
  Singing as I go.

Whose the fate that with me flies?
  Neither know I, aye nor care
  Haply a courtier debonair
Haply only a drummer dies,
  Sobbing a childish prayer.

Harry LeRoy Hawthorne

Compiled by June Gossler Anderson
Anoka Chapter NSDAR

Eli Lundy Huggins 1842-1929

Medal of Honor
Conflict: O'Fallon Creek, Montana
Date: April 1, 1880

Early Years

Eli Lundy Huggins was born on August 1, 1842 in Schuyler County, Illinois. One of eight children he was the son of Rev. Alexander Huggins and Lydia Pettijohn. The family moved to Nicolet County, Minnesota, being one of the first settlers in the county. His father and mother served as missionary assistants at the Dakota Indian Missions at Lac qui Parle and Traverse des Sioux. At 18, Eli left Hamline University to enlist during the call for troops at the beginning of the Civil War. He entered as a private and then corporal of Company E, Second Minnesota Infantry on July 5, 1861.

Civil War

The second Minnesota left the state for Washington on October 14. Corporal Huggins fought in the Battle at Mill Springs, Kentucky on January 19, 1862. Here the Confederate army was completely overrun. The regiment was later involved with the siege at Corinth, Mississippi in May of 1862. In October of that year, Huggins fought in the Battle at Perryville, Kentucky, under the command of Major General Alexander McDowell McCook against General Braxton Bragg. In late March of 1863, Huggins participated in the two-day battle at Chapel Hill, Tennessee, and then at Chickamauga on September 10. At Chickamauga, Eli Huggins was wounded and captured by the Confederates. He was discharged from the army at Nashville, Tennessee on September 27, 1865.

Indian Campaign

Huggins reenlisted in late February 1866 and received an appointment in the Regular Army as Lieutenant in the Second Artillery. He served several years on the Pacific Coast, Alaska, and later on the Atlantic Coast. In 1867, after the United States purchased Alaska from Russia, Huggins was transferred to Fort Kodiak in Alaska. It is here that he met his partner, Aleksandra Kashevarova, in 1868. On October 5, 1869, his first and only child, Zinovil Zenoa Huggins, was born on Kodiak Island, Alaska. Eli was transferred to the Second Cavalry on April 11, 1879, becoming captain of the unit later that month. The unit primarily served in Montana dealing with hostile Indians. Huggins was stationed at Fort Keogh through November of 1880.

On April 1, 1880, Captain Huggins was in command of troops in an engagement with Indians at O'Fallon Creek, Montana. He described the campaign, "in one of these pursuits in March of 1880 in the region between Missouri and Yellowstone, every member of my troop was frozen, some of them seriously...brought into Fort Keogh at different times more than a thousand Indians, who surrendered in the forks of the Missouri and Yellowstone. Among these Indians were Rain-in-the Face, Spotted Eagle, and Iron Shield." It is for this that Captain Huggins was awarded the Medal of Honor in action against the hostile Ogallala Sioux at O'Fallon Creek.

General Philip Sheridan wrote on March 24, 1880, concerning Huggins, "A party of 30-40 Sioux ran off about 30 ponies belonging to enlisted Crow scouts at Fort Custer, Montana. Forty- four officers and men went in pursuit and they traveled sixty-five miles in eleven hours. They overtook and engaged the hostiles, recaptured sixteen of the stolen stock. Captain Huggins with Troop E of the Second Cavalry surprised the Indian camp on April 1, captured five Indians, forty-six ponies, and some arms."

The illustrious military career of Eli Huggins continued until his retirement in 1903. He served special duty for the Adjutant General's office in Washington until January of 1881. He commanded an escort for a surveying party in Montana from May through October of 1862.

At the outbreak of the Spanish-American War in 1898, Eli Huggins applied for and was granted an appointment as Colonel of a volunteer regiment composed of men immune to yellow fever. He was mustered out the following year and returned to the Regular Army as Major of the Sixth Calvary.

Photo of *Winona, A Dakota Legend and Other Poems* by Eli L Huggins. 1890.

In August of 1900, Huggins sailed to China to participant in subduing the Boxer Uprising. Through 1901 he served in the Philippines as Lieutenant Colonel of the Third Calvary. On November 6, 1901, Huggins was transferred to the Thirteenth Cavalry and later that month, became Colonel to the Second Cavalry, stationed at Fort Meyer, Virginia. The day before his retirement on February 23, 1903, he was commissioned a Brigadier General.

Post Military Life

After his retirement, General Huggins and his sister, Jane Sloan Huggins Holtsclaw (1834 – 1920), moved to Muskogee, Indian Territory. He had invested heavily in real estate in the area.

In 1910, his residence was listed as Mission, San Diego, California. In 1920 he had moved to East San Diego, California. The 1920 census lists his sister Jane, a boarder, Cecile M. Alexander, and Eli's grandnephew, Alfred Alexander, living with him in East San Diego.

Throughout his life, Eli Huggins was a writer and published author. He wrote an article titled Men and Things in Alaska that appeared in the Minnesota periodical, The Citizen Magazine, in late November of 1874. In 1890, Huggins published his most famous work; a volume of poems called Winona, A Dakota Legend and Other Poems. In total, 31 works, categorized as Folklore, Poetry, History, Legends, Registers, Records, and Correspondence are attributed to Eli Lundy Higgins

It should also be noted that he spoke French, Spanish, Portuguese, and Russian as well as being fluent in the language of the Sioux.

Eli Lundy Huggins died on October 22, 1929 and was buried in the Mountain View Cemetery, Oakland, California. Upon his death, the Chief of Staff of the U.S Army, General C.P. Summerall, wrote of General Huggins saying, "the career of General Huggins, extending over a period of more than forty years, was distinguished by gallantry in action, devotion to duty, and efficiency and reliability in the performance of all tasks assigned to him.

The Medal of Honor awarded him bears ample testimony to his bravery and fearlessness as a soldier. His death marked the passing of another officer from the rapidly disappearing ranks of veterans of the Civil War."

Compiled by Cynthia Jorgenrud , Anoka Chapter NSDAR

Albert Walter McMillan 1862-1948

Medal of Honor
Conflict: Wounded Knee Creek, South Dakota
Date: December 29, 1890

Early Years

Albert Walter McMillan was born on October 13, 1862 along with his twin brother, Thomas Erskine, to Judge Samuel James Renwick McMillan and Harriet Elizabeth Butler in Stillwater, Washington County, Minnesota. The twins had nine siblings. Thomas died at the age of four. Albert outlived all of his siblings, dying in 1948.

An intelligent young man and son of a sitting senator, Albert McMillan studied at Princeton College and during his sophomore year was president of the Class of 1884. In the summer of 1883, he worked as a clerk for the Senate Judiciary Committee but did not return to Princeton for his senior year. According to that college's annual, *The Nassau Herald,* "His restless spirit took him west for more 'action' than a college course afforded."

Indian Conflict

McMillan's travels west saw him enlist in the Army at Jefferson Barracks, Missouri, on August 15, 1887. He listed his age as twenty-five, birthplace as Baltimore, Maryland and profession as school teacher. Albert was assigned as a private in Captain Isley's E Troop, 7th Cavalry where the young man's intelligence and drive saw him quickly rise to the rank of sergeant in his troop and was later promoted to Sergeant Major of his Regiment when the Regiment's Sergeant Major, Richard W. Corwine was killed along with 29 other soldiers on December 29, 1890 and Colonel Forsyth saw fit to recommend to the adjutant general of the Army that Albert fill the vacancy.

A number of soldiers' actions on 29 December, particularly regarding dislodging Indians from the ravine, caught the attention of the officers of E Troop, especially two privates, Mosheim Feaster and Thomas Sullivan. On March 26, Sergeant Major McMillan and Sergeant William G. Austin, both of E Troop during the battle, provided depositions regarding the conduct of Sullivan and Feaster. On April 17 and 18, 1891, 1st Lt Horatio G. Sickel and 2nd Lt. Sedgwick Rice wrote recommendations not only for Sullivan and Feaster for the Medal of Honor, but for three of their non-commissioned officers as well, including McMillan. Curiously, five days after Sickel recommended that

McMillan be awarded a Medal of Honor, the regiment's Sergeant Major voluntarily requested that he be reduced to the rank of private. Regardless of McMillan's request for reduction, on May 5, Captain Isley and Colonel Forsyth endorsed Sickel's recommendation for a medal. The department commander, Brigadier General Wesley Merritt, forwarded the request on to the adjutant general with no endorsement, presumably because he played no role in the previous winter's campaign. The adjutant general's office prepared the following summation and forwarded it to the commanding general of the Army, Major General John M. Schofield, who recommended approval:

"Case of Sergt. Albert W. McMillan, Troop E, 7th Cavalry, For a medal of honor. 1st Lieut. H. G. Sickel, 7th Cavy., recommends this man for a medal of honor for conspicuous bravery at Wounded Knee, S.D., Dec. 29, 1890, as follows: 'Troop E being engaged, dismounted, with Indians concealed in a ravine, McMillan, by his coolness and bravery attracted the attention of his troop commander, rendering him much assistance by placing the men on the skirmish line in good positions, directing their fire and encouraging them by good example; he frequently (exposed) himself to close fire from the ravine in order to obtain an advantage over the concealed Indians and made every effort to dislodge them.

Approved by the troop and regimental commanders and forwarded by the department commander. Application appears to be made under A.R. 175, which says 'medals of honor will be awarded, by the President, to officers or enlisted men who have distinguished themselves in action.' If awarded, the medal should be engraved as follows:
'The congress to Sergt. Albert W. McMillan, Troop "E", 7th Cavalry, For bravery at Wounded Knee Creek, S.D., Dec. 29, 1890" 4th Indorsement War Department. June 16th 1891. Let the medal of honor be issued. L. A. Grant (Lewis A. Grant) Assistant Secretary of War."

Medal of Honor citation: "Sergeant Albert Walter McMillan, United States Army, for extraordinary heroism on 29 December 1890, while serving with Company E, 7th U.S. Cavalry, in action at Wounded Knee Creek, South Dakota. While engaged with Indians concealed in a ravine, Sergeant McMillan assisted the men on the skirmish line, directed their fire, encouraged them by example, and used every effort to dislodge the enemy. Awarded on 23 June 1891."

In the spring of 1892, Private McMillan ran afoul of military justice. He had been arrested, convicted, and jailed for "using vile and insulting language to a lady." During this time he was listed as absent without leave from his unit and faced a general court martial upon his return to Fort Riley. He plead guilty and faced his sentence and extended his service to "make good time" for the period in which he was absent without leave. He mustered out on September 21, 1892.

Post Military Life

Albert returned to St. Paul, Minnesota and entered the University of Minnesota where he earned a Bachelor of Law degree in 1894. He worked for West Publishing Company for a time as the legal editor. During this time he suffered a breakdown, what we would probably refer to now as Post Traumatic Stress Disorder (PTSD). Before 1900 he moved to Blaine, Washington and later to Brawley, California. He fell on hard times and never recovered, working as a hired man, teamster, farmer and truck driver.

During World War I, he served with the American Red Cross traveling to England in September 1918. Following WWI he returned to Los Angeles and eventually retired in Sacramento, California. Albert never married.

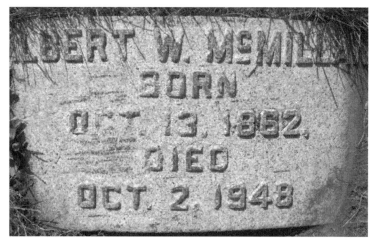

Albert Walter McMillan died in Sacramento on October 2, 1948. His body was returned to St. Paul where he was buried in a plot next to his father, mother and twin brother Thomas in Oakland Cemetery, St. Paul, Ramsey County, Minnesota.

Compiled by Merrilee Carlson, Nathan Hale Chapter NSDAR

Charles H. Montrose 1853-1913

Medal of Honor
Conflict: Battle of Cedar Creek, Montana
Dates: October 21, 1876-January 8, 1877

Early Years
Charles Montrose was born in St. Paul, Minnesota in 1853 but was residing in St. Louis, Missouri on June 21, 1876 when he entered the Army at the age of twenty-two, serving in the U.S. Army, Company I of the 5th Infantry. He was part of the reinforcements sent to battle the Lakota Sioux (Chief Sitting Bull) after the losses at the Battle of Little Bighorn (Custer).

Indian Conflict
When talks between Colonel Nelson Appleton Miles, Commander of the 5th Infantry Regiment, Companies A, B, C, D, E, F, H and I and Chief Sitting Bull broke down on October 21, 1876 at Cedar Creek, the Battle of Cedar Creek (aka Big Dry Creek or Big Dry River) ensued, whereby the Indians were essentially driven north to Canada.

With the entire 5th Infantry, 15 officers and 434 enlisted men, Col. Nelson A. Miles tracked Sitting Bull's Hunkpapas through the eastern Yellowstone country. On October 20th, Miles finally ran them down on the headwaters of the East Fork of Cedar Creek, about 20 miles northwest of present-day Terry, Montana. A parley was arranged between Miles and Sitting Bull, with nearly 300 warriors perched on a nearby hill watching the proceedings. The council was long and agitated, and Miles was wary. When the talks broke off, both sides returned to their camps with the understanding that the next day fighting would replace talking.

Miles struck first, bringing his 5th Infantry up to Sitting Bull's camp on the East Fork of Cedar Creek. Another talk was attempted, but Sitting Bull abruptly left the parley. Miles moved his men forward through the valley, Capt. James S. Casey taking his Company A to the Bluffs on the left and Lt. Mason Carter taking his Company K to a knoll on the right. Flanks secured, Miles moved the rest of the 5th Infantry toward the Indian camp.

About 900 warriors were there to confront the advance, but their hearts were not in the fight. Miles' skirmishers pushed them back and the howitzers blasted them. The soldiers pushed through and gained the Lakota encampment. The Indians fell back toward Bad Route Creek and eventually fled downstream to the Yellowstone River.

Miles had only two soldiers wounded. He found five Lakota bodies on the field, and perhaps five more were wounded. By early spring of 1877 due to the continuous military campaigns and intensive diplomatic efforts most of the remaining bands had surrendered.

Pvt. Montrose was one of thirty Medal of Honor recipients from the eight Companies at the Battle of Cedar Creek. He received his Medal of Honor on April 27, 1877. His Citation read: "Gallantry in Action."

Post Military Life
Pvt. Montrose left the Army July 17, 1877. He died on October 13, 1913 and was cremated at Fresh Pond Crematorium, Middle Village, New York City, New York. His ashes were retained by his family.

Compiled by Beth Iseminger,
Associate Member Maria Sanford Chapter NSDAR

George Horace Morgan 1855-1948

Medal of Honor
Conflict: Big Dry Fork, Arizona
Date: July 17, 1882

CAPTAIN GEORGE H. MORGAN
1899

Early Years
On January 1, 1855 in St. Catherine, Quebec, Canada, George Horace Morgan was born to Delia Elizabeth Warner Morgan and Brigadier General George Nelson Morgan who became an American citizen and commander of the 1st Minnesota Volunteers during the Civil War. George was a year old when his family moved to St. Anthony, Minnesota, a small town, whose falls were to attract first a milling industry and then a change of name—Minneapolis. He was twenty-one years of age and a school teacher when he passed a competitive examination and was appointed to the United States Military Academy at West Point in 1876.

Indian Conflict
George Horace Morgan graduated from the US Military Academy, Class of 1880. These were the days of the Indian Wars, and young Lieutenant Morgan learned about the Utes and the Apaches. He entered the service in Minneapolis, Hennepin County, Minnesota in 1880 and joined the 3rd Cavalry at Fort Washakie, Wyoming as a second lieutenant in the United States Army. Having a way with animals, human and otherwise, he was a popular officer. He knew horses, which was well for a cavalryman, and he also had a pet bear. "Best pet I ever had." he said. "It terrified a young lady alighting from a stage to visit friends at the Post. I rescued her gallantly and she later became my wife."

Lieutenant Morgan's first service was frontier duty at Fort Washakie, serving as a scout from October 1880 to May 1886. He spent the summer of 1882 in the field and at Whipple Barracks, Arizona. In the spring of 1882, a party of about 60 White Mountain Apache warriors coalesced under the leadership of a warrior called Na-tio-tish. In early July some of the warriors ambushed and killed four San Carlos policemen, including the police chief. After the ambush, Na-tio-tish led his band of warriors northwest through the Tonto Basin. Local Arizona settlers were greatly alarmed and demanded protection from the army which immediately sent out fourteen companies of cavalry from forts in the region. The ensuing Battle of Big Dry Wash was fought on July 17, 1882, between troops of the United States Army's 3rd Cavalry Regiment and 6th Cavalry Regiment and members of the White Mountain Apache tribe. Although the location of the battle was called "*Big Dry Wash*" in the official report, later maps called it "*Big Dry Fork,*" which is how it is cited in the four Medal of Honor citations that resulted from the battle

The first shots were fired around 3:00 pm and the battle lasted until nightfall, when a heavy thunderstorm struck, bringing rain and hail. Chief scout Al Sieber, together with fellow scout Tom Horn and soldier Lt. George H. Morgan, slipped to the banks opposite of the Apache line, and provided rifle fire for the cavalry. On the ridge overlooking the wash Lieutenant George H. Morgan, commanding the first major engagement of the battle, was exposed to enemy fire. A bullet ripped through his arm and into his body. He carried the bullet near his heart for the rest of his life.

Pressured and outgunned, the remaining Apache warriors, under the cover of darkness and the storm, slipped away on foot and retreated to a nearby Apache reservation, about 20 miles away. The site of the battle is now a historical park, in Coconino County, Arizona.

The citation accompanying George Horace Morgan's Medal of Honor reads: "For distinguished conduct in action against hostile Apache Indians at the Big Dry Wash, Arizona, July 17, 1882, by gallantly holding his ground at a critical moment and firing upon the advancing enemy until himself disabled by a shot; while 2nd Lieutenant, 3rd Cavalry, and serving as a volunteer with Lieutenant West's command of Indian scouts and Troop I, 6th Cavalry"

The lead that disabled him was a dumdum; he carried it for the rest of his life and, in the end, it killed him after all. The Indian? "When he got me," Morgan said, "he was so pleased he started to jump around and do a sort of victory dance. He was an easy target."

George Morgan was presented the Medal of Honor on July 15, 1892.

Post Military Life
George Morgan's marksmanship, that had proved so valuable that day, distinguished him in many a rifle competition from Arizona to Texas, for after he had recovered from his severe wounds—a convalescence that enabled him to continue his courtship and wed Molly Brownson of Omaha, Nebraska,—Lieutenant Morgan's duty with the Third Cavalry took him to most of the frontier posts of an expanding United States. During that time, from 1883 to 1896, five children joined the family.

Morgan served in the Spanish American War, Philippine Insurrection, Mexican Intervention, and World War I. From October 10, 1891, to October 1, 1895, he was Professor of Military Science and Tactics at the University of Minnesota. He was student as well as teacher for during this time he studied law and was admitted to the Minnesota Bar in 1895. The following year he was promoted to Captain, commanding Troup H of the Third Cavalry, which he led up San Juan Hill in the Spanish War on July 1, 1898, winning a Silver Star for gallantry and a promotion to Brevet Major.

In January 1899, he rejoined his troop and regiment at Augusta, Georgia, where he was instrumental in quelling a mutiny of volunteers. Then followed a few months of comparative quiet in assignment to Fort Myer, Virginia.

On November 23, 1899 Morgan arrived in Manila in command of the 1st Battalion, 28th U.S. Volunteer Infantry and for the next two years was in almost continual action. At Putol Bridge, Luzon, Morgan he again distinguished himself and won his second Silver Star.

After he had been mustered out of the volunteer service with his regiment, Morgan rejoined the Third Cavalry. He was aide to General Bell and Chief Commissary of the brigade in the Malavar campaign, December 1901 to April 1902. In April, he returned home and the following year was assigned as Major, 9th Cavalry, to Fort Assiniboine, Montana.

For the next two years, Major Morgan was again Professor of Military Science and Tactics at the University of Minnesota. Then he rejoined his squadron of the 9th Cavalry at Fort Riley, Kansas on October 3, 1905. While on duty there, he was member and President of the Cavalry Board, President of the Cavalry Examining Board, and at times director of the school.

From the following June until August 1909 he performed a tour of duty in the Philippines as Adjutant General at Fort William McKinley and as Justice of the Peace. Back in the United States he received his lieutenant colonelcy in the 11th Cavalry on 3 March 1911, and after a tour of duty at Fort Oglethorpe, Georgia, he was assigned to Fort Leavenworth to take the Field Officer's Course, and then in August 1913 to the Army War College.

Promoted to colonel on April 26, 1914, he commanded the 15th Cavalry at Fort Bliss, Texas, until August, when he was assigned first to the 7th Cavalry and then, in October, to the 8th Cavalry.

Morgan was chief of staff of the 13th Militia District from December 1915 until August 1916, and when the United States entered the First World War he was in command of a provisional cavalry regiment of the 10th Provisional Division. Although he was greatly disappointed that he was unable to take a regiment overseas, Colonel Morgan's experience in past wars made him invaluable in training the rapidly mobilized troops. Training and selecting cantonment sites occupied his energies, and in 1917 he again assumed command of a regiment, the 17th Cavalry at Douglas, Arizona, a command he held until his retirement on New Year's Day of 1919, five short years before the death of his beloved wife.

After retirement George Morgan settled in San Diego, California where his wife, Molly, died in 1924; then he moved to Washington, DC. He died there at age 93 when the bullet he received in the 1882 Battle of Big Dry Wash moved and struck his heart. He is buried in Section 3 of Arlington National Cemetery. The US Army honored him in 1998 by naming Camp Morgan in Bosnia after him.

Compiled by June Gossler Anderson, Anoka Chapter NSDAR

Samuel D. Phillips 1845-1915

Medal of Honor
Conflict: Muddy Creek, Montana
Date: May 7, 1877

Early Years

Samuel D. Phillips was born 28 January 1845 on a farm in Butler County, Ohio to parents John Phillips and Elizabeth McClain. In 1850, the Phillips family was living in Morgan Township, Butler County, Ohio. John Phillips was a farmer who owned land valued at $3,000. The family was large. There were eight children including 6-year-old Samuel. Also living with the family was Elizabeth's brother, William McClain. John Phillips died in October 1859. In 1860, Samuel age 15 was living with his widowed mother and three older siblings in Butler County, Illinois.

Civil War Years

On 1 September 1861, 16-year-old Samuel enlisted during the Civil War in Company B, 29th Illinois Volunteer Infantry at Cairo, Illinois. On 3 April 1862, after serving for seven months and three days, Samuel was honorably discharged for medical reasons at Pittsburg Landing, Tennessee. The medical record in Samuel's disability pension revealed that from December 27, 1861 to February 23, 1862 he was treated for pneumonia, diarrhea and typhoid fever. It is interesting to note that the Battle of Shiloh, also known as the Battle of Pittsburg Landing, was fought April 6-7, 1862. Seventeen-year-old Samuel just missed fighting in this two-day battle that resulted in more than 23,000 casualties. It was the bloodiest battle in American history at that time.

Samuel returned to civilian life and farming for fourteen years and lived in Indiana, Ohio and Illinois.

Indian Campaign

Samuel reenlisted on September 23, 1876 at St. Louis Missouri as a private in Company H, 2nd U.S. Cavalry, also known as the "Montana Battalion". A few months later, on 7 May 1877, Private Samuel D. Phillips was engaged in a battle "with hostile Sioux" for which he received the Congressional Medal of Honor for bravery.

The following excerpt from the regimental *History of the Second United States Cavalry, Part 6: 1865 to 1898, Back to the Frontier* tells the story of this battle and how Samuel won the Medal of Honor. "By April 1877, most of the cavalry Regiments of the United States was engaged in warfare with several small bands of Indians. The Cheyenne surrendered in December. Although Sitting Bull escaped into Canada, Crazy Horse surrendered in April of 1878. This left only a chief named Lame Deer and his warriors on soil claimed by the U.S. government, but the U.S. Cavalry, including the "Montana Battalion" of the Second Cavalry, was in pursuit. Marching day and night with only short breaks, the cavalrymen reached the area of an Indian encampment near Little Muddy Creek, Montana, on 6 May. At 0100 hours, 7 May 1877, after only a few hours' rest, the troopers broke camp and marched for the remainder of the night. At dawn they surprised Lame Deer's warriors. Company H charged through the village and stampeded the horses, and then the other cavalry troops charged, thoroughly routing the Indians. The village was one of the richest Indian encampments ever captured. The soldiers found many artifacts of Custer's Seventh Cavalry, including uniforms, guidons [cavalry unit pennants], and weapons. At the height of the battle, Private William Leonard became isolated from his command and defended himself for over two hours against the Indians from a position behind a rock before he was rescued. For gallantry in action, Privates William Leonard of L Troop and Samuel D. Phillips of H Troop were awarded the Medal of Honor."

Samuel was injured twice while in serving with the Second Cavalry at Fort Ellis Montana. On April 4, 1878 his hand was cut by circular saw and on July 1, 1878 his wrist was broken when he was thrown from a mule. The following year on May 22, 1879, he was honorably discharged for disability at Fort Assiniboine, Montana.

Post Military Life

On June 13, 1891, 46-year-old Samuel Phillips married 48-year-old widow Margaret Jane Murphy in Madison, Wisconsin. It was Samuel's first marriage and Margaret's third. She was twice a widow. Margaret and Samuel had no children. By 1900 the couple was living at 973 Hudson Avenue, St. Paul, Minnesota and Samuel was working as a janitor.

Private Samuel Phillips filed for a disability pension on August 15, 1892. He reported a fracture of right wrist, injury to ring finger left hand, heart trouble, asthma, deafness left ear, rheumatism and general debility. His pension was finally granted on May 19, 1899 at a rate of $6 a month. It was increased several times over the intervening years and he was receiving $22.50 a month at the time of his death in 1915.

A photograph of Samuel was not found but a pension form dated March 30, 1915, when he was 70, described him as "5' 4", dark eyes, grey hair with a florid [ruddy] complexion, weighing 180 pounds, with a right wrist that was enlarged and bent." An earlier pension form reported his hair was black.

The couple remained in St. Paul for the rest of their lives. Margaret preceded Samuel in death on January 18, 1914. She was 71 years old. Samuel D. Phillips died November 12,

1915 at the age of 70. Samuel and Margaret are buried side by side in block 46, lot 57, at St. Paul's Historic Oakland Cemetery in Ramsey County.

Compiled by Shirleen Ann Hoffman
Lake Minnetonka Chapter NSDAR

Wilbur Nelson Taylor 1846-1903

Wilbur Nelson Taylor

Medal of Honor
Conflict: Arizona Indian Campaigns.
Date: 1868 and 1869

Early Years

Wilbur Nelson Taylor, son of Thomas and Lydia (Knowles) Taylor, was born near Hampden, Maine, on December 2, 1846. He was the youngest son in a family of four boys and four girls. His life in Maine centered around Nealy's Corner, now a small crossroads but in the mid-1800s, the center of an agricultural community in the western part of Hampden.

Much of this biography was drawn from a 1966 family history written by Wilbur Nelson Taylor's son, Harold. Consistent with Harold's statement that everyone called his father Nelson, that is how this biography will refer to him.

During Nelson's teen years (ages 14-18), several of his relatives served in the Civil War: On June 6, 1864 Rodney J. Taylor died of wounds received in the Battle of the Wilderness; John W. Knowles died in Franklin, Louisiana, on April 28, 1863; and Nelson's brother Albert served in the 17th Regiment of the U.S. Infantry and later in the 7th.

Nelson worked on the family farm until after his father's death in 1865. Likely seeking adventure, he left Maine in 1866 and moved to Boston.

Indian Campaigns

Soon after arriving in Boston, Nelson enlisted in the Army and was assigned to the 8th U.S. Cavalry. He was sent to Arizona via ship to the Isthmus of Panama crossing this by land, then by ship to California, and by horseback to Arizona.

Nelson was likely among the first soldiers assigned to the 8th U.S. Cavalry. According to its history, the 8th Cavalry was organized on 21 September 1866 at Angel Island, California, following Congressional action to restore and maintain peace on the western frontier. The "Indian Wars" resulted from the clash between the hordes of settlers moving west and the Indians trying to preserve their ancestral lands and way of life. Only military means - specifically the cavalry - was perceived as an effective force against the Plains Indians and recalcitrant outlaws.

By December 1866, the Regiment Headquarters was moved from Angel Island to Camp Whipple, Arizona. It remained there for one year until moving to temporary locations at Churchill Barracks, Nevada, during December 1867 and January 1868. It left for temporary quarters at Camp Halleck, Nevada, in May 1868 and stayed there until 5 May 1870. This Arizona service was especially difficult for it involved covering vast distances with little support. It was also dangerous. The Indians were fierce fighters and were experts in conducting ambushes. The Troopers of the Eighth met every challenge.

Corporal Wilbur Nelson Taylor was one of eight members of the 8th U.S. Cavalry (five from Company K and three from Company E) to be cited for "Bravery in scouts and actions against Indians" during the Arizona Indian Campaigns in 1868 and 1869. The Medals of Honor (MOH) were presented to the men on September 6, 1869. The seven other members of his regiment receiving Medals of Honor included Francis C. Green, Jacob Gunther, David A. Matthews, James McNally, James Moriarity, Samuel Richman and Otto Smith.

Although we have been unable to find an official record describing Nelson's actions, his son Harold G. Taylor provided the following account in his family history: "...As a boy I remember my father telling about being in charge of a detachment of soldiers who were escorting a high Washington, D.C. official between two Arizona Army Posts during a tour of inspection. While the group was passing through a canyon, Indians, hidden behind rocks high on the side of the canyon, began firing on the soldiers and the man they were escorting. Father spurred his horse up the side of the canyon, in the face of the fire, and killed the Indians. Whether it was this exploit which earned the Medal, I do not know."

Nelson served with Company K, 8th U.S. Cavalry, for his entire five-year enlistment and achieved the rank of First Sergeant. Despite the encouragement of his captain to stay with the Army, Nelson opted not to re-enlist and completed his Army service in 1871.

Post-Military Life

Nelson returned to Boston where he met a man named Monroe, whom he much admired and through whose influence he learned the paper-hanger trade. During this period Nelson met his future wife, Araminta H. Seavey, while taking meals at the Boston boarding house where both resided. Araminta had grown up in York Harbor, Maine. She, too, had deep roots in Maine, including a Revolutionary Patriot in her ancestry. (In 1938 their son Harold submitted an application for membership in the Sons of the American Revolution based on his mother's Seavey line to Patriot Palatiah Perkins.) Araminta was employed as a typesetter on *The Boston Transcript* newspaper. The job required significant skills, and the pay was relatively high for a woman's job during that period.

In about 1876 Nelson moved from Boston to Minneapolis. Nelson and Araminta were engaged to be married, but agreed he would go west and get established first. Nelson worked busily through spring, summer and fall as a paper-hanger. In the winter, he worked in Minnesota's woods as a "lumber jack." By keeping busy year-round and carefully saving his money, he was able in a few years to acquire enough to go into business for himself. He opened a store with a stock of wallpaper and employed several men to work for him. He purchased a home on 19th Street and Clinton Ave in Minneapolis.

Nelson and Araminta ("Minta" in the Cook County, Illinois, marriage index) were married in Chicago on April 28, 1883. Nelson brought his bride back to Minneapolis, to the home he'd bought and furnished before her arrival. There, two sons were born to them, Harold on November 1, 1884, and in 1887, Monroe, named after Nelson's friend in Boston. After the Taylor family moved to larger quarters at 2628 5th Ave, a third son, Paul, was born in 1889.

Nelson operated his business under the name W. N. Taylor & Company. Despite the ups and downs of the economy, Nelson's business thrived. According to Harold's family history, his father "built up a high-grade clientele who respected him for the good advice he gave in the selections of wallpaper and paint, and the high standard of his workmanship. Although originally a paper hanger, after he opened his own business he did no actual paperhanging himself. He employed paper hangers who could do the kind of high grade work he insisted on."

Harold remembered his father as a cheerful, happy man who loved to fish. Nelson had a reputation as an excellent poker player, having learned the game during his five years in the Army.

At age 56 Nelson was diagnosed with an aneurysm in an artery near the heart, a condition that was inoperable in those days. He was confined to his bed for nine months before his death on November 20, 1903. Harold's family history indicates his father's investments enabled his mother "to live comfortably in the old home until her death in 1930 at the age of eighty." Nelson and Ariminta Taylor are buried at Lakewood Cemetery in Minneapolis, Minnesota.

Compiled by Georgetta "Gigi" Hickey
Lake Minnetonka Chapter NSDAR

Charles Henry Welch 1845-1915

Medal of Honor
Conflict: Little Big Horn Montana
Date: June 25-25, 1876

Early Years

Charles Henry Welch was born March 16, 1845 in New York City, New York, although his Medal of Honor gravestone shows his birth date as March 16, 1840. While the funeral home record lists the birth year as 1840, the document also shows Welch's age at death (on June 22, 1915) as 70 years, 3 months, 6 days, consistent with a birth year of 1840. The funeral home error likely caused the wrong year to be entered on the MOH gravestone. The gravestone he shares with his wife reflects his birth year as 1845. His parents may have been James and Alice Welch, but we have been unable to confirm any facts about his growing-up years.

Indian Campaign

Charles H. Welch enlisted in the Army on June 8, 1873 at Fort Snelling, Minnesota, and was assigned to Company D, 7th U.S. Cavalry. The Seventh Cavalry Regiment patrolled the plains of Kansas, Montana and Dakota Territory to protect the western movement of pioneers.

In June 1876 the Battle of Little Big Horn was waged against northern tribes of Indians including the Cheyenne, Sioux, and Arapaho as the Cavalry was attempting to force the Indians back to their reservations. One of the columns, led by Lt. Colonel George Custer, was effectively trapped, and 268 soldiers killed in less than an hour.

E. A. Brininstool and J. W. Vaughn, *Troopers with Custer: Incidents of the Battle of the Little Big Horn*. State in Chapter 14: "That greatest of Indian fights on the American continent, which occurred June 25-26, 1876, known variously as "Custer's last battle," and erroneously as "The Custer Massacre," developed many heroes, but none to whom the title is more apropos than the twenty-four troopers of the Seventh Cavalry who won Medals of Honor for extraordinarily-hazardous duty during two days of this remarkable and thrilling engagement.

"Five men received awards for direct combat actions...nineteen men (were) cited for heroism in obtaining critical water for the wounded. Four brave troopers exposed themselves to the enemy for four hours from a position ahead of the line while Sergeant Welch and fourteen of his comrades slipped out of the right wing of Captain Benteen's line to cross eighty yards of fire-swept ground to reach a deep ravine. With camp kettles, the fifteen brave men made repeated trips to the river while under protective fire from the four troopers at the head of the line. Despite the great danger, and Indian warriors who concealed themselves in bushes along the river in order to ambush the party, only one of these men was wounded. Had not the critical supply of water been obtained, many more of the wounded would have died."

Another, matter-of-fact and extremely understated account of Welch's experience at Little Big Horn was published in a Weld County, Colorado, local history: "Charlie Welch, a resident of the Godfrey Bottom area, was with Custer's forces at the Little Big Horn. The night before Custer's Last Stand, Charlie and two others, sent out to scout, were fired upon by some Indians, and Charlie was hit in the leg. He was taken to the rear for care. So, he could not participate in the battle. Charlie considered the wound a definite asset, as a lame leg was a small price to pay for saving his life." Sgt. Charles H. Welch was discharged on June 2, 1878, "for disability" at Fort Rice (Dakota Territory).

Post-Military Life
After his discharge, Charles settled in Weld County, Colorado, possibly near family members who had also settled there. A biographical sketch of Allen R. Godfrey states Godfrey "met and married Katie Welch, daughter of a pioneer family living in the Godfrey Bottoms, June 5, 1873." Katie and Charles were likely siblings.

In 1880 Charles married Allen Godfrey's 16-year-old sister, Carrie. They lived near her parents, and Charles farmed with his father-in-law, Holon Godfrey. Charles and Carrie

had nine children, five of whom survived to adulthood: They were Katie Augusta (b. 1881), Alice Maude (b. 1885), Elmer (b. 1889), Lyda/Lydia (b. 1892), and Charles Custer (b. 1896).

Charles Henry Welch died June 22, 1915 at LaSalle, Colorado. He and his wife Carrie are buried in Evans Cemetery, Evans, Colorado.

Submitted by Georgetta "Gigi" Hickey, Lake Minnetonka Chapter NSDAR

William Othello Wilson 1869-1928

Medal of Honor
Conflict: Sioux Campaign
Date: 1890

Early Years
I believe William Othello Wilson was born on September 16, 1869, although his birth date on the 1900 U.S. Federal Census is recorded as April 1867. We do know he was born in Hagerstown, Washington County, Maryland. Washington County records were destroyed by fire December 6, 1871. William O. Wilson's enlistment record states that he was 21 years, 4 months old when he enlisted. If I use the September date for his birth and his age on his enlistment record, it means his enlistment date was in January 1889. If he enlisted on August 21, 1889, his birth date would be in April. How, why or exactly when he came to Minnesota is a mystery.

Indian Campaign
William entered the United States Army at St. Paul, Ramsey County, Minnesota in 1889. He was 21 years, 4 months old, 5'7½" tall. He was assigned to Company I, 9th Calvary where he earned the rank of Corporal.

The 9th Cavalry, one of only four completely African-American United States army regiments during the Indian Wars Period, was informally called Buffalo Soldiers. The nickname was given to the "Negro Cavalry" by the Native American tribes they fought. The term eventually became synonymous with all of the African-American regiments formed in 1866. The four all-black military units in the Plains Indian Wars were the 9th & 10th Cavalry Regiments and the 24th & 25th Infantry Regiments.

"The 'Buffalo Soldiers' were established by Congress as the first peacetime all-black regiments in the regular U. S. Army. These regiments existed through WWII." The Buffalo Soldiers served in the Indian Wars on the Plains and in the Southwest. They often distinguished themselves in spite of being issued old horses, scanty ammunition and faulty equipment. In addition to controlling the Indians of the Plains and the Southwest, the soldiers built roads, discouraged illegal traders who sold guns and alcohol to the Indians, policed cattle rustlers and formed escorts for stagecoaches carrying military payroll or other valuables.

For many black soldiers, being a Buffalo Soldier was an attractive occupational choice in a society that only rarely and begrudgingly honored black achievement. Many were career soldiers in the United States Army and won Medals of Honor for their valor.

"On the morning of December 29, 1890, the Sioux chief, Big Foot and some 350 of his followers camped on the banks of Wounded Knee Creek, a tributary of the White River. Surrounding their camp was a force of U.S. troops charged with the responsibility of arresting Big Foot and disarming his warriors. In a frantic attempt to return to their glory days, many Sioux sought deliverance in a new mysticism preached by a Paiute shaman called Wovoka, and fought fiercely believing that their "Ghost Shirts" would protect them from the bluecoats' bullets. In this savage battle twenty-four soldiers distinguished themselves to the degree that they were awarded the Medal of Honor."

The 9th Calvary was stationed at Fort McKinney near Buffalo, Wyoming in the 1880's during the Plains Indian Campaign. In December 1890, Troops D, F, I and K of the 9th Cavalry, under the command of Major Guy V. Henry, made a forced march in harsh winter conditions from the fort to the Pine Ridge Agency, South Dakota. It was one of the greatest cavalry rides in recorded military history.

Corporal Wilson's unit, a battalion of the 9th Cavalry, had been sent in search of the Sioux band led by Big Foot and was about 50 miles from the Pine Ridge Reservation when news arrived about the battle at Wounded Knee. The courier with news of the battle also had orders for them to return to Pine Ridge as soon as possible. To expedite their return, the Lt. Colonel and the main part of the unit left immediately. Corporal William Wilson under Captain Loud, stayed with the slow supply wagons and a small detachment."

About two miles from Pine Ridge early on the morning of December 30, 1890, after the battle of Wounded Knee in South Dakota, a band of Burlé Lakota Warriors under Chief Two Strike attacked the 9th Cavalry supply train and cut off the wagons. Captain Loud wrote a message to send to Major Guy V. Henry for help, but Indian scouts refused to carry it. Wilson volunteered to ride to the agency for help and successfully delivered the message, despite being pursued by hostile Sioux Indians. The besieged soldiers were soon rescued by Major Henry's troops from the agency.

Corporal William Wilson's Medal of Honor was awarded for action during the Sioux Campaign in South Dakota. His award was for his heroism in action on the day after Wounded Knee, December 30, 1890, at White Clay Creek, a tributary of the White River. His Citation reads as follows: "William Wilson returned to Hagerstown, Maryland in 1898. For his voluntary action during the Indian Wars, William was cited for bravery. On September 17, 1891, nine months after his dash for help, William was awarded the Medal of Honor for "qualities of the most conspicuous bravery and gallantry." A more detailed citation was published in General Order 100 on December 17, 1891: "For gallantry in carrying a message for assistance through country occupied by the enemy when the wagon train under escort of Captain Loud was attacked by hostile Sioux Indians, near the Pine Ridge Agency, South Dakota."

Post Military Life

After his military service, William married Margaret Virginia (nee Jackson) Brown in 1898 in Hagerstown, Washington County, Maryland. Seven children were born to this couple: Percy born July 1899; Maroline born abt. 1902; C. Herman born 1903, died 1977; Elsie M. born 24 Nov, 1905, died Dec 5, 2001, William O. born abt. 1910, and Anna V. (Jones) born May 7, 1912 & died on May 20, 2008.

The 1900 United States Census shows William, his wife Margaret and son Percy, age 1, living with his in-laws, Peary and Hanna L. Jackson, their adopted son age 21, sister and nephew.   Margaret is age 30 and gives the information that they have been married two years and that she is the mother of two children, one living. The 1910 United States Census has William listed as a teacher. Other sources and census records have stated William worked at carpentry, upholstering, cooking and calligraphy; he was adept at many skills.

William's family knew of his distinguished military service. He is the only Washington County person to have received the Medal of Honor, but he received little recognition until recently. In 1988 a traffic triangle was named for him and a marker placed there. The triangle is located where Jonathan Street, Pennsylvania Avenue, Charles Street and Forest Drive meet. In May 2011 a flagpole was added during a ceremony attended by more than 100 neighborhood residents and participants.   Mary Jones, a great-granddaughter of Wilson, was present for the dedication. In 2015 a New Memorial Park and Hagerstown Circle of Achievement was dedicated. Among the nine honored was William Othello Wilson, 1867-1928.

William O. Wilson was the last American soldier to receive the Medal of Honor during the Indian Campaigns and on American soil. Twenty-four soldiers received the Medal of Honor for Wounded Knee. There were seventeen, not at Wounded Knee, black soldiers serving in the frontier Indian Campaigns who were awarded the Medal of Honor.

Wilson died January 18, 1928 at the age of 61. In 1997 his grave is located at Rose Hill Cemetery, Hagerstown, Maryland and the Veterans Administration has placed a military marker there.

Compiled by Susan Carleton Jirele
Anthony Wayne Chapter NSDAR

SPANISH-AMERICAN WAR/PHILIPPINES CAMPAIGN

"Remember the Maine!" was the rallying cry sparking the Spanish-American War (1898), a conflict between the United States and Spain that ended Spanish colonial rule in the Americas and resulted in U.S. acquisition of territories in the western Pacific and Latin America. The war originated in the Cuban struggle for independence from Spain, which began in February 1895. Spain's brutally repressive measures to halt the rebellion were graphically portrayed for the U.S. public by several sensational newspapers, and American sympathy for the rebels rose. The growing popular demand for U.S. intervention became an insistent chorus after the unexplained sinking in Havana harbor of the battleship USS Maine on February 15, 1898 which had been sent to protect U.S. citizens and property after anti-Spanish rioting in Havana.

Spain declared war on the United States on April 24, followed by a U.S. declaration of war on the 25th. The ensuing war was pathetically one-sided, since Spain had readied neither its army nor its navy for a distant war with the formidable power of the United States. The Battle for San Juan Hill in Cuba was the bloodiest and most famous battle of the war. It was also the location of the greatest victory for the Rough Riders, led by Theodore Roosevelt, who was posthumously awarded the Medal of Honor in 2001 for his actions in Cuba.

Commodore George Dewey led a U.S. naval squadron into Manila Bay in the Philippines on May 1, 1898, and destroyed the anchored Spanish fleet in a leisurely morning engagement that cost only seven American seamen wounded. Manila itself was occupied by U.S. troops by August.

By the Treaty of Paris, signed December.10, 1898, Spain renounced all claim to Cuba, ceded Guam and Puerto Rico to the United States, and transferred sovereignty over the Philippines to the United States for $20,000,000. The Spanish-American War was an important turning point in the history of both antagonists. Spain's defeat decisively turned the nation's attention away from its overseas colonial adventures and inward upon its domestic needs, a process that led to both a cultural and a literary renaissance and two decades of much-needed economic development. The victorious United States, on the other hand, emerged from the war a world power with far-flung overseas possessions and a new stake in international politics that would soon lead it to play a determining role in the affairs of Europe.

Although the United States achieved victory in the Spanish-American War, gaining new territory and establishing itself as an imperial power, it soon found itself engaged in another conflict as the Philippines began to rebel against its new American rulers. Shortly after President McKinley made it clear that the Philippines would not be granted independence, fighting broke out, and the subsequent war would cost the lives of over 4,000 American troops, 20,000 Filipino soldiers, and 500,000 Filipino civilians. As time progressed, the Filipinos continued to seek independence, which was eventually established in 1935 with the Commonwealth of the Philippines.

Wikipedia and http://www.history.com/topics/spanish-american-war.)

SPANISH AMERICAN WAR 1898

PHILIPPINES CAMPAIGN 1899

Harry Bell 1859-1938

Medal of Honor
Conflict: Philippine Insurrection
Battle for Luzon
Date: October 17, 1899

Early Years

Harry Bell was born September 21, 1859 in Milwaukee, Wisconsin to parents Adam Bell and Katherina Matilda (Boettinger) Bell. His father was born in England and his mother in Germany.

Spanish-American War- Philippines Campaign

Harry entered the service at Minneapolis, Hennepin County, Minnesota and served as a Captain in the U.S. Army, 36th Infantry, Volunteers. US Military and Naval Population Federal Census of 1900 shows that Captain Harry Bell was living "in the field" at the Manila Headquarters, District Department of Southern Luzon, Philippines.

After the Spanish-American War (1898) the Philippines came under the control of the United States. Many Filipinos wanted independence. On February 4, 1899, armed hostilities began between the Americans and the Filipinos. On November 24, 1899 U.S. troops secured control of central Luzon, the major island of the Philippines. Captain Harry Bell was awarded the Medal of Honor for his actions during the battle for Luzon. On 17 October 1899, Captain Bell "led a successful charge against a superior force, capturing and dispersing the enemy and relieving other members of his regiment from a perilous position."

Post War Years

Harry was 43 years old when he married 29-year-old Kate Reimers on August 3, 1904 in Davenport, Scott County, Iowa. The couple's first child, John Morris Bell, was born June 17, 1905 in Davenport. Harry moved his young family from Iowa to Kansas about 1906. In 1910 Harry was living on base at Fort Leavenworth with wife Kate and sons John M. age four, Harry F. age three and Walter H. age one. He worked as a Master Signal Electrician in the Army Service School. He retired from the military on July 7, 1915.

In 1920 Harry Bell, his wife and three sons were still living on base, where Harry was employed as a Chief Clerk at the Fort Leavenworth Military Prison.

By 1930 Harry was living apart from his wife and children. He was a roomer in the household of 60-year-old widow Elizabeth Ertley in Columbus City, Franklin County, Ohio and employed as a civil service clerk for the U.S. government. The 1930 US census listed Harry as a widower, even though his wife Kate did not die until 11 July 1954. In 1930, Kate Bell was living with 19-year-old son Walter, at 1104 Spruce, Leavenworth, Kansas. She, too, was listed as widowed in the census.

Apparently the couple had experienced marital problems and, as was usual for the time, lived apart and declared their spouse to be deceased. Youngest son Walter was employed as a carpenter at this time and he likely provided support for his mother.

Harry Bell died November 6, 1938 in Proviso Township, Cook County, Illinois. He was buried November 8, 1938 in Section R, Lot 168, at Fort Leavenworth National Cemetery. Even though Harry and Kate Bell experienced several years of separation, when Kate died in 1954, she was buried next to her husband in Fort Leavenworth National Cemetery in Lot 168.

Compiled by Shirleen Ann Hoffman
Lake Minnetonka Chapter NSDAR

Otto A. Boehler 1873-1910

Medal of Honor
Conflict: San Isidro, Luzon, Philippine Islands
Date: May 16, 1899

Early Years

Otto A. Boehler, was born on October 15, 1873 in Germany. His occupation was a carpenter. He entered service in the US Army-Air Force from Wahpeton, North Dakota. He served in Company I, 1st North Dakota Volunteer Infantry.

Spanish-American War- Philippine Campaign

Private Otto Boehler was one of a hand-picked group of soldiers known as "Young's Scouts," tasked with being at the forefront of movement in rebel-controlled areas. On May 16, 1899, eleven of these scouts under Captain William Birkhimer of the 3rd US Artillery earned Medals of Honor in a frontal attack on 300 enemies. Three days later the scouts were looking for water when they encountered a large enemy force of at San Isidro. The rebel forces set fire to the strategic bridge over the Rio Grande de Pampanga. Three Scouts immediately sprinted across the bridge, firing at the enemy from point-blank range, while the remaining Scouts took cover and returned fire on the enemy trenches on the opposite bank, only fifty yards distant. Private Boehler was one of twenty-two Scouts that braved the hail of fire to rush the burning, wooden bridge and extinguish the flames, though constantly under fire. They then attacked and routed the enemy forces numbering 600 men. Private Boehler and six other Scouts earned the Medal of Honor for this action. In all, thirteen of Young's Scouts earned Medals of Honor in the three-day period for heroism on May 16, 1899 at San Isidro, Luzon, Philippine Islands.

Post War Years

Otto Boehler, married Bernardina Smart in 1902 (per 1910 United States Census, Breckenridge, Wilkin County, Minnesota Census). Also listed was the following; Son, Charles, age 8, daughter, Elizabeth M, age 6, and son, Fredrick B Boehler, age 3.

Otto Boehler, died on October 15, 1910 in Breckenridge, Wilkin Co., Minnesota. He is buried in the St. Mary's Catholic Church in Breckenridge, Minnesota.

Compiled by DeAnn Caddy, Captain Robert Orr Chapter NSDAR

Charles P. Davis 1872-1943

Medal of Honor
Conflict: San Isidro, Luzon
          Philippine Islands
Date: May 16 1899

Early Years

Charles P. Davis was born June 5, 1872 in Long Prairie, Todd County, Minnesota to Silas J. Davis and Philino (Rambo) Davis. Charles was the eldest of the Davis' thirteen children, eleven of whom survived. Charles completed 8th grade elementary education.

Spanish-American War – Philippines Campaign

Charles entered the service as a Private in Company G, 1st North Dakota Volunteer Infantry, at Valley City, Barnes County, North Dakota. During the Spanish American War, on May 16, 1899 near San Isidro, Philippine Islands with 21 other scouts, Charles charged across a burning bridge, under heavy fire, and completely routed 600 of the enemy who were entrenched in a strongly fortified position. Nearly seven years after his distinguished gallantry Charles P. Davis was issued the Medal of Honor on April 28, 1906.

Post War Years

At the age of 28 years, Charles married Ruth Mary Butterfield in 1902. They had no children.

The 1910 US Federal Census shows that Charles worked as a clerk in a poolroom in North Dakota, Barnes, Valley Ward 1, District 0016. In the 1920 US Federal Census, Charles was self-employed as a detective in North Dakota, Barnes, Valley Ward 1, District 16. In 1930, according to the US Federal Census, Charles was found to be working as a Patrolman for Railroad Industry in North Dakota, McHenry, Drake, District 15. The 1940 US Federal census shows that Charles was not working but collecting compensation.

Charles passed away on May 28, 1943 in Valley City, Barnes County, North Dakota. He is buried in North Dakota Veterans Cemetery, Mandan, Morton County, North Dakota.

Compiled by Susan Duff-Erkel
Captain Robert Orr Chapter NSDAR

MEXICAN EXPEDITION MARCH 14, 1914 TO FEBRUARY 7, 1917

MEXICAN EXPEDITION

The Pancho Villa Expedition—now known officially in the United States as the Mexican Expedition but originally referred to as the "Punitive Expedition, U.S. Army"—was a military operation conducted by the United States Army against the paramilitary forces of Mexican revolutionary Francisco "Pancho" Villa from March 14, 1916, to February 7, 1917, during the Mexican Revolution 1910–1920.

Pancho Villa, the Mexican revolutionary leader, controlled much of northeastern Mexico during 1914 and 1915. He experienced military setbacks after breaking with the Carranza government and being subjected to a U.S. arms embargo. The Wilson Administration supported Carranza as the legitimate Mexican head of state and hoped that U.S. support could end Mexican political instability during the revolutionary period.

The Punitive Expedition into Mexico that the United States Government undertook in 1916 against Mexican Revolutionary leader Pancho Villa threatened to bring the United States and Mexico into direct conflict with one another. However, careful diplomatic maneuvering by Mexican President Venustiano Carranza and U.S. President Woodrow Wilson successfully resolved the crisis.

Wikipedia

Albertus Wright Catlin 1868-1933

Medal of Honor
Action: Vera Cruz
        Mexico
Date: April 22, 1914

Early Career

Albertus Wright Catlin was born December 1, 1868, in Gowanda, New York. He was appointed to the U.S Naval Academy in May 1886 from Minnesota and was the captain of the football team and played left halfback at Annapolis for three years. He graduated with the Class of 1890. To fulfill the required two years of sea duty, he served on board the USS Charleston as a Midshipman.

Catlin applied for the Marine Corps and was commissioned a second lieutenant on July 1, 1892. That September he reported for duty at the Marine Corps School of Application and graduated first in his class in April 1893. Then he was promoted to First Lieutenant and transferred to Marine Barracks, League Island, Philadelphia Navy Yard, Pennsylvania, in December. In August 1895, he reported to USS Cincinnati.

Spanish-American War

He then transferred to the USS Maine and was in command of the Marine Corps Guard when the USS Maine was blown up in Havana Harbor in February 1898. This was the catalyst that started the Spanish-American War. During that war, he served on board the auxiliary cruiser the "USS St. Louis", which participated in the blockade of the harbor at Santiago de Cuba, and led the first Marines to land in the occupation of Cuba. The Marines and Sailors attempted to cut the undersea telegraph linking Cuba with Jamaica.

On June 1911, Catlin's Mamaluke Sword was recovered "in a fair state of preservation" along with a penknife from his quarters in the salvaging operation of the Maine.

Interim

After the Spanish-American War, Catlin's orders sent him to the Marine Barracks at the Brooklyn Navy Yard, New York. In March 1899, he was promoted to Captain and assigned to the Marine Barracks at Port Royal, South Carolina. In 1902, Catlin received orders to the Marine Barracks at Cavite, Philippines. From that February to July 1904, he was the first commanding officer of the Marine Barracks, Naval Station, Honolulu,

Territory of Hawaii. After that he served in recruiting duty at Buffalo, New York until the following spring when he returned to the Marine Barracks at the Brooklyn Navy Yard. He was promoted to Major in June 1905. June 30, 1906, Major Catlin was in command of a battalion of Marines consisting of 7 officers and 204 enlisted men on board the USS Dixie, from the League Island Navy Yard for Monte Cristi. From the fall of 1906 until May 1909, he served with the First Provisional Regiment in Guantanamo Bay, Cuba.

After this, he served the Post Quartermaster at the Marine Barracks at Boston, Massachusetts. Later he was transferred back to the Marine Barracks at the Philadelphia Navy Yard. In 1911, he returned to serve in Cuba in command of the 1st Regiment, which formed at Guantanamo Bay on March 8, 1911. After this in the fall of 1911, Catlin served in succession on board USS Connecticut, USS Utah, and USS Wyoming.

Mexican Campaign

Catlin served as a Major during the 1914 Vera Cruz, Mexican Campaign, on board the USS Wyoming. He was awarded the Congressional Medal of Honor for his bravery on April 22, 1914. His citation reads: "For distinguished conduct in battle, engagement of Vera Cruz, 22 April 1914. Eminent and conspicuous in command of his battalion, Maj. Catlin exhibited courage and skill in leading his men through the action of the 22nd and in the final occupation of the city". His Medal was awarded on December 4, 1915.

World War I

In December 1914, Catlin was in command at the Naval Prison, Portsmouth Navy Yard, Maine, and also had a temporary duty at the Army Service Schools at Fort Leavenworth, Kansas. In October 1915, he was promoted to Lieutenant Colonel and in February 1917 was promoted to Colonel.

He graduated from the Army War College one month after the outbreak of World War I. Due to his graduation, he was placed in charge of the Marine overseas training camp at Quantico, Virginia. He was sent to France in October 1917 as the commanding officer of the 6th Marine Regiment, 4th Brigade, 2nd Division, AEF. From June 1 – 6, 1918, the 6th Regiment was in action in the front lines from Paris-Metz Road through Lucy-le-Bocage to Hill 142. On June 6, 1918, when the 6th Regiment was attacking Bois de Belleau, (the Battle of Belleau Wood), Catlin was wounded in the chest by a sniper and evacuated to a hospital the next day. It was the first time he had been wounded in 28 years of active service. He was awarded the Croix de Guerre with Palm and the French Legion of Honor by France for his service in their country.

In addition to the Medal of Honor, Catlin was awarded two Croix de Guerre, one with palms and one with gilt star for gallantry in action against the enemy at Belleau Wood. He was also made an Officer of the Legion of Honor for his services in the same sector.

Soon after his return from France, he summarized his war experiences in a book called *With the Help of God and a Few Marines.*

Post War Years

When Colonel Catlin returned to the United States, he served at Headquarters Marine Corps and was appointed brigadier general on August 30, 1918. After his tour at Headquarters, he was assigned to the Marine Barracks at Quantico. In November 1918, he assumed command of the First Brigade of Marines in Haiti until September 1919.

Brigadier General Catlin retired from the Marine Corps in December 1919. He was in ill health as a result of his wound and died in Culpeper, Virginia, on May 31, 1933. Brigadier General Catlin is buried in Arlington National Cemetery along with his wife, Martha Ellen Catlin. His grave is located in Section 7, Site 10038

Added by: Don Morfe

After his death Brigadier General Catlin was honored in several ways:

The base headquarters building in Lejeune Hall on Marine Corps Base Quantico, Virginia is on Catlin Avenue is named for him. During World War II, in the Salt Lake area of Oahu, Hawai'i, Camp Catlin was formed to train Marines for fighting in the Pacific and became the first home for Headquarters, Fleet Marine Force, Pacific and the SS *George Washington* was renamed the *USS Catlin* (AP-19) in his honor. On December 1, 2006, Rear Admiral Harry Harris Jr., Captain Mark Leary, and Marine Major George Nunez, unveiled a monument dedicating Quarters M101 on Guantanamo Bay to the memory of Catlin. From that day forward, the flag quarters at the Marine Site will be known as Catlin House.

Compiled by Glynae Deschene
Maria Sanford Chapter NSDAR

Jesse Farley Dyer 1877-1955

Medal of Honor
Conflict: Vera Cruz
          Mexico
 Date: April 21- 22, 1914

Early Years
Jesse Farley Dyer, son of Frank W. Dyer and Rachel D. (Gibson), was born December 2, 1877 in St. Paul, Ramsey County, Minnesota. He had one brother, John. Their parents, Frank and Rachel were married September 21, 1871, in Osage, Iowa and moved to Minnesota prior to their children's births. Jesse's very early years are not clearly documented.

He entered service in Minnesota in 1903 as a Marine in the 8th Co. 2nd Battalion, 2nd Regiment. Seven years later the *Oakland Tribune*, Oakland California, announced on March 20, 1910, "Lieutenant Jesse Farley Dyer, U. S. Marine Corps, will be married this summer to Miss Nellie M. Murphy, daughter of Mr. and Mrs. Ira F. Murphy, of Grand Rapids, Mich. Lieutenant Dyer is now stationed in Washington. Both of the young people were formerly residents of Minneapolis. Lieutenant Dyer, who is on duty in the office of the judge advocate general of the navy, will be maintained in Washington. After his marriage, he and his wife will reside there."

Mexican Campaign
On April 9, 1914, U.S. sailors from the USS Dolphin, stationed off Mexican waters near the port of Tampico, landed at the port. They were arrested and later released. According to the Mexican version of events, the soldiers had entered a restricted area, but were found to have done so accidentally. Elements in the U.S., however, considered it to be Mexican harassment of the U.S. Military.

The local Mexican military commander apologized verbally to Admiral Henry Mayo, in charge of the American naval squadron in question. However, Mayo, with the backing of President Wilson, declined the apology. He instead insisted that those responsible for the arrests be punished, and that the Mexican military on shore issue a twenty-one gun salute to the U.S. flag. The commander responded with a written apology, and General Huerta himself expressed his regret, but the U.S. demand for a salute to the flag was turned down.

On April 22, 1914, President Wilson received the backing of Congress for the use of military force to resolve the issue. He ordered the U.S. Navy to seize the port of Veracruz, which was preparing to receive a German ship loaded with ammunition intended for Huerta's troops. In response, Mexican congressmen criticized the U.S. and mobs burned the American flag and looted American businesses in Mexico. The U.S. occupation of Veracruz lasted until November 1914 and was a primary cause of Huerta's resignation in August of that year as his southern armies' supplies ran out.

Jesse Dyer was recognized for his service in the Vera Cruz incident that led to his Medal of Honor recognition. His Citation read: "The President of the United States of America, in the name of Congress, takes pleasure in presenting the Medal of Honor to Captain Jesse Farley Dyer, United States Marine Corps, for distinguished conduct in battle, engagements of Vera Cruz, 21 and 22 April 1914, while commanding of a Company of Marines. Captain Dyer was in both days fighting at the head of his company, and was eminent and conspicuous in his conduct, leading his men with skill and courage."

Post War Years

After the Vera Cruz conflict, Jesse and his family, consisting of wife, Nellie, daughter, Julia and mother in law, Julia Murphy, were located in the Virgin Islands. Marine Captain Dyer had been promoted to Major and had been appointed as an aid to Rear Admiral James H. Oliver, United States Navy, who was to become the first governor appointed by the President to administer government to the islands. Major Dyer held this position for two years.

Upon returning to the United States, Major Jesse F. Dyer was living for some time in New York City; then in 1930 the Dyer family was found to be living in Washington, DC. The household now consisted of Jesse F. Dyer and wife Nellie, daughters, Louise C. and Marcia A. Dyer and Jesse's father, Frank. By late June of 1937, Jesse and his wife moved to their home in Redondo Beach, California, looking forward to retirement.

By the year 1940, Jesse and his wife and youngest daughter, Marcia, were living in Inglewood, California. Jesse had risen to the rank of Colonel of the USMC. At the time of his death on March 31, 1955 in Riverside County, Corona, California, Jesse F Dyer had been honored with the official rank of Brigadier General. He is buried at Fort Rosecrans National Cemetery, San Diego County, San Diego, California, Section P, Site 1606. He had served his country for 39 years, from 1903-1942.

Compiled by Dianne Lawson, Josiah Edson Chapter NSDAR

WORLD WAR I

The assassination of Austrian Archduke Franz Ferdinand on June 28, 1914 in the Bosnian capital, Sarajevo was the spark that set off the First World War declared on July 28, 1914. More than 70 million military personnel, including 60 million Europeans, were mobilized in one of the largest wars in history. It drew in all the world's economic great powers, assembled in two opposing alliances: the Allies (based on the Triple Entente of the British Empire, France and the Russian Empire) versus the Central Powers of Germany and Austria-Hungary. These alliances were reorganized and expanded as more nations entered the war: Italy, Japan and the United States joined the Allies, while the Ottoman Empire and Bulgaria joined the Central Powers.

At the outbreak of the war, the United States pursued a policy of non-intervention, avoiding conflict while trying to broker a peace. However, there were two major events that changed American public opinion about the war. The first occurred in 1915, when a German U-boat sank the British ocean liner *RMS Lusitania*. Considered by Americans to be a neutral ship that carried mostly passengers, Americans were furious when the Germans sank it, especially since 159 of the passengers were Americans.

The second was the Zimmermann Telegram. In early 1917, Germany sent Mexico a coded message promising portions of U.S. land in return for Mexico joining World War I against the United States. The message was intercepted by Britain, translated, and shown to the United States. This brought the war to U.S. soil, giving the U.S. a real reason to enter the war on the side of the Allies. On April 6, 1917, the United States officially declared war on Germany.

By the time the war was over on November 11, 1918, over 9 million combatants and 7 million civilians had died (including the victims of a number of genocides). It was one of the deadliest conflicts in history, and paved the way for major political changes, including revolutions in many of the nations involved. The Treaty of Versailles, officially ended World War I. Its punitive terms would ensure a future Global Conflict.

Excerpts from Wikipedia and http://history1900s.about.com/od/worldwari/p/World-War-I.htm

WORLD WAR I

1914-1918

Louis Cukela 1888-1956

Medal of Honor: Army and Navy
Action: Soissons engagement.
　　　　　Villers-Cotterest, France
Date:　　July 18, 1918

Early Years

Louis Cukela was born in Spalato, Croatia, May 1, 1888, the son of George and Johanna (Bubrich) Cukela. He attended grade schools in Spalato, and then attended the Merchant Academy for two years and the Royal Gymnasium for two years. In 1890 his mother passed away. In 1913, Louis and his brother immigrated to the United States and settled in Minneapolis, Minnesota. His father and three sisters remained in Serbia.

World War I Years

On September 21, 1914, he enlisted in the U.S. Army. With war raging in Europe, based on a spark touched off in Cukela's native Serbia, he enlisted in the U.S. Marine Corps in 1917. Following the United States' entry into the conflict, he went to France and took part in the engagements of the 5th Marine Division.

Major Cukela is a double recipient of the Medal of Honor, one by the Army and one by the Navy, for the same action in World War I. The event occurred near Villers-Cotterest, France on the morning of July 18, 1918, during the Soissons engagement. The 66th Company, 5th Marines, in which Major Cukela was a gunnery sergeant, was moving through Forest de Retz when it was held up by an enemy strong point.

His citation reads: "When his company, advancing through a wood, met with strong resistance from an enemy strong point, Sgt. Cukela crawled out from the flank and made his way toward the German lines in the face of heavy fire, disregarding the warnings of his comrades. He succeeded in getting behind the enemy position and rushed a machinegun emplacement, killing or driving off the crew with his bayonet. With German hand grenades he then bombed out the remaining portion of the strong point, capturing 4 men and 2 damaged machineguns."

This now-famous Marine was wounded in action twice, but there is no record in the Navy's Bureau of Medicine and Surgery, so he was never awarded the Purple Heart. The first wound was on September 16, 1918 at Jaulny, France during the Mihiel engagement.

He was wounded again during the fighting in the Champagne sector. Neither wound was serious.

Major Cukela received a field appointment to the rank of second lieutenant in the Marine Corps Reserve on September 26, 1918, and was selected for a commission in the regular Marine Corps on March 31, 1919. He was promoted to first lieutenant on July 17, 1919, and the rank of captain on September 15, 1921.

Interim War Years
After WWI, Major Cukela served at bases in Haiti, Santo Domingo, the Philippines, and China, also at domestic posts at Quantico, Virginia; Philadelphia, Pennsylvania; Norfolk and Hampton Roads, Virginia; Mare Island, California, Washington, DC; Nashville, Indiana; and Fort Knox, Kentucky.

Louis married Minnie Myrtle Strayer of Mifflintown, PA, at Washington, DC, on December 22, 1923. They had no children. From June, 1933 to January, 1934, the major served as a company commander with the Civilian Conversation Corps. He was the post quartermaster at Norfolk from 1934 to 1940.

World War II Years
Cukela was retired as a major on June 30, 1940, but was recalled to active duty on July 30th of the same year. During World War II, Cukela served at Norfolk and Philadelphia. He returned to the inactive retired list on May 17, 1946, serving a few days less than 32 years of active duty in the Army and Marines.

Post War Years
The last surviving double recipient of the Medal of Honor, Major Cukela died at the U.S. Naval Hospital, Bethesda, Maryland, on March 15, 1956. After services at St. June Frances de Chantel Church, Bethesda, he was buried with full military honors in Arlington National Cemetery on March 22, 1956. Mrs. Minnie Cukela died five months later and is buried at his side.

At the time of his death, Major Cukela was survived by a sister, Mrs. Zorka Cukela Dvoracek of Sibenik, Croatia.

2nd Lt. Cukela receiving Medal of Honor from Gen. John Pershing, ca. 1918-19

[Image courtesy of http://www.croatia.org]

In addition to the two Medals of Honor, Major Cukela was awarded the Silver Star by the Army, the Medaille Militaire (he was the first Marine officer ever to receive this award), the Legion d'Honneur in the rank of Chevalier, the Croix de Guerre with two palms, another Croix de Guerre with silver star, all by France; the Croce al Merito di Guerra by Italy, and the Commander's Cross of the Royal Order of the Crown by Yugoslavia. He also received three Second Division citations.

Major Cukela also had the following decorations; Victory Medal with Aisne, Aisne-Marne, St. Mihiel, Meuse-Argonne, Defense Sector clasps and three silver stars, Haitian Campaign Medal, Expeditionary Medal with one star, Yangtze Service Medal, American Defense Service Medal, American Area Campaign Medal, World War II Victory Medal, and the French Fourragere.

Compiled by Jane Homme
St. Croix River Valley Chapter NSDAR

George Henry Mallon 1877-1934

Medal of Honor
Action: Forges Woods
France
Date: Sept. 26th, 1918

Early Years

George Henry Mallon was born on June 15th, 1877 in Ogden, Riley County, Kansas, the second child of ten and first son to parents Robert Currie Mallon and Emma L. Stephens. George's father, Robert C. had emigrated at ten years old with his parents and siblings from County Tyrone, Ulster, Ireland in 1850.

Spanish-American War /Philippines Campaign

Three days after George Mallon turned 21 years old he joined the military for the first time on June 18th, 1898 as a member of the 22nd Kansas Volunteer Infantry serving until November 3rd of the same year in the Spanish-American War as a private.

His second enlistment was on January 7, 1899 at Fort Riley, Kansas when he enlisted for the Philippines Campaign. George was 22 years, 6 months old. His occupation was listed as farmer. He had blue eyes, dark brown hair, a fair complexion and stood 5'8 ¼". George was Number 17 in the register, 12th U.S. Infantry, Company K and "discharged on January 6th, 1902 at sea on the Warren by expiration of service, [rank] Sergt. [Sergeant]", and notation of his service record was: "Excellent." On January 29, 1902, he was listed as an invalid.

Interim War Years

At age 29 George married Effie Gladys Campbell in Kansas City, Wyandotte County, Kansas on December 22, 1906. They moved to Minneapolis, Minnesota in 1907 and George worked installing automatic sprinklers systems for a fire extinguisher company. From May 15th, 1917 to August 15th, 1917 he was in the R.O.T.C.

World War I

After the U.S. entered WWI, the government called for candidates for officers' training camps. George volunteered. He was 40 years old at the time. After a three-month training period at the first Fort Snelling camp, George was commissioned a Captain in the infantry section of the National Army. He was assigned to "E" Company, 132nd

Regiment, 33rd Division and stationed at Camp Logan, Texas from September 6th, 1917 until May 5th, 1918 when his unit was sent to Hoboken, New Jersey.

They embarked from Hoboken on the ship Mt. Vernon on May 16th and arrived at Brest, France on May 26th, 1918 as part of the American Expeditionary Force. Captain Mallon was on the Western Front in France from June 1918 to August 1918 and they first went into battle on July 4th, 1918 at Hamel, France. From August 1918 to October 1918, they were part of the American Front in France.

Capt. Mallon participated in battles at Hamel, the Somme Offensive, Boise de Forges and Meuse Argonne. "The Meuse-Argonne Offensive, also known as the Mass-Argonne Offensive and the Battle of the Argonne Forest, was a major part of the final Allied Offensive of World War I that stretched along the entire Western Front. The Americans faced the most difficult natural obstacle, the dense Argonne Forest. General John Pershing's opening surprise attack advanced 5 miles (8 km) along the Meuse River but only 2 miles (3 km) in the difficult Argonne Forest sector. It was fought from September 26, 1918, until the Armistice of November 11, 1918, a total of 47 days. The Meuse-Argonne Offensive was the largest in United States military history."

On the first day of this offensive, September 26th, 1918, "in the Bois-de-Forge campaign at the battle of Forges Woods, 41 year-old Captain Mallon along with nine men became separated from the balance of their company because of a fog. Captain Mallon, with his nine soldiers, pushed forward and attacked nine active hostile machineguns, capturing all of them without the loss of a man. Continuing on through the woods, he led his men in attacking a battery of four 155-millimeter howitzers, which were in action, rushing the position and capturing the battery and its crew. In this encounter Captain Mallon personally attacked one of the enemy with his fists. Later, when the party came upon two more machineguns, this officer sent men to the flanks while he rushed forward directly in the face of the fire and silenced the guns, being the first one of the party to reach the nest. The exceptional gallantry and determination displayed by Captain Mallon resulted in the capture of 100 prisoners, eleven machineguns, four 155-millimeter howitzers and one antiaircraft gun.

Five days later on October 1st, 1918, one of the casualties of this battle was Captain Mallon as he was wounded by a high explosive in his right thigh at Meuse River. He was under medical care at Base Hospital 35#, in Mars, France from October 1st to January 14th, 1919. Not permanently disabled he arrived at Hoboken, New Jersey on May 17th, 1919 and was discharged from service at Camp Grant, Illinois on June 20th, 1919 as a Captain. He had turned 41 years old five days earlier. Captain Mallon was placed on the Emergency Officers Retirement List June 11, 1928.

Before Captain Mallon left France, on January 22, 1919, he was named one of General John J. Pershing's 100 heroes' of World War I. "On February 2, 1919 General Pershing presented to Captain Mallon the: "Congressional Medal of Honor" for conspicuous gallantry on Sept. 26th, 1918 at the battle of Forges Woods. He received the "French Legion of Honor" and the French "Croix de Guerre with Palm" and was decorated by Vice Admiral Mabeau of the French Navy for the above acts."

Post War Years

Captain Mallon returned to Minneapolis, Minnesota but did not resume his former activities in civil life, as his injured leg was not strong. Instead he accepted a position with the Building Trades Council of Minneapolis.

Capt. Mallon also became involved in politics and ran for Lieutenant Governor on the Republican ticket. The Working People's Non-partisan Political League endorsed him and those on his ballot on June 21, 1920. Capt. Mallon's ticket lost the primary by 15% of the vote.

The League promoted an alternative veterans organization. Based in Minneapolis - and sustained by the Nonpartisan League - the World War Veterans hoped to be a more sympathetic version of the American Legion. Capt. Mallon became the most prominent member. Last mention of Capt. Mallon's political activities for unionizing the common man was when he was manager of the NPL in Kansas and worked to get the farmers to organize.

Captain Mallon was a Hennepin County Commissioner for eight years In December 1920, the commission's activities organized a strong county war records committee, which included Captain Mallon.

Early in 1934, Captain Mallon had a stroke and was taken to the Veteran's hospital at Fort Snelling. On March 1st he was transferred to the St. Cloud VA Hospital where he died August 2, 1934 at age 57. Two different obituaries were published for Captain Mallon's funeral. The first, published on Saturday, August 4, 1934, gave the information that his funeral was on Monday morning, August 6th at St. Ann's Catholic Church and mentioned his wife, Effie Mallon, and two sons, George H. Jr., 14, and Robert, 9. "Captain Mallon belonged to the Russell Gaylord post of the Veterans of Foreign Wars, and was a member of the Disabled American Veterans. He was a charter member of the order of the Purple Heart." This obituary also included these lines: "His heroism in the World war won Captain Mallon the Congressional Medal of Honor, the most distinguished military honor the United States can bestow. He also was honored by England, France, Italy and other countries."

The second obituary published on Sunday, August 5, stated: "Captain George H. Mallon will be accorded military honors at funeral services to be conducted Monday under auspices of Gaylord Post, Veterans of Foreign Wars, and the Disabled American Veterans. Short services will be at 8:30 a.m. in the home, 3601 Washburn Avenue North, to be followed by requiem mass at St.

Ann's Church, 1213 Twenty-sixth Avenue North. There will be a firing squad and guard of honor from the Third infantry at the grave in St. Mary's cemetery."

The remainder of this second obituary lists the names of the seven active pallbearers, one being a general; another, a lieutenant. This is followed by the names of 72 honorary pallbearers. This second list of prominent men included four generals, three colonels, one captain, one lieutenant, three doctors, five reverends, four judges, Mayor Bainbridge of Minneapolis and Minnesota Governor Floyd B. Olson.

Five years later in 1939, Fort Snelling National Cemetery was established in Minnesota. Captain Mallon's body, which had been buried in a private cemetery, was reinterred. His was the first burial in this National Cemetery on July 5, 1939 with Capt. Mallon being burial #1 and the main street in the cemetery, Mallon Blvd, named after him. Ogden, Kansas honored their native son by naming Mallon Road for Captain George Henry Mallon.

Captain Mallon's wife, Effie Campbell Mallon, died on December 31, 1970 in Johnson County, Kansas at age 82, thirty-six years after her husband's death. Their oldest son, George Henry Jr. died on December 17, 1988. Son Robert Currie Mallon died January 14, 2009 in Kandiyohi County, Minnesota.

Captain Mallon's award documents are at the Military Historical Society of Minnesota's Museum at Camp Ripley, Little Falls and have been restored and conserved. According to a granddaughter in Kansas, Captain Mallon's medals were on display at Ft. Riley, Ogden, Kansas and were included in a traveling display around the United States some years ago.

Captain George H. Mallon is one of only two WWI Medal of Honor recipients from Minnesota. He is one of General John J. Pershing's top 100 heroes of World War I.

His awards include: Congressional Medal of Honor, Purple Heart, Philippine Campaign Medal, World War I Legion of Honor (France) Croix de Guerre with palm

Compiled by Joyce Rohloff Gardner, Anthony Wayne Chapter NSDAR

Nels T. Wold 1895-1918

Medal of Honor awarded posthumously
Action: Cheppy
France
Date: September 26, 1918

Early Years

Nels T. Wold was born December 24, 1895 in Winger, Polk County, Minnesota, the 8th of 10 children, to Tidemand E. and Klara (Tharaldsrud) Wold who both immigrated to the United States from Norway in 1883. After Klara died when Nels was just six years old, Tidemand remarried and had an 11th child with his second wife, Osse Lee. Tidemand died when Nels was 16.

When Nels registered for the draft on June 5, 1917 he was living in Akron, Ohio, and working for Goodyear Rubber Company. He was described as tall, with blue eyes and light hair. He was living in Minnewaukan, North Dakota when he enlisted in the Army. He was inducted at Crookston, Minnesota on April 2, 1918, and sent to Camp Dodge, Iowa. His emergency contact was his stepmother who was living in McIntosh, Minnesota at the time.

World War I

During World War I Nels served in Company M, 163rd Depot Brigade from his induction until April 21, 1918. He was promoted to Pvt. 1st class, transferred to Company I, 138th Infantry, and sent overseas on May 3, 1918. After a short layover in England, the company was sent on to France on May 19, 1918.

Nels wrote to his sister, Inga, from France: "I am lying in the grass under a big shade tree and taking a good rest. It is very pleasant and beautiful around here now." Soon after, he was positioned at the spear point of the long Meuse-Argonne Front; he was one of 400,000 American soldiers flanked across France by millions of British, French, and other Allied troops.

According to the records of the American Expeditionary Force, 35th Division 138th Infantry, Company I. Records, 1917-1976: "The men of Company I spent most of the next two months training, marching, and camping at various locations in the Vosges region of France. On July 17, 1918, they saw their first action in the trenches of France when Company I relieved another unit on the Collette front. Two days later, Company I itself was relieved, and the men began another period of marching, training, and camping. In early September, Company I, along with the rest of the 35th Division, was sent to the Saint-Mihiel area, where it was held in reserve during the Allied offensive in that region. Later in that month, after being sent into the Argonne forest region of northeastern France, the company took part in the Battle of the Argonne from September 26 through September 30. Here, near the town of Cheppy, Company I's commanding officer, Captain Alexander R. Skinker, was killed on September 26 while trying to knock out a German machine gun emplacement. For this action, Skinker was posthumously awarded the Congressional Medal of Honor."

This was the same day that Nels was killed, also trying to knock out a German machine gun nest. Nels had already disabled four enemy machine guns, but his luck ran out attacking the fifth.

"When Nels' army comrades realized that the invincible fighter had been downed by German machine guns, two men carried Nels one mile to a safe place to die. One man was from Rutland, North Dakota. Chris Antonson (his July 26, 1920 letter can be read behind the glass display case at the American Legion) wrote out the last words Nels supposedly said as he lay dying, 'Pray for me boys, and write my folks and tell them I love them all.'"

Photos courtesy of Kathrine (Vargaso) and Jerry Kaupang

Nels was initially buried near Cheppy, France. His remains were later moved to Elim Cemetery in Winger, Minnesota.

Post War Years
On December 31, 1919, Nels T. Wold was posthumously awarded the Congressional Medal of Honor. The commendation reads: "Nels Wold, Pvt, Co. I, 138th Inf. For conspicuous gallantry and intrepidity above and beyond the call of duty in action with

the enemy near Cheppy, France, September 26th, 1918. He rendered most gallant service in aiding the advance of his company, which had been held up by machine gun nests, advancing, with one other soldier and silencing the guns, bringing with him upon his return, 11 prisoners. Later the same day he jumped from a trench and rescued a comrade who was about to be shot by a German officer, killing the officer during the exploit. His actions were entirely voluntary and it was while attempting to rush a fifth machine gun nest that he was killed. The advance of his company was mainly due to his great courage and devotion to duty."

"Wold was one of the 100 named by General Pershing as America's bravest and who were awarded the Congressional Medal of Honor. Corporal O. G. Birkeland of McIntosh, who was a chum of Wold, said, 'Nels was a typical fighter and feared no danger.'"

On June 5, 1919, the new American Legion Post in Crookston was named the Nels T. Wold Post. Ione (Vraa) Ostgarden, the daughter of Nels' sister Alma (Wold) Vraa, was a life member, and held several leadership positions in the Auxiliary of Nels T. Wold American Legion Post #20.

Compiled by Leslie Hartz Sprott
Anthony Wayne Chapter NSDAR

WORLD WAR II

World War II was inevitable. The terms of the Treaty of Versailles were so punitive that it left Germany impoverished and destitute. Then a madman came to his country's rescue—a man whose promise to "make Germany great again" left most of western Europe a shambles for the second time in a little over twenty years. Still reeling from Germany's defeat in World War I, Hitler's government had envisioned a vast, new empire of "living space" in eastern Europe. This would require German dominance in Europe, which, in turn, would require war

It was the most widespread war in history, and directly involved more than 100 million people from over 30 countries. In a state of "total war", the major participants threw their entire economic, industrial, and scientific capabilities behind the war effort, erasing the distinction between civilian and military resources. Marked by mass deaths of civilians, including the Holocaust (in which approximately 11 million people were killed) and the strategic bombing of industrial and population centers (in which approximately one million were killed, and which included the atomic bombings of Hiroshima and Nagasaki), it resulted in an estimated 50 million to 85 million fatalities. This made World War II the deadliest conflict in human history.

The War in Europe began in 1939. The United States hoped to stay out of the war. Drawing on its experience from World War I, Congress passed a series of Neutrality Acts between 1935 and 1939. Americans in general, however, while not wanting to fight the war, were definitely not neutral in their sympathies. America's isolation from war ended on December 7, 1941 when Japan staged a surprise attack on Pearl Harbor, Hawaii. On December 8, President Roosevelt asked Congress to declare war against Japan. Three days later, Germany and Italy, allied with Japan, declared war on the United States. America was now drawn into a global war along with its allies, Great Britain and the Soviet Union.

Excerpts from: http://www.nationalww2museum.org; http://www.u-s-history.com

WORLD WAR II

1941-1945

Willibald Charles Bianchi 1915-1945

Medal of Honor awarded posthumously
Action: Bagac, Province of Bataan,
Philippine Islands
Date: February 3, 1942,

Early Years

Willibald Charles Bianchi, son of Joseph and
Caroline "Carrie" (Eibner) Bianchi was born on
March 12, 1915, in New Ulm, Minnesota. He was
the second child, and the only son, born to Joseph
and Carrie. Willibald "Bill" had an older sister,
Josephine, and three younger sisters, Magdalene,
Jermayn and Mary Louise.

Bill grew up on a 73 acre poultry farm south of New Ulm where he helped his father
with many farm chores including milking cows and tending to chickens and turkeys.
While he was still in high school, his father, Joseph, died in an accident on their
farm. Bill had to leave school and take over the responsibility of running the farm to
support his family. He later completed his high school studies at the University of
Minnesota farm school in St. Paul, MN. At age 21, Bill Bianchi enrolled at South
Dakota State University (SDSU) where he majored in animal science, was active as
an Army ROTC cadet major, and played on the college football team. He worked his
way through college by cleaning and sweeping out the college print shop and
classrooms, and doing furnace work. His fellow students started calling him
"Medals" because he wore his ROTC uniform a lot, even when he went home on
weekends, partly because he could not afford much clothing, but also because he
liked soldiering. He was very proud of his ROTC decorations. Upon graduation
from SDSU in 1940 he was commissioned a second lieutenant in the United States
Army. He requested foreign service in order to see action at the earliest possible
date.

World War II Years

Bill Bianchi enlisted as a 2nd Lieutenant, Officer Reserve Corps at New Ulm, Brown
County, Minnesota on June 3, 1940. In April, 1941, now a 1st Lieutenant in the U.S.
Army, he left for the Philippines to serve in the U.S. Army, 45th Infantry Division,
Philippine Scouts. His first task was to convert Philippine natives into trained
soldiers. Bianchi distinguished himself by transforming these natives into fearless
jungle fighters. He and the other officers who made up our first expeditionary force

of World War II, worked against time to create an army that could withstand Japanese aggression. In the end, there wasn't enough time. The U.S. didn't have enough trained troops, airplanes and tanks to oppose the Japanese landings, so all they could do was try to delay the enemy as their armies converged on Manila. U.S. troops retreated into the Bataan Peninsula to keep a foothold in the Philippines until reinforcements came. These soldiers didn't have the equipment and ordinance of the customary World War II soldier—these refinements were to come later. The men on Bataan were the pioneers. They were the men who held the line while the country was getting ready.

The Congressional Medal of Honor was awarded to Bianchi for his bravery in battle during the famous Tuol River pocket on West Bataan on February 3, 1942. This took place prior to the fall of the Philippines during the early stages of World War II. He was wounded early in the action when 2 bullets passed through his left hand. He was wounded a second time by 2 machine gun bullets through the chest. His third wound was severe when he was blown off the top of an American tank by either a mortar explosion or a grenade blast. Bill lay unconscious on the ground. It was some time later that Bill's mother, Carrie Bianchi, received a telegram from the Adjutant General of the United States Army. It reads: "Deeply regret to inform you that your son, 1st Lt. Willibald Charles Bianchi, was seriously wounded in action in the Philippines on February 3. Progress reports will be forwarded as received." Bill returned to active duty after just one month and was promoted to Captain. His actions succeeded in weakening the Japanese position so that it was later captured by infantrymen with little or no loss of life.

On April 9, 1942, Bill Bianchi was captured by the Japanese with some 75,000 other American and Filipino soldiers, in the fall of Bataan. The Allied troops were interned for 24 hours without food or water, and then they were forced on the infamous 65-mile Bataan Death March from Mariveles to San Fernando. Many soldiers died along the way from disease and mistreatment. Bodies crushed by Japanese transports littered the line of march. The prisoners were half crazed by hunger, thirst, and the heat. In spite of Bianchi suffering from the same horrible conditions, he was up and down the line helping the men, spurring them on, and sharing their burdens, saving many from being killed by the Japanese.

Bianchi was moved to several prison camps, each with conditions worse than the one before. There were no medical supplies, clean clothes, or sanitary facilities, and little food. Prisoners slept on mud-floored huts, soaked by rain. Bianchi's reputation as a caregiver continued as he did what he could to aid his fellow men who, like himself, were suffering from the effects of the starvation diet, work, and dreadful living conditions. He bartered with his captors and managed to get food from their mess halls to aid hundreds of starving prisoners. Brigadier General Ted Spaulding, Huron, SD, served with Bianchi, and witnessed this first-hand. Many servicemen wrote to Bianchi's mother following the war, telling her that they owed their lives to her son.

One of Bill's most difficult assignments was to fairly distribute the scanty rations that were issued by the captors. All too often, those put in charge of food distribution used their position to better the lot for themselves and their friends at the expense of the overall group. It took a man of great character and determination, such as Bianchi, to first see that all men received a fair share.

On October 16, 1944, Bianchi was transferred to Bilibid prison in Luzon, where conditions were even worse than at O'Donnell (April/May 1942) and Cabanatuan (June 1942-October 1944). He left Bilibid on December 12, 1944, aboard the Japanese ship Orokyo Maru, anchored at Subic Bay, where he again provided assistance to his buddies. That ship was sunk a few days later and he was transferred to an unmarked prison ship anchored off Formosa. On the morning of January 9, 1945, an American plane dropped a 1,000 pound bomb into the hold of the anchored ship. The U.S. was unaware the target was filled with American prisoners of war. Bianchi was killed instantly. He was 29 years old. Comrades who knew him said that he was probably in the ship's hold aiding the sick.

Captain Willibald C. Bianchi was one of three men awarded the Congressional Medal of Honor for achievements prior to the fall of the Philippines in 1942, and was probably the most outstanding American soldier on Bataan in the early months of the War. His name will live long in the memories of the prisoners of Camp O'Donnell, Cabanatuan and Bilibid, for in addition to being a war hero, Bianchi was their No. 1 Benefactor through those three terrible years.

The Congressional Medal of Honor was awarded posthumously to Captain Bianchi's mother, Carrie Bianchi, on June 7, 1945 at Fort Snelling, Minnesota, along with other awards and citations including Bronze Star and the Purple Heart with 3 Oak Clusters.   Bianchi is the only Congressional Medal of Honor recipient from New Ulm, Minnesota, and the only soldier originally from Brown County, Minnesota, to receive our country's highest military award for his acts of bravery during World War II.

Bianchi's mother received the following letter dated October 25, 1945, from General Douglas MacArthur. "Dear Mrs. Bianchi: My deepest sympathy goes to you in the death of your son, Captain Willibald C. Bianchi, who died in action against the enemy. You may have some consolation in the memory that he, along with his comrades in arms who died on Bataan and Corregidor and in prison camps, gave his life for his country. It was largely their magnificent courage and sacrifices which stopped the enemy in the Philippines and gave us the time to arm ourselves for our return to the Philippines and the final defeat of Japan. Their names will be enshrined in our country's glory forever. In your son's death I have lost a gallant comrade and mourn with you. Very faithfully, General Douglas MacArthur."

Wilibald Bianchi' Citation for Medal of Honor reads as follows: "For conspicuous gallantry and intrepidity above and beyond the call of duty in action with the enemy on 3 February 1942, near Bagac, Province of Bataan, Philippine Islands. When the rifle platoon of another company was ordered to wipe out 2 strong enemy machinegun nests, 1st Lt. Bianchi voluntarily and of his own initiative, advanced with the platoon leading part of the men. When wounded early in the action by 2 bullets through the left hand, he did not stop for first aid but discarded his rifle and began firing a pistol. He located a machinegun nest and personally silenced it with grenades. When wounded the second time by 2 machinegun bullets through the chest muscles, 1st Lt. Bianchi climbed to the top of an American tank, manned its antiaircraft machinegun, and fired into strongly held enemy position until knocked completely off the tank by a third severe wound."

Carrie Bianchi wrote that, "As a mother, I am proud to be able to give to this generation and to our beloved America the most precious gift that life makes possible, my only son."

Post War Years

Captain Willibald C. Bianchi was just 29 years old when he was very tragically killed on January 9, 1945. Bill never married so he left no descendents to honor him for his acts of valor and bravery in war. However, Bill's four sisters and their families have kept his memory alive. They have honored him by donating his Congressional Medal of Honor award and his other medals to the Brown County Historical Society along with the supporting documentation for each award. Thanks to the family, the public can actually view the medals and appreciate the significance of his sacrifice for generations to come.

The City of New Ulm honored him in 1955 by naming a new street Bianchi Drive in the new hilltop residential area. In 1990 the American Legion Post in New Ulm changed its name from Ben J. Seifert Post #132 to Seifert-Bianchi Post #132 to honor the only Congressional Medal of Honor recipient from New Ulm. Captain Bianchi was honored by his alma mater, South Dakota State University, Brookings, SD, in 1998, when the Bianchi memorial in the University Student Union was dedicated and the Scholarship for ROTC and New Ulm natives attending SDSU was established. He was honored again in 2000 when the "Cpt. Willibald C. Bianchi Medal of Honor Monument" was dedicated.

.

Captain Willibald C. Bianchi was buried at the National Memorial Cemetery of the Pacific (Punchbowl) (MA-39) (MH) Honolulu, Hawaii (marker only). He is also remembered on the Wall of the Missing at the Manila American Cemetery and Memorial in Manila, The Philippines.

Compiled by Marilyn Grothem Wilkus, Anthony Wayne Chapter NSDAR

Michael Colalillo 1925-2011

Medal of Honor
Action Utergriesheim
       Germany
Date: January 9, 1946

Early Years:

Let me introduce you to a special American, Mike Colalillo. The second of nine children, Mike was born on December 1, 1925 in Hibbing, Minnesota shortly after his parents emigrated from Italy. He grew up in a tough neighborhood in western Duluth, Minnesota and left Denfeld High School without graduating. It was a hard time in the Colalillo household. Mike was a young boy whose family struggled through the Great Depression and a teenager who left school in order to help support his family by working in a neighborhood bakery after the death of his mother. He was the smallest and fastest member of the Raleigh Street Kids. They were rough and tough; they made their presence known. Mike was a pretty tough guy, and he was nicknamed "Egan" after a well- known Chicago bad guy. However, this boy was a softy and always willing to share with and assist his friends.

He made many touchdowns in football and was a pretty good hockey player. Perhaps a little more exuberant than most and was often called for boarding. The referee would blow the whistle and Mike would yell, "What for?" It became quite a frequent scene and soon, every time the referee would blow the whistle and point at Mike, the whole crowd of spectators in unison, would yell. "What for?"

Because of trying times, a person either becomes strong or becomes passive. Mike, a street smart young boy, is described as having a quiet dignity, surprising shyness and a touch of greatness. His records in the service attest that Mike overcame the adversities of a poor upbringing.

World War II

Mike was eighteen years old, when he was drafted in 1944. This 5 foot 11 inch, 145 pound recruit was a private when he landed with the 100th Army Infantry Division at Marseille, France. The episode that changed the young soldier's life took place early on the morning of April 7, 1945, in the vicinity of Untergriesheim, Germany, where German resistance to the American advance was particularly heavy. On that day he encouraged his comrades to follow him into enemy fire, manned an exposed machine gun, and helped a wounded soldier back to friendly lines. For his actions during the battle, he was awarded the Medal of Honor on January 9, 1946.

Private Colalillo's official Medal of Honor citation reads: "Private First Class Mike Colalillo, 2d Squad, 2d Platoon, Co. C, 1st Battalion, 398th Infantry, 100th Infantry Division was pinned down with other members of his company during an attack against strong enemy positions on 7 April 1945 in the vicinity of Untergriesheim, Germany. Heavy artillery, mortar, and machine gun fire made any move hazardous when he stood up, shouted to his company to follow, and ran forward in the wake of a supporting tank, firing his machine pistol. Inspired by his example his comrades advanced in the face of savage enemy fire. When his weapon was struck by shrapnel and rendered useless, he climbed to the deck of a friendly tank, manned an exposed machine gun on the turret of the vehicle, and, while bullets rattled around him, fired at an enemy emplacement with such devastating accuracy that he killed or wounded at least 10 hostile soldiers and destroyed their machine gun. Maintaining his extremely dangerous post as the tank forged ahead, he blasted three more positions, destroyed another machine gun emplacement and silenced all resistance in this area, killing at least three and wounding an undetermined number of riflemen as they fled. His machine gun eventually jammed; so he secured a submachine gun from the tank crew to continue his attack on foot. When our armored forces exhausted their ammunition and the order to withdraw was given, he remained behind to help a seriously wounded comrade over several hundred yards of open terrain rocked by an intense enemy artillery and mortar barrage. By his intrepidity and inspiring courage Private First Class Colalillo gave tremendous impetus to his company's attack, killed or wounded 25 of the enemy in bitter fighting, and assisted a wounded soldier in reaching the American lines at great risk to his own life."

Mike was discharged from an Army base in Wisconsin, returning by train to Minneapolis and then home, sharing a memorable bus ride to Duluth with his friend and fellow World War II veteran, Tom Dougherty. It was now a time of victory, a time to shed the shadow of death, a time to celebrate all the good things in life.

Not long after his discharge he received the Medal of Honor. He was now 20 years old.

At the white House, Mike recalled that

while President Harry Truman was pinning the Congressional Medal of Honor on his chest, the President said, "I would have rather gotten his Medal of Honor than be the President of the United States."

What does Colalillo remember about that devastating day in 1945? "I don't like to remember it to tell you the truth. I was scared--very scared. The feeling I had was to shoot or they'd shoot me. It was something you had to do. I think of how your friends got killed alongside you. That comes back to you once in a while."

Mike Colalillo's decorations and awards include: The Combat Infantryman Badge, European-African-Middle East Campaign Service Medal with Bronze Star, Good Conduct Medal, Purple Heart, World War II Victory Medal, Two Bronze Stars, Silver Star and a French Campaign Ribbon.

Post War

Other honors include a Bronze sculpture of Mike Colalillo given to Duluth City Hall in 1978, plaques in various veterans' memorials, a street named in his honor, and induction into the Duluth Hall of Fame. Displays of Mike's citation and portrait hang at two museums. The Duluth Depot Veteran's Memorial Hall and the Bong Museum in Superior, Wisconsin. The Mike Colalillo Medal of Honor scholarship Fund," a Scholarship fund of $25,000 was invested to present an award each year to a student from St. Louis County who is enrolled in a higher education institution.

After returning to Duluth, Mike married Lina Nissila on November 16, 1945. They had two daughters and a son and lived in the western end of Duluth for many years. Mike was employed by Interlake Iron Works Company in 1946. In 1950, he caught his left hand in a conveyor belt which caused a permanent injury, making his hand nearly useless. After his injury he became a longshoreman, and years later retired from the Duluth Port Authority.

Mike's life was filled with many friends and family members. He died on Friday December 30, 2011 at the Ecumen Bayshore Care Center and is buried at Forest Hill Cemetery in Duluth. The church was filled with not only these friends and family but, those of us who stood in awe of an everyday neighbor, fellow worker, a gentle giant in our eyes and a man who deeply loved his country. The streets were lined with people standing holding their hands over their hearts and flags flying as his funeral procession slowly passed. I wish that our citizens would honor all of our brave veterans in similar ways.

Mike Colalillo's story is one of countless stories that paint an important and very individual picture of the patriotic effort made by legions of veterans but, there are many more human experiences that are invaluable in portraying the whole picture of war. We need to preserve, protect and remember so that future generations will understand the way life was in those difficult challenging times.

Preserve in honor the United States veterans who served in harms-way and the heroes who never made it home. Our friend, Mike stands in the midst of all young men and woman who also had fought so gallantly.

Submitted by Royleen Newman
Greysolon Daughters of Liberty Chapter NSDAR

Henry Courtney 1916-1945

Medal of Honor awarded posthumously
Action: Battle on Sugar Loaf Hill
Okinawa, Shima, Ryukyu Islands
Date: May 14, 1945.

Early Years

Henry Courtney was born to Henry A. Courtney Sr. and Florence E. on January 6, 1916. He had one brother, John G., Washington D. C.; two sisters, Mrs. Benjamin Storey, St. Paul, MN and Mrs. Joseph C. Bean, Darien, Connecticut. He attended Duluth Central High school, graduated from the University of Minnesota, and attained a law degree from Loyola University in Chicago, Illinois. He was a member of the Minnesota and Illinois Bar. Before going into active military service he was associated with the law firm of Courtney & Courtney in Duluth. Henry was known as "Bob" to family and friends.

World War II

Henry Courtney had barely qualified to practice law when he was called to active duty as a Commissioned Second Lieutenant in the Marine Corps Reserve, February 1940. He organized Company C of the Marine Corps Reserve in Duluth. In March of that year he was placed in command of the Duluth unit of the Marine Corps Reserve which was mobilized and sent to San Diego for training. He then served in Iceland for ten months between 1941 and 1942. While Courtney was stationed in Iceland, the Japanese attacked Pearl Harbor.

From August of 1942 to June 1943 he served on Guadalcanal Solomon Islands, where he was assigned to the staff of the Twenty Second Marine Regiment, Sixth Marine Division. He participated in the first U.S. offensive invasion of the Solomon Islands in World War II, commanding a company of the First Marine Division.

He taught in the Marine School at Quantico just before leaving for Okinawa. His next and last battle was on Sugar Loaf Hill, Okinawa, Japan.

Sugar Loaf Hill is no more than 50 feet high. Yet, the brutal struggle to secure this hellish rise cost the 6th Marine Division 2,662 casualties and ranked among the bloodiest of battles. The fight for Sugar Loaf Hill has largely been forgotten outside the Corps. Sugar Loaf Hill is squatted on a shell blasted plateau like a trash heap; its rocky slopes were barren, honeycombed with caves and tunnels that the enemy would use with skill and advantage. Okinawa, barely the size of Rhode Island, sixty-seven miles long and 18 miles wide at its widest point, is located only 350 nautical miles from the Japanese homeland. It is a powerful tribute to those who fought and died there in the spring of 1945.

Courtney had suffered a slight shrapnel wound in the right thigh on the 9th of May. Regardless of his wound he stayed with his battalion. He also spent the night with the frontline troops after "G" company's bloodletting on 12 May, apparently feeling his presence might help steady the men.

An eyewitness account: "He led his men by example rather than by command. He pushed ahead with unrelenting aggressiveness, hurling grenades into cave openings, having devastating effects on the enemy." One of the survivors recalled Courtney's words, "Take all the grenades you can carry and when you get over the top throw them and dig in." The gallant words of Major Courtney will go down in history of the Marine Corps, "I want volunteers for a Bonzai of our own. If it works, we'll take the top of the hill tomorrow."

On the 15th of May, 1945 Major Henry A. Courtney was killed when a shell severed his jugular vein.

Weeks after May, 1945 the place looked like a garbage dump. Litter of the battle remained strewn on the torn and battered hill—helmets, discarded ammunition, paper, clothing, letters and pictures of loved ones. To a disinterested observer it was just so much assorted "rubbish" littering the ground, but to the marines, this was and is "Hallowed Ground".

His Citation from the president tells of the action and "conspicuous gallantry and intrepidity of the risk of his life above and beyond the call of duty."

Henry Courtney is nearly forgotten except by those who knew him during his short life

and by the few living marines who followed him up the slopes of Sugar Loaf Hill. Only 15 of the original 46 who bravely followed Courtney lived to tell us about it.

The Major's remains were buried at the cemetery dedicated by the Sixth Marine Division. His body was brought home to his family and reburied at Calvary Cemetery in Duluth on March 29 1949.

Major Courtney was also decorated with the

following: Two Purple Hearts, Presidential Unit (ribbon bar with gold star), American Defense Service Medal, European-African-Middle Eastern Campaign Medal, Asiatic-Pacific Campaign Medal, Victory Medal of World War II, The Gold Star.

Post War

In 1993 the Okinawans began work to develop the area. Bulldozers working around Sugar Loaf Hill unearthed human remains, old canteens, and various rusted pieces of equipment. The narrow gauge railroad bed is now a four lane highway. A new water tower was proposed to be placed at the top of the hill. At this point an Okinawan artist came forward with a suggestion for a park-like setting for a peace monument and history display at Sugar Loaf Hill. In 1994 their city fathers approved the park.

Charlie Hill, The Horse Shoe Ridge, Half Moon, Motobu Peninsula, Ishikaw Isthmus, Naha and Conica Hill are remote spots on which men died in battle in 1945 that are now covered with fast food franchises, outlet stores, pawnshops and used car lots. The irony of it brings to mind the line that Shakespeare wrote, "In thy faint slumbers I by thee have watched and heard thee murmur tales of Iron wars."

The Sixth Marine Division has dedicated a cemetery to Courtney on Okinawa near where they stormed ashore Easter Sunday. There are 1,697 brave souls buried at this site. The Sixth Marine Division was later honored with a Presidential Unit Citation, the highest unit award conferred by the United States, for their actions on Okinawa. Not very many of the brave souls that fought against the enemy are alive today. But, neither time nor even death itself can sever the blood bonds between the men who have fought so bravely. Again, as Shakespeare wrote," We few, we happy few, we band of brothers; for he today that sheds his blood with me shall be my brother."

In 1955 an Escort Vessel was built for the U.S. Navy at Bay City, Michigan. It was named in Major Courtney's honor. The statement of dedication presented at the launching stated, "Major Henry A. Courtney, Jr. once described by his Commanding General as Marine Corps' greatest hero, died on Okinawa Island 10 years ago last May. But his name soon will be in active duty again with the U.S. Armed Forces."

A news release in 1956 stated, "Okinawa Camp to honor Courtney. A U.S. Marine Corps base on Okinawa has been renamed in honor of Major Henry A. Courtney Jr., Duluth World War II Congressional Medal of Honor Recipient." And a Duluth news release in 2006 states: "Marine's display gets makeover. A new memorial for Medal of Honor Recipient"

The following books refer to the Battle on Sugar Loaf Hill. They include many accounts regarding Courtney's heroic actions: *Killing Ground on Okinawa -- The battle of Sugar Loaf Hill* written by James H. Hallas; Goodbye *Darkness* by William R. Manchester; *Once a Marine* by Robert B. Asprey; and *The Conquest of Okinawa--An account of the Sixth Marine Division* by Phillips D. Carleton.

Many other books and periodicals were written of the gallant men who fought on Sugar Loaf Hill. Major Henry A. Courtney stands among them as a symbol of the bravery of the defenders of our nation.

Compiled by Royleen Newman
Greysolon Daughters of Liberty Chapter NSDAR

Richard Eugene Fleming 1917-1942

Medal of Honor awarded posthumously
Action: Battle of Midway Island
Date: June 5, 1942

Early Years

Richard Eugene Fleming was born on November 11, 1917, a cold day in Minnesota, to Richard Fleming, the English-born vice president of a wholesale collier (coal dealer) and Octavia Fleming. He attended St. Thomas Military Academy, a Roman Catholic military prep school in St. Paul. After graduating as Top Student Officer from St. Thomas in 1935 he enrolled in the University of Minnesota and joined the Delta Kappa Epsilon fraternity where he became its president. In 1939 he received his Bachelor of Arts degree.

World War II Years

Soon after graduating from the University of Minnesota, Fleming, then 22 years old, enlisted in the Marine Corps Reserve on December 15, 1939 and applied for flight training. He was accepted as an aviation cadet on January 25, 1940 and sent to the Naval Air Station in Pensacola, Florida for training, finishing at the top of his class in 1940. He received his wings and commission on December 6, 1940. The Naval Air Base at San Diego became his first duty station. He was posted to VMF-214, a Marine dive-bombing squadron known as the "Black Sheep Squadron" where he piloted a Vough SB2U-3 Vindicator out of San Diego, and then out of Ewa Field in Hawaii.

Fleming's father died the following year leaving Octavia Fleming as the matriarch of the clan. Richard's letter to her dated December 3, 1941 stated, "This is the last time I'll be able to write for probably some time. I'm sorry I can't give you any details. It's that secret." The secret was that eighteen of his squadron were flying their Vindicators out to sea for a touchdown on the US Lexington. They continued on to Midway Island where they were two days later when the Japanese attacked Pearl Harbor, destroying their home field, Ewa, in Hawaii.

The pilots returned to Ewa shortly after the attack and on December 17 were ordered to proceed to Midway where Fleming would later engage in the Battle of Midway as Flight

Officer of Marine Scout Bombing Squadron 241. He was promoted to first lieutenant in April 1942 and on May 25th he and five other lieutenants were promoted to captain.

Early in the morning of June 4, 1942 the aviators on Midway got the word to stand by and warm up their aircraft. Led by their squadron commander, Lofton Henderson, they roared off to intercept waves of incoming Japanese aircraft. Then, climbing into the sky, they headed towards the spot where the Japanese fleet was believed to be lurking. When Major Henderson was shot down during the initial attack on a Japanese aircraft carrier, Fleming took command of the unit. Leaving the remainder of his formation, he dove to the perilously low altitude of 400 feet exposing himself to enemy fire in order to score a hit on the ship. After failing to drop a bomb on the aircraft carrier, Akagi, his aircraft limped back to base with 179 holes in it.

Captain Fleming was promoted to squadron commander the following day, June 5, 1942. He returned to battle after four hours of sleep to direct his squadron in a coordinated glide-bombing dive-bombing assault upon the Japanese. Pressing his aircraft to an altitude of 500 feet he put his plane into an approach glide for a screaming dive at the Japanese cruiser Mikuma. Diving low he succeeded in scoring a near-miss on the objective. His plane, hit by anti-aircraft fire, caught fire but Captain Fleming managed to keep his burning aircraft on course until he could release his bomb. Unable to pull out of his dive, Fleming, his plane a mass of flames, crashed into the sea. He, along with his gunner, Private First Class George Albert Toms, was killed. There is some inconclusive evidence that Fleming might have deliberately crashed his plane into the battleship, Kamikaze, style gutting the Mikuma which sank the next day.

For "extraordinary heroism and conspicuous gallantry above and beyond the call of duty," Captain Fleming was posthumously awarded the nation's highest military decoration — the Medal of Honor, while Pfc. Toms received the Distinguished Flying Cross. On November 24, 1942, President Franklin Roosevelt presented the Medal of Honor to Fleming's mother. Fleming's citation, signed by President Franklin D. Roosevelt reads:

"The President of the United States takes pride in presenting the MEDAL OF HONOR to Captain Richard E. Fleming, United States Marine Corps Reserve: For extraordinary heroism and conspicuous intrepidity above and beyond the call of duty as Flight Officer, Marine Scout-Bombing Squadron Two Forty One during action against enemy Japanese forces in the Battle of Midway on June 4 and 5, 1942. When his squadron Commander was shot down during the initial attack upon an enemy aircraft carrier, Captain Fleming led the remainder of the division with such fearless determination that he dived his own plane to the perilously low altitude of four hundred feet before releasing his bomb. Although his craft was riddled by 179 hits in the blistering hail of fire that burst upon him from Japanese fighter guns and antiaircraft batteries, he pulled out with only two minor wounds inflicted upon himself. On the night of June 4, when the Squadron Commander lost his way and became separated from the others, Captain Fleming brought his own plane in for a safe landing at its base despite hazardous weather conditions and total darkness. The following day, after less than four hours' sleep, he led the second division of his squadron in a coordinated glide-bombing and dive-bombing assault upon a Japanese battleship. Undeterred by a fateful approach glide, during which his ship was struck and set afire, he grimly pressed home his attack to an altitude of five hundred feet, released his bomb to score a near-miss on the stern of his target; then crashed to the sea in flames. His dauntless perseverance and unyielding devotion to duty were in keeping with the highest traditions of the United States Naval Service."

Captain Richard Fleming was the only person to receive the Congressional Medal of Honor for action in this crucial battle

Post War
Although Captain Richard Eugene Fleming is officially listed as "missing in action" his name lives on. The United States Navy ship, the USS *Fleming*, commissioned on September 18, 1943, was named in his honor, and his name is listed on the "Tablets of the Missing" at Honolulu Memorial in Honolulu, Hawaii.

Closer to home Richard Fleming is memorialized each year at his high school alma mater, Saint Thomas Academy, during the Cadet Colonel Promotion ceremony when he is remembered by the presentation of the "Fleming Saber," to the Cadet Colonel. In 2008 this military academy added another award, "The Fleming Alumni Veterans Award." Since 2014 Governor Mark Dayton has proclaimed March 25th as Minnesota Medal of Honor Day. The proclamation specifically names Richard Fleming along with three other MOH recipients. Fleming has also been memorialized in his home town. The former South St. Paul Municipal Airport was renamed the Richard E. Fleming Field in his honor. Though his body is not there, a memorial marker to Captain Fleming has been placed at Fort Snelling National Cemetery.

Compiled by June Gossler Anderson
Anoka Chapter NSDAR

Louis James Hauge Jr. 1924-1945

Medal of Honor awarded posthumously
Action: Okinawa Shima in the Ryūkyū Chain
Date: May 14, 1945.

Early Years

Louis Hauge Jr. was born on December 12, 1924 in Ada, Minnesota. He was active in all athletics, but left high school after his first year and worked in a canning factory in Ada where he became assistant foreman. He later was employed by a ship yard in Tacoma, Washington as a painter.

World War II Years

Louis Hauge was inducted into the Marine Corps Reserve on April 23, 1943 and completed light-machine gun school at Camp Elliott, California before serving with the 1st Marine Division at New Caledonia and New Guinea. Later, he saw combat action on Peleliu as a message runner with Headquarters Company, 1st Battalion, 1st Marines. In this capacity, he distinguished himself for his bravery under fire and was given a meritorious promotion to corporal.

Corporal Hauge was killed in action on May 14, 1945, while serving on Okinawa as a member of the 1st Marine Division. For his heroic actions on that day, he was awarded the Medal of Honor. At the time of his death, Corporal Hauge was squad leader of a machine gun squad in Southern Okinawa engaged in an assault against a heavily fortified Japanese hill. It was during the evening that the left flank of Company C, 1st Battalion, 1st Marines, was pinned down by a barrage of mortar and machine gun fire. The enemy was pouring enfilade fire into the ranks of the Marines. Quickly spotting the two guns responsible for the damage, Corporal Hauge boldly rushed across an open area, heaving hand grenades as he ran. Wounded before he reached the first gun, he nevertheless continued his one-man assault and completely destroyed the position. Without stopping, he pushed forward and attacked the second gun with grenades and demolished it before falling from the deadly fire of the Japanese snipers. Inspired by his actions, his company rose from their besieged position and pressed home the attack.

Louis Hauge's Medal of Honor was presented to his father on June 14, 1946 by Col Norman E. True, USMC, who represented the Commandant of the Marine Corps. His Medal of Honor citation reads: "For conspicuous gallantry and intrepidity at the risk of his life above and beyond the call of duty as Leader of a Machine-Gun Squad serving with Company C, First Battalion, First Marines, First Marine Division, in action against enemy Japanese forces on Okinawa Shima in the Ryūkyū Chain on 14 May 1945. Alert and aggressive during a determined assault against a strongly fortified Japanese Hill position, Corporal Hauge boldly took the initiative when his company's left flank was pinned down under a heavy machine-gun and mortar barrage with resultant severe casualties and, quickly locating the two machine guns which were delivering the uninterrupted stream of enfilade fire, ordered his squad to maintain a covering barrage as he rushed across an exposed area toward the furiously blazing enemy weapons. Although painfully wounded as he charged the first machine-gun, he launched a vigorous single-handed grenade attack, destroyed the entire hostile gun position and moved relentlessly forward toward the other emplacement despite his wounds and the increasingly heavy Japanese fire. Undaunted by the savage opposition, he again hurled his deadly grenades with unerring aim and succeeded in demolishing the second enemy gun before he fell under the slashing fury of Japanese sniper fire. By his ready grasp of the critical situation and his heroic one-man assault tactics, Corporal Hauge had eliminated two strategically placed enemy weapons, thereby releasing the besieged troops from an overwhelming volume of hostile fire and enabling his company to advance. His indomitable fighting spirit and decisive valor in the face of almost certain death reflect the highest credit upon Corporal Hauge and the United States Naval Service. He gallantly gave his life in the service of his country." Signed HARRY S. TRUMAN

Corporal Hauge's remains were eventually returned to the United States and interred in the National Memorial Cemetery of the Pacific in Honolulu, Hawaii. His marker is in Ada Cemetery, Ada, Norman County, Minnesota, Plot: Block 4, Row 1, in Fenced area.

Post War Years

The United States Navy container & roll-on/roll-off ship, MV *Cpl Louis J. Hauge Jr.* (T-AK-3000), commissioned on September 7, 1984, is named in honor of Cpl. Hauge. This ship is the lead ship of its class of five maritime prepositioning ships. The Cpl. Louis J. Hauge Jr. class is the original class of MPS ships chartered by Military Sealift Command. A Marine Corps installation on the island of Okinawa was named Camp Louis J. Hauge Jr. During the Vietnam War, Camp Hauge served as a staging installation for Marines in transit to and from Vietnam. The camp was decommissioned following the return of Okinawa to the Japanese government.

Compiled by DeAnn Caddy, Captain Robert Orr Chapter NSDAR

Lloyd Cortez Hawks 1911-1953

Medal of Honor
Action: Carano, Italy
Date: January 30, 1944

Early Years

Lloyd was born January 30, 1911 to Leroy and Rachael (Hickman) Hawks while they were temporarily living in Green Valley Township, Becker, Minnesota. He was the youngest of seven children. At age 8 the family moved back to Watervliet, Berrien County, Michigan where Lloyd's childhood and formative years were spent on the family farm. In 1930, Lloyd, with the nickname "Goldie," graduated from Watervliet High School. Although, the family's homestead, history, and traditions, were based in Southwestern Michigan, Lloyd moved back to Minnesota as an adult. He was residing in Carlisle Township, Otter Tail County, Minnesota in the 1940 census.

He went into service at Fort Snelling, Minnesota, and was assigned to the 98th Field Artillery at Fort Lewis, Washington. His initial training was as a mule driver. After six weeks with the mules, Hawks was transferred to the 30th Medical Detachment at Fort Lewis. In October 1941, he was transferred to the enlisted Reserve Corps. He spent five and a half months as a civilian working as a patrolman guarding Army warehouses at Fort Mason, San Francisco before being recalled to active duty.

World War II Years

Lloyd was finally able to enter into service in May 1942. Lloyd returned to the Army's Third Division, Thirtieth Infantry Medical Detachment. On October 23, 1942 he left on the U.S.S. Joseph T. Dickman from Hampton Roads, Newport News, Virginia. He landed with his division in North Africa on November 8, 1942. Hawks made his second amphibious landing on Sicily's D Day, July 10, 1943. In December 1943 his unit saw fierce combat. Hawks proved himself a brave and capable medic, winning the Silver Star for heroic actions.

On January 30, 1944, at 3 p.m., near Carano, Italy, Pfc. Hawks braved an enemy counterattack in order to rescue two wounded men who, unable to move, were lying in an exposed position within 30 yards of the enemy. After crawling only ten yards toward the casualties two riflemen attempting the rescue had been forced to return to their fighting holes by extremely severe enemy machinegun fire. An aid man, whom the enemy could plainly identify as such, had been critically wounded in a similar attempt. Pfc. Hawks, nevertheless, crawled 50 yards through a veritable hail of machinegun bullets and flying mortar fragments to a small ditch, administered first aid to his fellow aid man who had sought cover therein, and continued toward the two wounded men 50 yards distant. An enemy machinegun bullet penetrated his helmet, knocking it from his head, momentarily stunning him. Thirteen bullets passed through his helmet as it lay on the ground within six inches of his body. Pfc. Hawks, crawled to the casualties, administered first aid to the more seriously wounded man and dragged him to a covered position 25 yards distant. Despite continuous automatic fire from positions only 30 yards away and shells which exploded within 25 yards, Pfc. Hawks returned to the second man and administered first aid to him. As he raised himself to obtain bandages from his medical kit his right hip was shattered by a burst of machinegun fire and a second burst splintered his left forearm. Displaying dogged determination and extreme self-control, Pfc. Hawks, despite severe pain and his dangling left arm, completed the task of bandaging the remaining casualty and with superhuman effort dragged him to the same depression to which he had brought the first man. Finding insufficient cover for three men at this point, Pfc. Hawks crawled 75 yards in an effort to regain his company, reaching the ditch in which his fellow aid man was lying. Six hours after being wounded Hawks was evacuated.

"For gallantry and intrepidity at the risk of life, and above and beyond the call of duty," Lloyd Cortez Hawks was awarded the Medal of Honor by Franklin Roosevelt on January 10, 1945. The medal was placed around his neck by his niece Phyllis Hawks, a Navy Wave.

Hawks is quoted as saying, "Sure, I gave aid to a good many wounded men under fire, but there's nothing remarkable about that. After all that's what a medical soldier is supposed to do, isn't it?"

The Post War Years
While he lay in an Army Hospital recovering from his wounds, he received a letter of encouragement and support from one Cora Marian Torkelson. Back in the states, an acquaintance led to romance and they were married on January 13, 1946. The couple had three children Leroy George (1947-2000ₓ), David Langdon (1949-1970), and Charlotte Ann, who was born in 1952 while the family was stationed in Japan.

Hawks chose to remain in the Army after World War II. He also served in the Korean War, working his way up to the rank of Sergeant First Class. Hawks, despite an initial Army assessment that he was not fit enough or too old to serve in combat, showed an almost superhuman physical effort and courage in saving the lives of his three comrades.

During his military career, Hawks also received the Italian Military Medal of Valor Cross (comparable to the Medal of Honor), the Silver Star with two oak leaf clusters, the Bronze Star with one oak leaf cluster, the Purple Heart with two oak leaf clusters, the Meritorious Service Award Insignia, the World War II Victory Medal, the American Theater Ribbon, the American Defense Medal, the European African Middle Eastern Campaign Ribbon, the Distinguished Unit Medal, the Japanese Occupation Medal and the Combat Medical Badge. He died of a heart attack at the age of 42 years in 1953, and is buried in Greenwood Cemetery, Park Rapids, Hubbard County, Minnesota.

On January 18, 2007 Fort Stewart, Georgia, dedicated the Hawks Troop Medical Clinic honoring the Army's most-decorated combat medic, Lloyd Cortez Hawks.

A dedication ceremony was held on May 18, 2012 at his gravesite, unveiling a monument with Mr. Hawks wearing his Medal of Honor, a listing of his medals, and on the reverse side the inscription of how he earned the Medal of Honor.

Compiled by Susan Duff-Erkel
Captain Robert Orr Chapter NSDAR

Richard Edward Kraus 1925-1944

Medal of Honor awarded posthumously
Action: Peleliu, Palau Islands
Date: October 5, 1944

Early Years
Richard Edward Kraus was born to Hazel M. (Peters) and August Nicholas Kraus, November 24, 1925 in Cook County, Chicago, Illinois. In the following years, the family, consisting of Richard and his sister, Yvonne, moved to Minnesota, possibly because August was originally from Minnesota and Hazel was from North Dakota.

World War II Years
Richard E. Kraus moved to Minneapolis, Minnesota, when he was seven years old. He attended Edison High School there and was inducted into the Marine Corps on his 18th birthday after previously trying to enlist. His first combat action was during the Marine Corps' assault on Peleliu in the fall of 1944 as part of a unit attached to the 1st Marine Division. Extensive training for Marines was necessary to enable them to cope with the psychological and physical shock and stress encountered on Peleliu. Combat conditions for the Marines were considered the most extreme of the southern Pacific conflicts. The lack of clean water, high temperature and humidity, on an island that were mainly consisted of coral, made for nearly unbearable conditions.

On the occasion of his heroism and death, he was serving as an amphibious tractor driver with the 8th Amphibious Tractor Battalion, Fleet Marine Force, which participated in the D-Day landings on Peleliu. He and his three companions had accepted a volunteer mission to evacuate a wounded fellow Marine from the front lines. With a stretcher, the four penetrated the lines over some distance being met with an intense shower of hand grenade fire, which forced them to take cover. Upon returning to the rear, the party of four was approached by two men, who they believed to be Marines. Requesting the password and with no vocal response, they proved to be Japanese, and one of the enemy responded by throwing a hand grenade towards the four Marines. PFC Kraus unhesitatingly used his body to block the force of the grenade, giving his life to save his three comrades. He had been overseas for only three months at the time of his death.

Post War Years

Private Richard Edward Kraus was a posthumous recipient of the Nation's highest military tribute. The official citation for Private Richard E. Kraus was signed by President Harry S, Truman. It read: "The President of the United States of America, in the name of Congress, takes pride in presenting the Medal of Honor (Posthumously) to Private First Class Richard Edward Kraus, United States Marine Corps Reserve, for conspicuous gallantry and intrepidity at the risk of his life above and beyond the call of duty while serving with the Eighth Amphibian Tractor Battalion, Fleet Marine Force, in action against enemy Japanese forces on Peleliu, Palau Islands, on 5 October 1944. Unhesitatingly volunteering for the extremely hazardous mission of evacuating a wounded comrade from the front lines, Private First Class Kraus and three companions courageously made their way forward and successfully penetrated the lines for some distance before the enemy opened with an intense, devastating barrage of hand grenades which forced the stretcher party to take cover and subsequently abandon the mission. While returning to the rear, they observed two men approaching who appeared to be Marines and immediately demanded the password. When, instead of answering, one of the two Japanese threw a hand grenade into the midst of the group, Private First Class Kraus heroically flung himself upon the grenade and, covering it with his body, absorbed the full impact of the explosion and was instantly killed. By his prompt action and great personal valor in the face of almost certain death, he saved the lives of his three companions, and his loyal spirit of self-sacrifice reflects the highest credit upon himself and the United States Naval Service. He gallantly gave his life for his comrades."

This award was presented to his mother on August 2 1945, by Col. Norman E. True, District Marine Officer for the North Naval District. PFC Kraus was also awarded the Purple Heart

Private Kraus was initially buried in the U.S. Armed forces Cemetery on Peleliu, Palau Islands. His parent requested his body to be transferred to the U.S. and on November 8, 1948, Fort Snelling National Cemetery in Minneapolis, Minnesota, became his final resting place in Section DS, Site 61-N.

The USS Richard E. Kraus (DD849)

The Gearing-class destroyer USS Richard E. Kraus (DD-849) was named in his memory and served with the United States Navy from 1946 to 1976.

PFC Richard E. Kraus is one of three Minnesota Medal of Honor recipients from the Northeast Twin Cities who are named on the Anoka County Veteran's memorial at Bunker Hills, an Anoka County Park in Coon Rapids, Minnesota.

Compiled by Dianne Lawson, Josiah Edson Chapter NSDAR

James Dennis LaBelle 1925-1945

Medal of Honor awarded posthumously
Action: Iwo Jima in the Volcano Islands
Date: March 8, 1945.

Early Years

James LaBelle was born in Columbia Heights, Minnesota on November 25, 1925. He attended grammar school and played basketball and baseball. His favorite hobby was raising homing pigeons. At Columbia Heights High School, he starred on the basketball, baseball and boxing teams. His vocational courses were in woodwork and metalwork. During summer vacations, he worked as an apprentice acetylene welder for a local air conditioning corporation.

World War II

At 17 years of age, with his mother's permission, LaBelle enlisted in the United States Marine Corps Reserve in Minneapolis, Minnesota. His recruit training was at the Marine Corps Base in San Diego, California. At Camp Pendleton, California he qualified in the intensive combat training course before embarking for overseas. He joined the regimental Weapons Company, 27th Marines, 5th Marine Division, on June 30, 1944. In August, he sailed on board the USS George F. Elliott, bound for Hilo, Hawaii and eventually to Iwo Jima. At Camp Tarawa, a Marine camp in Hawaii, the regimental Weapons Company, he engaged in more indoctrination and training preparatory to actual combat.

Private LaBelle's first battle was taking part in the assault on Iwo Jima, which began on February 19, 1945. This was after aerial and naval forces had pounded its desolate surface for many days; the island of Iwo Jima felt the sting of invading Marine amphibious forces. One of thousands, PFC LaBelle fought continuously from the initial landing until March 8, 1945. At this time, PFC LaBelle jumped onto a live grenade to protect two other soldiers in his foxhole. He gallantly gave his life and earned the highest honor his nation could bestow. He was only nineteen years old. The family did not receive official word of his death for another three months.

Private James LaBelle was awarded the Congressional Medal of Honor. It was presented to his mother by General William E. Riley, then Director of Marine Corps

Public Information, in a ceremony at Minneapolis's Powderhorn Park on July 21, 1946. Private First Class James D. LaBelle's citation reads: "For conspicuous gallantry and intrepidity at the risk of his life above and beyond the call of duty while serving with the Weapons Company, Twenty-seventh Marines, Fifth Marine Division, in action against enemy Japanese forces during the seizure of Iwo Jima in the Volcano Islands, 8 March 1945. Filling a gap in the front lines during a critical phase of the battle, Private First Class LaBelle had dug into a foxhole with two other Marines and grimly aware of the enemy's persistent attempts to blast a way through our lines with hand grenades, applied himself with steady concentration to maintaining a sharply vigilant watch during the hazardous night hours. Suddenly a hostile grenade landed beyond reach in his foxhole. Quickly estimating the situation, he determined to save the others if possible, shouted a warning and instantly dived on the missile, absorbing the exploding charge in his own body and thereby protecting his comrades from serious injury. Stouthearted and indomitable, he had unhesitatingly relinquished his own chance of survival that his fellow Marines might carry on the relentless fight against a fanatic enemy and, his dauntless courage, cool decision and valiant spirit of self-sacrifice in the face of certain death reflect the highest credit upon Private First Class LaBelle and the United States Naval Service. He gallantly gave his life in the service of his country."

Private First Class LaBelle's remains were returned to the United States in late 1948, and were reinterred in the cemetery in Fort Snelling National Cemetery, Minneapolis, Hennepin County, Minnesota, Plot: Section B1, Grave 422-S.

James D. La Belle is one of three Minnesota Medal of Honor Recipients from the Northeast Twin Cities who are named on the Anoka County Veteran's memorial at Bunker Hills Anoka County Park in Coon Rapids, Minnesota. The other two are Richard E. Kraus and Richard K. Sorenson.

Compiled by Glynae Deschene,
Maria Sanford Chapter NSDAR

Arlo Laverne Olson 1918-1943

Medal of Honor awarded posthumously
Action: Voltumo River, Italy
Date: October 13, 1943

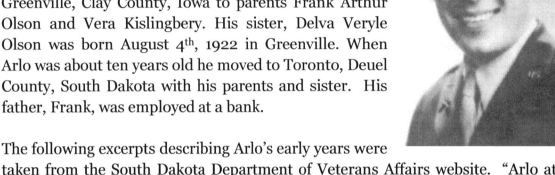

Early Years

Arlo Laverne Olson was born April 20th, 1918 in Greenville, Clay County, Iowa to parents Frank Arthur Olson and Vera Kislingbery. His sister, Delva Veryle Olson was born August 4th, 1922 in Greenville. When Arlo was about ten years old he moved to Toronto, Deuel County, South Dakota with his parents and sister. His father, Frank, was employed at a bank.

The following excerpts describing Arlo's early years were taken from the South Dakota Department of Veterans Affairs website. "Arlo attended school in Toronto and was an active student. He was an avid reader of Zane Grey books, participated in basketball and pole-vaulting, and played the clarinet in band. He also achieved the level of Eagle Scout, something only about two percent of all Scouts attain. After graduating from high school in 1936, he attended the University of South Dakota, where he was an ROTC cadet. In 1940, Arlo graduated from USD and went to work in a bank in Hallock, Minnesota. A year later he joined the Army. His pastor said 'Arlo went to war fearless.'

World War II Years

Arlo entered the Army on June 28, 1941 in Toronto, South Dakota as a 2nd Lieutenant with the 15th Infantry, 3d Infantry Division. His qualifications as a leader of men were soon evident, and he quickly rose in rank. He made 1st Lieutenant on February 1, 1942, and he was promoted to Captain on December 1 of that same year. On Christmas Day in 1942, he married Myra Bordeaux of Baton Rouge, Louisiana. They wed in Natchez, Mississippi where she was a radio announcer. After a few short months together, Capt. Arlo Olson was shipped overseas. He never returned.

General Louis E. Hibbs presented the Medal of Honor to Arlo's widow (Mrs. Myna Olson) at Camp Ban Dom, Mississippi on 16 September1944. The citation read: "For conspicuous gallantry and intrepidity at the risk of his life above and beyond the call of duty. On October 13th, 1943 when the drive across the Volturno River began, Capt. Olson and his company spearheaded the advance of the regiment through 30 miles of mountainous enemy territory in 13 days. Placing himself at the head of his men, Capt.

Olson waded into the chest-deep water of the raging Volturno River and despite point blank machine gun fire aimed directly at him made his way to the opposite bank and threw 2 hand grenades into the gun position, killing the crew. When an enemy machine gun 150 yards distant opened fire on his company, Capt. Olson advanced upon the position in a slow, deliberate walk. Although 5 German soldiers threw hand grenades at him from a range of 5 yards, Capt. Olson dispatched them all, picked up a machine pistol and continued toward the enemy. Advancing to within 15 yards of the position he shot it out with the foe, killing 9 and seizing the post. Throughout the next 13 clays, Capt. Olson led combat patrols, acted as company No. 1 scout and maintained unbroken contact with the enemy. On 27 October 1943, Capt. Olson conducted a platoon in attack on a strongpoint, crawling to within 25 yards of the enemy and then charging the position. Despite continuous machine gun fire which barely missed him, Capt. Olson made his way to the gun and killed the crew with his pistol. When the men saw their leader make this desperate attack they followed him and overran the position. Continuing the advance, Capt. Olson led his company to the next objective at the summit of Monte San Nicola. Although the company was forced to take cover from the furious automatic and small arms fire, which was directed upon him and his men with equal intensity, Capt. Olson waved his company into a skirmish line and, despite the fire of a machine gun which singled him out as its sole target, led the assault which drove the enemy away. While making a reconnaissance for defensive positions, Capt. Olson was fatally wounded. Ignoring his severe pain, this intrepid officer completed his reconnaissance, supervised the location of his men in the best defense positions, refused medical aid until all of his men had been cared for, and died as he was being carried clown the mountain.

For his conspicuous gallantry and intrepidity at the risk of his life and beyond the call of duty, Captain Arlo Olson was also awarded the Silver Star and the Italian Cross of Valor.

Arlo never got to meet his little girl, Myra (Sandra) Lavern Olson, who was born in December of 1943. He died on October 28, 1943 at Mount San Nicola, Italy at age 25. His remains were returned to the United States and buried in Fort Snelling National Cemetery, Minneapolis, Minnesota (MH) (C-24-13787).

Post War Years
The U.S. Navy named a transport ship in his honor. To preserve his memory, the local Legion Post #81, Toronto, South Dakota, was renamed the Erickson-Olson Post in 1943.

Compiled by Shirleen Ann Hoffman, Lake Minnetonka Chapter NSDAR

Donald Eugene Rudolph 1921-2006

Medal of Honor
Action Munoz, Luzon
          Philippine Islands
Date: February 5, 1945

Early Years
A career soldier, Donald Eugene Rudolph was born on February 21, 1921 in South Haven, Wright County, Minnesota. He entered the service in the U.S. Army in Hennepin County, Minnesota on February. 17, 1941 serving through December 4, 1945. He reenlisted on February. 2, 1948 serving through February 7, 1950, and re-upped for a third time on June 12, 1960 serving through July 31, 1963.

World War II Years
On Jan. 9, 1945, nearly three years after the Bataan Death March and the fall of Corregidor, United States forces launched the invasion of Luzon, the main Philippine island, going ashore at Lingayen Gulf for a drive on Manila, about 110 miles to the south. On Feb. 5, Sergeant Rudolph, a platoon leader in the 20th Infantry, Sixth Infantry Division, was administering first aid in the battle for the heavily defended Luzon town of Muñoz when his men came under fire from Japanese soldiers concealed in a culvert. With riflemen covering him, Sergeant Rudolph moved forward alone, carrying his rifle and grenades.

According to the Medal of Honor citation, Donald Eugene Rudolph killed three Japanese soldiers in the culvert, then worked his way across open ground and attacked pillboxes housing machine guns. He hurled a grenade through an opening in the first pillbox, tore away the wood and tin covering with his bare hands, and then dropped another grenade inside. He then grabbed a pickax and used it to pierce a second pillbox, which he took out with rifle fire and a grenade. He destroyed six more pillboxes, and when his platoon was attacked by a Japanese tank, he climbed to its top and dropped a white phosphorus grenade through the turret, killing the crew.

He was given a battlefield commission as a lieutenant, and on Aug. 23, 1945, he was awarded the Medal of Honor by President Harry S. Truman. He was cited for acting in "complete disregard for his own safety" and having "cleared a path for an advance which culminated in one of the most decisive victories of the Philippine campaign."

His Medal of Honor citation reads as follows: "2d Lt. Rudolph (then T/Sgt.) was acting as platoon leader at Munoz, Luzon, Philippine Islands. While administering first aid on the battlefield, he observed enemy fire issuing from a nearby culvert. Crawling to the culvert with rifle and grenades, he killed 3 of the enemy concealed there. He then worked his way across open terrain toward a line of enemy pillboxes which had immobilized his company. Nearing the first pillbox, he hurled a grenade through its embrasure and charged the position. With his bare hands he tore away the wood and tin covering, and then dropped a grenade through the opening, killing the enemy gunners and destroying their machinegun. Ordering several riflemen to cover his further advance, 2d Lt. Rudolph seized a pick mattock and made his way to the second pillbox. Piercing its top with the mattock, he dropped a grenade through the hole, fired several rounds from his rifle into it and smothered any surviving enemy by sealing the hole and the embrasure with earth. In quick succession he attacked and neutralized 6 more pillboxes. Later, when his platoon was attacked by an enemy tank, he advanced under covering fire, climbed to the top of the tank and dropped a white phosphorus grenade through the turret, destroying the crew. Through his outstanding heroism, superb courage, and leadership, and complete disregard for his own safety, 2d Lt. Rudolph cleared a path for an advance which culminated in one of the most decisive victories of the Philippine campaign." He was also awarded the Purple Heart with oak leaf cluster, Asiatic Pacific ribbon, Bronze Star and a Good Conduct Medal.

Post War Years

After retiring from the Army in 1963, Donald Rudolph worked for the Veterans Administration as a Benefits Counselor in both Minneapolis and St. Cloud until retiring 1976. Then he and his wife, Helen, moved to Shamrock Lake north of Bovey, Minnesota. Lt. Rudolph was a member of the Medal of Honor Society, Legion of Valor, Veteran of Foreign Wars Post 159 in Minneapolis, American Legion of Grand Rapids, Legion of Honor, National Sojourners-Minnesota Chapter # 25 in Minneapolis, the National Order of Battlefield Commissions plus other civic organizations.

He died on May 25, 2006 in Bovey, Itasca County, Minnesota. His obituary stated: "Donald Rudolph an Army sergeant in World War II who received the Medal of Honor for single-handedly destroying Japanese machine-gun positions in the battle to recapture the Philippines, died Thursday, 25 May 2006, at a nursing home in Grand Rapids, Minnesota. He was 85." He is buried at Fort Snelling National Cemetery; Section DS Site 22-S.

Compiled by Beth Iseminger, Associate Member Maria Sanford Chapter NSDAR

Richard K. Sorenson 1924-2004

Medal of Honor
Action: Namur, Kwajalein
Date: February 1, 1944

Early Years

A native of Anoka, Minnesota, Richard Keith "Rick" Sorenson was born the son of a WWI Navy veteran, Carl Siren Sorenson and his wife, Virginia A. Mox, on 28 August 1924. Hailing from a family of Norwegian immigrants, his grandfather, Nels, was the only child in his family to be born in America, in 1859. On his mother's side, his grandparents listed their birthplaces as "Poland Russian" and "Poland Germany" on the 1920 US Census for Duluth, Minnesota, having been naturalized in the 1880s. Sorenson's father was a machinist for the Buick

Corporation and the family lived for a time in Flint, Michigan. They returned to Anoka, where Richard graduated from Anoka High School in 1942.

Upon hearing the news of Pearl Harbor with his family on the radio as a 17 year-old, Richard had gone to the Navy recruiting station the next day, even completing the papers, but his parents wouldn't sign. He enlisted the following fall, after football season, at age eighteen in Anoka. When he traveled to San Diego for basic training, it not only was his first trip away from home, but his first time on a train.

World War II Years

Richard Sorenson enlisted in the Marine Corps in December of 1942 and, in 1943, joined Company M, 3rd Battalion, 24th Marines at Camp Pendleton. Early in 1944 he departed for combat duty in WWII's Pacific theatre.

He earned the Medal of Honor for his heroism during the Marine landing at Namur, Kwajalein on the night of February 1, 1944 when, as a 19 year-old private, he threw himself on an exploding Japanese grenade in order to save the lives of five fellow marines. He was severely injured, with fragments of the grenade piercing his thighs, hip, and right arm. At the time, he was not expected to survive. Ironically, as he was being evacuated one of his stretcher bearers was killed by a Japanese sniper. Sorenson was removed to Hawaii and underwent six surgeries over the course of nine months.

Richard Sorenson was awarded his medal by Major General Joseph C. Fegan, then commanding officer of the Department of the Pacific, while in the U.S. Naval Hospital in Seattle, Washington on 19 July 1944, "in front of all the other applauding patients, doctors and nurses." Sorenson's citation reads:

"For conspicuous gallantry and intrepidity at the risk of his life above and beyond the call of duty while serving with an assault battalion attached to the 4th Marine Division during the battle of Namur Island, Kwajalein Atoll, Marshall Islands, on 1-2 February 1944. Putting up a brave defense against a particularly violent counterattack by the enemy during invasion operations, Pvt. Sorenson and 5 other marines occupying a shell hole were endangered by a Japanese grenade thrown into their midst. Unhesitatingly, and with complete disregard for his own safety, Pvt. Sorenson hurled himself upon the deadly weapon, heroically taking the full impact of the explosion. As a result of his gallant action, he was severely wounded, but the lives of his comrades were saved. His great personal valor and exceptional spirit of self-sacrifice in the face of almost certain death were in keeping with the highest traditions of the U.S. Naval Service."

Sorenson was not only awarded a Congressional Medal of Honor, but also a Purple Heart.

After his recovery, Sorenson went on to serve in the Marine Corps. He was assigned to the Marine Air Detachment at the Naval Air Station at Minneapolis, Minnesota and promoted to Corporal. The following month, he was ordered to the headquarters of the Central Recruiting Division in Chicago, Illinois and was promoted to Sergeant. Remaining on recruiting duty, he was ordered to the Midwestern Recruiting Division in St. Louis, Missouri, with additional duty at Fargo, North Dakota. Receiving orders to Great Lakes, Illinois, he remained there until honorably discharged in February 1946.

Following his discharge, he went to work as a contract representative with the Veteran's Administration in Minneapolis. He studied business at St. John's University at Collegeville, Minnesota in 1948. While attending college, he met his wife and lifelong companion of 55 years, Mildred Snow, on a blind date. They were married on 26 November 1949.

In 1950 Sorenson was recalled to active duty during the Korean War, receiving orders to the Marine Corps Recruiting Station in Minneapolis. While at the station, he was promoted to Staff Sergeant in May 1951 and to Master Sergeant in June 1953. In

October 1953, Sorenson was appointed a Second Lieutenant and reported for training at the Basic School at Marine Corps Schools, Quantico, Virginia. In April 1954, he was assigned as the Assistant Supply Officer of the Seventh Engineer Battalion at Camp Pendleton and was promoted to First Lieutenant in the fall. Early the next year, he joined the Second Replacement Battalion and was ordered overseas to Okinawa, Japan with the Third Engineer Battalion, Third Marine Division.

In November 1955, he returned to the United States, resigned his commission, and resumed civilian life.

Post War Years

Sorenson returned to the Veterans Administration until 1957, served as an insurance underwriter for the next decade, and then returned once again to the V.A. and retired as Director of Veterans Affairs for the state of Nevada and nine counties of California in 1985. He remained active in his community in public service.

He and Mildred went on to raise a family five children, three sons and two daughters, Robert, Wendy, Debbie, James and Thomas.

When interviewed by the Anoka Historical Society in 1991, Sorenson was asked if he had any words of wisdom to share. He said: "Well, I think that really what we have to do in future generations, we have to be concerned about our freedom. We won our freedom in just one generation, and in one generation, we could lose it. That freedom is a very dear and precious thing, and I really don't think people understand how valuable it is until they lose it." He is one of Anoka's WWII heroes for whom a park in the city is dedicated.

Sorenson died suddenly on October, 9, 2004 in Reno, Nevada, where he had lived since 1978. His widow still resides in Reno, as do many members of his family. He was buried with full military honors at Fort Snelling National Cemetery in Minneapolis, Minnesota. His father and mother are also buried at Fort Snelling.

Compiled by Kathleen M. Barrett Huston
Lake Minnetonka Chapter NSDAR

Franklin Van Valkenburgh 1888-1941

Medal of Honor awarded posthumously
Action: U.S.S Arizona, Pearl Harbor
Hawaii
Date: December 7, 1941

Early Years

Franklin Van Valkenburgh was born on April 5, 1888 in Hennepin County, Minneapolis, Minnesota. He graduated from the U.S. Naval Academy, June of 1909. From 1911-1914, he was with the Asiatic Squadron and Franklin served as an instructor at the Naval Academy intermittently 1920-1925.

The United States entry to WWI found Van Valkenburgh serving as the battleship USS Rhode Island's engineering officer. On June 1, 1920, Van Valkenburgh reported on

board the USS Minnesota for duty as engineer officer. He held that post until the battleship was decommissioned in November, 1921. He again served as an instructor at the Naval Academy until May 15, 1925 before he joined the USS Maryland on June 26, 1925.

His postgraduate education was in the field of steam engineering, and during this time he served on the battleships Minnesota and Maryland. In 1928 he was assigned to the Office of the Chief of Naval Operations in Washington DC.

In the early 1930s, Franklin was Commander of the Destroyer Talbot and Destroyer Squadron Five. He was a student at the Naval War College and Inspector of Naval Material at the New York Navy Yard before again serving at sea during 1936-1938 as Commanding Officer of the Destroyer Melville. Then he spent time ashore with the Third Naval District. In February 1941, Captain Van Valkenburgh became commanding officer of the battleship Arizona.

War Years

On February 5, 1941, Van Valkenburgh relieved Capt. Harold C. Train as commanding officer of USS *Arizona* (BB-39). Newly refitted at Puget Sound Naval Shipyard, *Arizona* served as flagship of Battleship Division 1 for the remainder of the year, based primarily at Pearl Harbor with two trips to the west coast.

In a letter to a relative, Faith Van Valkenburgh Vilas, dated November 4, 1941, Captain Van Valkenburgh wrote: "We are training, preparing, maneuvering, doing everything we can do to be ready. The work is intensive, continuous, and carefully planned. We never go to sea without being completely ready to move on to Singapore if need be, without further preparation. Most of our work we are not allowed to talk about off of the ship. I have spent

The USS *Arizona's* Memorial Wall

16 to 20 hours a day on the bridge for a week at a time, then a week of rest, then at it again. Our eyes are constantly trained Westward, and we keep the guns ready for instant use against aircraft or submarines whenever we are at sea. We have no intention of being caught napping."

On December 4, the battleship went to sea in company with USS *Nevada* and USS *Oklahoma* for night surface practice and, after conducting these gunnery exercises, returned to Pearl Harbor independently on the 6th to moor at berth F-7 alongside Ford Island.

The USS *Arizona's* forward magazines explode

Both Captain Van Valkenburgh and the embarked division commander, Rear Admiral Isaac C. Kidd, spent the next Saturday evening, December 6, on board. Suddenly, shortly before 08:00 on December 7, Japanese planes roared overhead, shattering the Sunday peace and punctuating it with the explosion of bombs and the staccato hammering of machine guns. Captain Van Valkenburgh ran from his cabin and arrived on the navigation bridge where he immediately began to direct his ship's defense. A quartermaster in the pilot house asked if the captain wanted to go to the conning tower—a less-exposed position in view of the Japanese strafing— but Van Valkenburgh refused to do so and continued to man a telephone, fighting for his ship's life. A violent explosion suddenly shook the ship, throwing the three occupants of the bridge—Captain Van Valkenburgh, an ensign, and the quartermaster, to the deck, and blowing out all of the bridge windows. Dazed, battered and shaken, the ensign stumbled through the flames and smoke of the shattered bridge's interior and escaped, but Captain Van Valkenburgh and the quartermaster were never seen again. A continuing fire, fed by ammunition and oil, blazed for two days until finally being extinguished on December 9. Despite a thorough search, Captain Van Valkenburgh's body was never found. All that was ever retrieved was his Annapolis class ring.

Post War Years

Captain Van Valkenburgh died on December 7 1941 at Pearl Harbor Hawaii. His memorial is in the National Memorial Cemetery of the Pacific. A memorial was built above the sunken ship as an active U.S. Military Cemetery with a shrine room listing the names of the lost crew members on a marble wall. Franklin's name is engraved on that wall.

Captain Franklin Van Valkenburgh received the Medal of Honor posthumously. The citation reads "For conspicuous devotion to duty, extraordinary courage and complete disregard of his own life." In 1943, the destroyer USS Van Valkenburgh was named in his honor

Arizona Memorial Wall

Compiled by Diana Myers Keewaydin Chapter NSDAR

Dirk Jan Cornelius Vlug 1916-1996

Medal of Honor
Action: Ormoc Road
Limon, province of Leyte
Philippines.
Date: December 15, 1944

Early Years
Few people earn a moniker during their lifetime, but that was the case with Dirk Vlug. At the time of his passing in 1996, he was known as the man who single-handedly destroyed five Japanese tanks. Like so many of our Medal of Honor winners, Mr. Vlug's beginnings were humble.

Dirk Jan Cornelius Vlug was born in the Township of Corrina, Maple Lake, Wright County, Minnesota on August 20, 1916 to 30-year old Dutch immigrants from the Netherlands. The second son and fourth child of Isaac Vlug and Mietje (pronounced Met-cha), Dekker joined siblings Peter (born 1909), Alida (born 1912) and Wesselina (born 1914). Farmers in Minnesota, the Vlugs had two more children after Dirk, Gertrude born in 1918 and Marian born in 1922. However, when Dirk was six years old the family moved to Michigan. By 1930 Isaac Vlug had settled the family in Grand Rapids, Michigan taking up carpentry as a trade to support them.

World War II Years
Like many of the greatest generation, Mr. Vlug answered his country's call to service on April 21 1941 at Kalamazoo, Michigan. Enlisting in the United States Army as a Private First Class, Mr. Vlug was assigned to the 126th infantry, 32d Infantry Division. A cannoneer in the "Red Arrow" Brigade, he was soon sent to the Pacific theatre to participate in several campaigns and by December 15, 1944 Mr. Vlug was stationed in the Philippines guarding the American road block on the Ormoc Road near Limon Province of Leyte in the Philippines. Alone in a foxhole armed with his rocket launcher and only six rounds of ammunition, Mr. Vlug heard the slow rumble of eight Japanese tanks coming towards his battalion.

Without hesitation or concern for his personal safety, Mr. Vlug "destroyed the first tank killing its occupants with a single round. As the crew of the second tank started to dismount and attack him, he killed one foe with his pistol and forced the others to return to their vehicle which he destroyed with a second round." As three more tanks approached Mr. Vlug "flanked the first and eliminated it, then despite hail enemy fire pressed forward to destroy another. With his last round of ammunition, he struck the remaining vehicle, causing it to crash down a steep embankment." This created an opening for his fellow soldiers to rush through and attack the enemy.

According to a 1992 interview with the Grand Rapids Press, Mr. Vlug said "I would load, take a shot and dive back in the hole. I felt that anytime I could die, and it would only take one shot in the right place." Lasting only 30 minutes and with only six rounds of ammunition, Mr. Vlug single-handedly destroyed five Japanese tanks. Along with his time in Leyte, Mr. Vlug also participated in the campaigns of New Guinea, Papuan, Southern Philippines and Luzon.

Post War Years

Following his discharge from the service on June 14, 1945, Mr. Vlug returned home to his parents. Less than a year later on May 23, 1946, the War Department announced that due to his "single-handed destruction of five Japanese tanks in the Philippines" Dirk Vlug would be awarded the Congressional Medal of Honor. That honor was bestowed on him by President Harry S. Truman on June 7, 1946 at the White House.

After his release from the United States Army, Dirk Vlug's service to his country continued. He entered the Michigan Army National Guard serving from May 23, 1949 until being honorably discharged as a Master Sergeant on January 25, 1951. Soon after the war's end he would find time to marry. On August 16, 1946 Dirk Vlug married Angie Sikkema in McBain, Missaukee County, Michigan. Together they raised three daughters: Carol, Margie and Meribeth.

In 1950 to support his young family Mr. Vlug became a postal carrier in Grand Rapids retiring his position in 1976. On Veteran's Day 1992, He received Michigan's highest military honor, the Distinguished Service Medal. Lt. Col. Brian Downey, spokesman for Michigan's Department of Public Affairs declared "The state wanted to do something to recognize the service of its veterans who epitomize valor, and that kind of service to state and country."

In retirement Mr. Vlug enjoyed such hobbies as golfing, bowling and making bird houses, but perhaps his favorite activity was staying in contact with his fellow veterans. He and Angie hosted monthly picnics in an effort to stay in touch with those he served with. Mr. Vlug enjoyed traveling too. In 1994, he and his wife went to Leyte to commemorate the 50th anniversary of the Battle of the Philippines. According to Angie Vlug both she and her husband were "treated like royalty" during their visit to the island.

In 1996 the Military Order of Foreign Wars of the United States bestowed upon Mr. Vlug an honorary membership. Shortly thereafter on June 25, 1996, he passed away in Grand Rapids. Remembered by his friends as an intensely humble man who rarely spoke of his heroics, Angie Vlug was quoted

as saying, "A lot of other people flaunt it, and he was very upset about other Medal of Honor Winners who flaunted it. He just wasn't that way." At the time of his passing Mr. Vlug was survived by his three daughters and sons-in-law Carol and David Shirk, Margie and Bernie deWit, and Meribeth and Victor Eerkes as well as 7 grandchildren and one great grandchild. By the time of her death on January 7, 2013, Angie Vlug had seen 16 great grandchildren added to the family since Dirk's passing.

In October 1999 another honor was given posthumously to Mr. Vlug. The United Veteran's Council sought and received permission from the Grand Rapids City Commission to rename a street along Veterans Memorial Park "Dirk Vlug Way."

Dirk Vlug and his wife Angie are interred in Greenwood Cemetery in Grand Rapids, Michigan.

Compiled by Laura Gallup
Anoka Chapter NSDAR

KOREAN WAR

JUNE 25, 1950
TO
JULY 27, 1953

KOREAN WAR

Liberated from Japan in 1945 during the final days of World War II, Korea was divided by the Allies with the United States occupying the territory to the south of the 38th Parallel and the Soviet Union the land to the north. Later that year it was decided that the country would be reunited and made independent after a five-year period. This was later shortened and elections in North and South Korea were held in 1948. While the Communists under Kim Il-sung took power in the north, the south became democratic. Supported by their respective sponsors both governments wished to reunite the peninsula under their particular ideology. After several border skirmishes, North Korea invaded South Korea on June 25, 1950, opening the conflict.

Backed by the United Nations, with many of the troops furnished by the United States, South Korea resisted and fighting ebbed and flowed up and down the peninsula until the front stabilized just north of the 38th Parallel. A bitterly contested conflict, the Korean War saw the United States follow its policy of containment as it worked to block aggression and halt the spread of Communism. As such, the Korean War may be seen as one of the many proxy wars fought during the Cold War.

Negotiations at Panmunjom bore fruit in 1953 and an armistice went into effect on July 27. Though fighting ended, no formal peace treaty was concluded. Instead, both sides agreed to the creation of a demilitarized zone along the front. Approximately 250 miles long and 2.5 miles wide, it remains one of the most heavily militarized borders in the world with both sides manning their respective defenses. Casualties in the fighting numbered around 778,000 for UN/South Korean forces, while North Korea and China suffered around 1.1 to 1.5 million. In the wake of the conflict, South Korea developed one of the world's strongest economies while North Korea remains an isolated pariah state.

militaryhistory.about.com/od/battleswars1900s/tp/The-Korean-War.

John Upshur Dennis Page 1904-1950

Medal of Honor awarded posthumously
Action: Korean Conflict
        Chosen Reservoir, Korea (North)
Date: November 29, 1950-December 10, 1950

Early life

John U.D. Page was born February 8, 1904 on Malahi Island, Luzon, Philippine Islands and studied engineering at Princeton University. Princeton was Page's second choice, when his dream of attending West Point was thwarted by weak eyesight. He graduated from Princeton in 1926 with a varsity letter in pistol and a Reserve Officers' Training Corps (ROTC) commission. He entered Service in St. Paul, Minnesota in 1926 and was a part of U.S. Army X Corps Artillery while attached to 52nd Transportation Truck Battalion. He was called to duty in World War II as a reservist.

World War II

Trained in artillery, Page was considered an expert teacher, and he spent much of World War II training troops at Fort Sill, Oklahoma, much to his chagrin. He finally got to command an artillery battery in Germany, and remained in the military after World War II. Assigned to the prestigious Command and General Staff College at Fort Leavenworth, Kans., he pulled strings to go to Korea rather than to the classroom.

Korean War

Lieutenant Colonel Page's valor at the Chosin Reservoir was so incredible, the Marines among whom he served submitted him for the Navy Cross, making him one of only three Army recipients of that award in Korea.

The Medal of Honor awarded for his actions during the Korean War was presented on April 25, 1957. It reads: "The President of the United States of America, in the name of Congress, takes pride in presenting the Medal of Honor (Posthumously) to Lieutenant Colonel John Upshur Dennis Page (ASN: 0-29085), United States Army, for conspicuous gallantry and intrepidity in action above and beyond the call of duty in a series of exploits while attached to the 52d Transportation Truck Battalion, in action against enemy aggressor forces at the Chosin Reservoir, North Korea, from 29 November to 10 December 1950. On 29 November, Lieutenant Colonel Page left X Corps Headquarters at Hamhung with the mission of establishing traffic control on the main supply route to 1ˢᵗ Marine Division positions and those of some Army elements on the Chosin Reservoir plateau. Having completed his mission Lieutenant Colonel Page was free to return to the safety of Hamhung but chose to remain on the plateau to aid an isolated signal station, thus being cut off with elements of the Marine Division. After rescuing his jeep driver by breaking up an ambush near a destroyed bridge Lieutenant Colonel Page reached the lines of a surrounded Marine Garrison at Koto-ri. He then voluntarily developed and trained a reserve force of assorted army troops trapped with the marines. By exemplary leadership and tireless devotion he made an effective tactical unit available. In order that casualties might be evacuated, an airstrip was improvised on frozen ground partly outside of the Koto-ri defense perimeter which was continually under enemy attack. During two such attacks, Lieutenant Colonel Page exposed himself on the airstrip to direct fire on the enemy, and twice mounted the rear deck of a tank, manning the machinegun on the turret to drive the enemy back into a no man's land. On 3 December while being flown low over enemy lines in a light observation plane, Lieutenant Colonel Page dropped hand grenades on Chinese positions and sprayed foxholes with automatic fire from his carbine.

"After ten days of constant fighting the marine and army units in the vicinity of the Chosin Reservoir had succeeded in gathering at the edge of the plateau and Lieutenant Colonel Page was flown to Hamhung to arrange for artillery support of the beleaguered troops attempting to break out. Again Lieutenant Colonel Page refused an opportunity to remain in safety and returned to give every assistance to his comrades. As the column slowly moved south Lieutenant Colonel Page joined the rear guard. When it neared the entrance to a narrow pass it came under frequent attacks on both flanks. Mounting an abandoned tank Lieutenant Colonel Page manned the machinegun, braved heavy return fire, and covered the passing vehicles until the danger diminished. Later when another attack threatened his section of the convoy, then in the middle of the pass, Lieutenant Colonel Page took a machinegun to the hillside and delivered effective counter fire, remaining exposed while men and vehicles passed through the ambuscade. On the night of 10 December the convoy reached the bottom of the pass but was halted by a strong enemy force at the front and on both flanks. Deadly small-arms fire poured into the column. Realizing the danger to the column as it lay motionless, Lieutenant Colonel Page fought his way to the head of the column and plunged forward into the heart of the hostile position. His intrepid action so surprised the enemy that their ranks became disordered and suffered heavy casualties. Heedless of his safety, as he had been throughout the preceding ten days, Lieutenant Colonel Page remained forward, fiercely engaging the enemy single-handed until mortally wounded.

" By his valiant and aggressive spirit Lieutenant Colonel Page enabled friendly forces to stand off the enemy. His outstanding courage, unswerving devotion to duty, and supreme self-sacrifice reflect great credit upon Lieutenant Colonel Page and are in the highest tradition of the military service."

Lt. Colonel John Upshur Dennis Page was killed in action December 10, 1950. He was buried in Arlington National Cemetery on December 14, 1954.

In addition to the Medal of Honor, Lieutenant Colonel Page was awarded:

★ Combat Infantryman Badge
★ Korean Service Medal
★ Medal of Honor
★ National Defense Service Medal
★ Navy Cross
★ Purple Heart
★ Republic of Korea Presidential
   Unit Citation
★ Republic of Korea War Service
   Medal
★ United Nations Service Medal
★ World War II Victory Medal

Lt. Col. Page has also been honored by the following:
The Military Sealift Command ship MV *LTC John U.D. Page* (T-AK-4543) is named in his honor. Prior to T-AK 4543, the only Beach Discharge Lighter, a 338-foot landing craft, in the US military was also named the USAV *Lt. Col. John U.D. Page* (BDL X1). Camp Page, near Chunchon, ROK, was the home of the Apache unit linked to the 2nd Infantry at the DMZ until it was closed in 2005.

Compiled by Beth Iseminger, Maria Sanford NSDAR Chapter, Associate Member

VIETNAM WAR

The Vietnam War was the longest war in United States history. Promises and commitments to the people and government of South Vietnam to keep communist forces from overtaking them reached back into the Truman Administration. Eisenhower placed military advisers and CIA operatives in Vietnam, and John F. Kennedy sent American soldiers to Vietnam. Lyndon Johnson ordered the first real combat by American troops, and Richard Nixon concluded the war.

Despite the decades of resolve, billions and billions of dollars, nearly 60,000 American lives and many more injuries, the United States failed to achieve its objectives. One factor that influenced the failure of the United States in Vietnam was lack of public support. The antiwar movement in 1965 was small, and news of its activities was buried in the inner pages of newspapers, if there was any mention at all. Only later in the war did public opinion sour. The enemy was hard to identify. The war was not fought between conventional army forces. The Viet Cong blended in with the native population and struck by ambush, often at night.

Massive American bombing campaigns hit their targets, but failed to make the North Vietnamese concede. Promises made by American military and political leaders that the war would soon be over were broken. And night after night, Americans turned on the news to see the bodies of their young flown home in bags. Draft injustices like college deferments surfaced, harkening back to the similar controversies of the Civil War. The average age of the American soldier in Vietnam was nineteen.

As the months of the war became years, the public became impatient. Many began to feel it was time to cut losses. President Nixon signed a ceasefire in January 1973 that formally ended the hostilities. At home, returning Vietnamese veterans found readjustment and even acceptance difficult. The scars of Vietnam would not heal quickly for the United States. The legacy of bitterness divided the American citizenry and influenced foreign policy into the 21st century.

The Vietnam War:ushistory.org

VIETNAM WAR

NOVEMBER 1, 1955 TO APRIL 30, 1975

Michael Reinert Blanchfield 1950-1969

Medal of Honor awarded posthumously
Action: Binh Dinh Province
            Republic of Vietnam
Date: July 3, 1969

Early Years

Michael Reinert Blanchfield was born on January 4, 1950 in Minneapolis, Hennepin County, Minnesota to Robert and Jeannette (Watson) Blanchfield. He had four siblings, brothers Bill and James and sisters Bobby Jo and Patricia. In 1961, his family moved to Arlington Heights, Illinois which is a suburb of Chicago. As a sophomore, Michael dropped out of high school. On September 25, 1968 at the age of 17 he enlisted in the Army at the age of 17 in Chicago, Illinois and earned his GED while in the Army.

Vietnam War Years

On February 20, 1969, Michael was sent to Vietnam as Specialist Fourth Class in Light Weapons Infantry in Company A, 4th Battalion, 503rd Infantry Regiment, 173rd Airborne Brigade. On July 3, 1969, in Binh Dinh Province, Michael smothered the blast of a hand grenade with his body, sacrificing himself to protect those around him.

For this action, Michael was posthumously awarded the Congressional Medal of Honor. The Medal of Honor citation reads: "For conspicuous gallantry and intrepidity in action at the risk of his life above and beyond the call of duty, Sp4c. Blanchfield distinguished himself while serving as a rifleman in Company A on a combat patrol. The patrol surrounded a group of houses to search for suspects. During the search of one of the huts, a man suddenly ran out toward a nearby tree line. Sp4c. Blanchfield, who was on guard outside the hut, saw the man, shouted for him to halt, and began firing at him as the man ignored the warning and continued to run. The suspect suddenly threw a grenade toward the hut and its occupants. Although the exploding grenade severely wounded Sp4c. Blanchfield and several others, he regained his feet to continue the pursuit of the enemy. The fleeing enemy threw a second grenade which landed near Sp4c. Blanchfield and several members of his patrol. Instantly realizing the danger, he shouted a warning to his comrades. Sp4c. Blanchfield unhesitatingly and with complete disregard for his safety, threw himself on the grenade, absorbing the full and fatal impact of the explosion. By his gallant action and self-sacrifice, he was able to save the lives and prevent injury to 4 members of the patrol and several Vietnamese civilians in the immediate area. Sp4c. Blanchfield's extraordinary courage and gallantry at the cost of his life above and beyond the call of duty are in keeping with the highest traditions of the military service and reflect great credit upon himself, his unit, and the U.S. Army."

In addition to the Medal of Honor, Michael was also awarded the National Defense Service Medal, Combat Infantryman Badge, Purple Heart, Vietnam Campaign Medal and Vietnam Service Medal.

Nineteen year old Michael died a hero on January 4, 1962 in Vietnam. He was buried in All Saints Catholic Cemetery, Des Plaines, Illinois. In addition to his family, he was survived by his fiancée, Miss Frances Ratz of Wheeling.

Post War Years
Michael made a difference in the lives of the soldiers he saved that day. His story continues to make a difference. On May 27, 2011, the Wheeling High School presented his family with an honorary diploma and a plaque signifying his induction as a distinguished alumnus. The ceremony took place with about 60 history students watching from within the theater, however the entire student body watched from their classrooms. The school administration scheduled the ceremony so that it could be used as a teaching tool as well as an honorary ceremony for Blanchfield. History teacher and Vietnam War veteran Bob Kupon said, "They've seen movies about war, but seeing the movies is not what this is. You touch history." On that day, Michael touched the lives of each of those students.

Compiled by Merrilee Carlson, Nathan Hale ChapterNSDAR

Kenneth Lee Olson 1945-1968

Medal of Honor awarded posthumously
Action: Long An
           Republic of Vietnam
Date: May 13, 1968,

*Greater love hath no man than this, that he
lay down his life for his friends. ~ John 15:13*

Kenneth Lee "Ken" Olson believed these words. In the
jungles of Vietnam in 1968, while a soldier in the U.S.
Army, Olson died by these words while saving the life
of a fellow soldier.

Early Years
The youngest of Ben and Lydia Olson's three sons,
Ken was born May 26, 1945 in Willmar, Minnesota. He grew up on the family farm on
the Meeker-Kandiyohi county line, south of Lake Koronis. With older brothers Philip
and Daniel, he grew up loving to hunt and fish.

He attended country school through the eighth grade and then attended Paynesville
High School. At PHS, he graduated cum laude, belonged to the National Honor Society,
served as senior class president and president of the FFA Chapter, played trumpet in the
band, played intramural sports, was a Homecoming candidate and starred in a drama
production.   As a young man, Ken was chosen as the Paynesville delegate to the
Minnesota American Legion Boys State program.

"He was one of my top students," recalled LeRoy Hillbrand, who taught agriculture and
was the advisor for the FFA Chapter in Paynesville for over 30 years. Olson had
outstanding scholastic ability as well as a friendly, outgoing personality, according to
Hillbrand. Ken was an active member of the Paynesville Gospel Tabernacle and served
as president of the youth group.

In June 1967 Ken was the first person in his family to graduate from college, earning a
Bachelor of Arts from the University of Minnesota College of Agriculture and the School
of Business. He had planned to continue his agriculture studies in graduate school at
Purdue University, but the Meeker County draft board informed him that his student
deferment would not be extended. On the basis of his college degree, Ken expected to
get a desk job instead of being sent to the front lines in Vietnam, recalled his sister-in-
law Juanita Olson.

Vietnam War Years

He was inducted into the United States Army on June 20, 1967 in Hennepin County, Minnesota. A Specialist Fourth Class, he was a member of Company A, 5th Battalion, 12th Infantry, 199th Brigade. Just before shipping out to Vietnam, Ken had one last visit home to Minnesota. Soon after shipping out, he ordered Mother's Day flowers for his mother.

Specialist Fourth Class Kenneth Olson arrived in Vietnam around April 1, 1968. Six weeks later, on May 13, 1968, his unit was reinforcing a reconnaissance platoon that was engaged by an entrenched Viet Cong force. His Medal of Honor citation describes his heroic act: "Sp4c. Olson and a fellow soldier moved forward of the platoon to investigate another suspected line of bunkers. As the two men advanced, they were pinned down by intense automatic weapons fire from an enemy position ten meters to their front. With complete disregard for his own safety, Specialist Olson exposed himself and hurled a hand grenade into the Viet Cong position. Failing to silence the fire, he again exposed himself to the intense fire in preparation to assault the position. As he prepared to hurl the grenade he was wounded, causing him to drop the activated device within his own position. Realizing that it would explode immediately, Specialist Olson threw himself upon the grenade and pulled it into his body to take the full force of the explosion. (Kenneth L. Olson Congressional Medal of Honor, 1970)"

By taking the full force of the grenade, Olson saved the life of Gary Lindley, the fellow soldier who had advanced with him to that forward position. Olson's sacrifice was not a surprise to people who knew him, his giving nature and his deep religious beliefs. "Hopefully," Edwin Schaumann, Jr. told the *Paynesville Press* in 1995, "we all have that in us."

Ken Olson died on Monday, May 13, 1968 in Long An Republic of Vietnam. Since Vietnam is across the International Date Line, it was still Mother's Day in Minnesota when he died. Perhaps his mother was wearing the flowers Ken had shipped to her. A week later two soldiers came to the family farm to inform Ben and Lydia Olson that Ken was missing in action. Because his body had not been recovered, he was not initially reported as deceased. However, family members were certain of Ken's death because of eye witness accounts from fellow soldiers.

Ken Olson is buried in the Paynesville, Minnesota Cemetery and memorialized on "The Wall," the Vietnam Veterans Memorial Panel 59E, Line 28

In April 1970, President Nixon presented Congressional Medals of Honor to 22 American heroes. Ken's family accepted the Medal at the White House ceremony. Ken Olson is the only Paynesville, Minnesota High School graduate to earn the Congressional Medal of Honor. He is the only University of Minnesota graduate to earn the Medal of Honor during the Vietnam War.

Post War Years

Olson's sacrifice and service are honored in several ways. At the University of Minnesota College of Food, Agriculture and Natural Resource Sciences, there is a Ken Olson Memorial Scholarship Endowment. In 2004, Ken was in the first class of inductees into the Paynesville High School Distinguished Alumni. Two identical bronze memorials designed by the late Minneapolis artist/veteran Rodger Brodin were cast. One of the plaques is displayed inside the front lobby of American Legion Post 271 in Paynesville, Minnesota. The other is on display in the Minnesota Commons Room on the first floor of the St. Paul Student Center on the University of Minnesota campus. Featuring a bas-relief portrait of Ken, the inscription reads:

"Kenneth L. Olson, Paynesville, MN, graduated June, 1967 with a BA from the College of Agriculture and the School of Business. Ken was drafted into the US Army on June 20, 1967. On May 13, 1968, in the Republic of Vietnam, Specialist Fourth Class Olson was serving with Company A, 5th Battalion, 12th Infantry, 199th Infantry Brigade. During a firefight with an enemy force Sp4c Olson threw himself upon a grenade and pulled it into his body to take the full force of the explosion. By this unselfish action, Sp4c Olson sacrificed his own life to save the lives of his fellow comrades-in-arms."

Greater love hath no one than this that a man lay down his life for his friends.
John 15: 13

Compiled by Karrie Louise-Norenberg Blees
Greysolon Daughters of Liberty Chapter
NSDAR

Robert Joseph Pruden 1949-1969

Medal of Honor awarded posthumously
Action: Quang Ngai Province
          Republic of Vietnam
Date: November 20, 1969,

Early Years

Robert Joseph Pruden, son of Lawrence and Marlys (Gitzen) Pruden, was born in St. Paul, Minnesota, on September 9, 1949. He was the second-oldest in a family of 13 children. He enjoyed sports and played baseball, football and hockey. He graduated from Harding High School in 1967 and aspiring "to make a difference in Vietnam" he enlisted in the U.S. Army.

Vietnam War Years

Robert entered the service in Minneapolis, Minnesota and completed the Non-Commissioned Officer Indoctrination Course at Harmony Church, Fort Benning, Georgia, in Class 2-69, 72nd Company, graduating on October 8, 1968. He then completed Ranger training at Fort Benning and Dahlonega, Georgia, before reporting for duty with G/75th Infantry (Rangers).

In November 1969 at the age of 20, Staff Sergeant Pruden was on a reconnaissance mission with the 75th Ranger Infantry Regiment (Airborne), American Division. Under threat in enemy territory, he left his concealed position to divert attention from his five team members. Suffering several gunshot wounds, Pruden directed his team to an evacuation helicopter before he died from his injuries.

On April 22, 1971, President Richard Nixon awarded the Medal of Honor to Robert's family for his actions. His mother, father, five brothers, and seven sisters were present at the private ceremony in the White House Blue Room. The citation reads: "For conspicuous gallantry and intrepidity in action at the risk of his life above and beyond the call of duty. S/Sgt. Pruden, Company G, distinguished himself while serving as a reconnaissance team leader during an ambush mission. The 6-man team was inserted by helicopter into enemy controlled territory to establish an ambush position and to obtain information concerning enemy movements. As the team moved into the preplanned area, S/Sgt. Pruden deployed his men into 2 groups on opposite sides of a well-used trail. As the groups were establishing their defensive positions, one member of the team was trapped in the open by the heavy fire from an enemy squad. Realizing that the ambush position had been compromised, S/Sgt. Pruden directed his team to open fire on the enemy force. Immediately, the team came under heavy fire from a second enemy element. S/Sgt. Pruden, with full knowledge of the extreme danger involved, left his concealed position and, firing as he ran, advanced toward the enemy to draw the hostile fire. He was seriously wounded twice but continued his attack until he fell for a third time in front of the enemy positions. S/Sgt. Pruden's actions resulted in several enemy casualties and withdrawal of the remaining enemy force. Although grievously wounded, he directed his men into defensive position and called for evacuation helicopters, which safely withdrew the members of the team. S/Sgt. Pruden's outstanding courage, selfless concern for the welfare of his men, and intrepidity in action at the cost of his life were in keeping with the highest tradition of the military service and reflect great credit upon himself, his Unit, and the United States Army. "

Post War Years

In addition to the Medal of Honor, Robert was awarded a Bronze Star and two Purple Hearts. He was an inaugural inductee to the U.S. Army Ranger Hall of Fame at Fort Benning, Georgia. The Army Rangers award the Pruden Trophy to the winner of its annual fitness challenge. Pruden Hall at Kelly Barracks, a U.S. military installation in Germany, is also named after him.

Robert Pruden is buried at Fort Snelling National Cemetery in Minneapolis, Minnesota.

Submitted by Georgetta "Gigi" Hickey
Lake Minnetonka Chapter NSDAR

Laszlo Rabel 1937-1968

Medal of Honor awarded posthumously
Action: Binh Dinh Province
          Republic of Vietnam
Date: November 13, 1968

Early Years

Staff Sergeant Laszlo Rabel was born in Budapest on September 21st 1937. He escaped from Hungary after participating in the failed 1956 revolution against Soviet-backed Hungarian Communist forces. Rabel is thought to have lost several family members and friends in the uprising and he eventually made it across the border into Austria and found refuge in the United States in 1957, enlisting in the Army in 1965. During his training he regaled his comrades with stories of his role in the uprising, one of which was retold in a letter written to him posthumously by a fellow soldier, Larry Warner, 173rd Airborne Brigade, 1966-1967, 5th Special Forces Group 1967-1968:

"Alas, Lazlo, I keep you in my mind and in my heart. I remember you well. When we were students together at the MACV Recondo School in Nha Trang in 1967, you were so much older than I was. I was only twenty years old, half way through the first of two tours In Country. You were 30.... On breaks, those of us who were students from the 173rd Airborne Brigade would gather together and tell stories. You regaled us with stories of the shock to your most innocent youth in Hungary in 1956, when you were a 19-year-old lad, being caught up in the Revolution that was brutally crushed. Your recounting of escaping and evading through Russian lines was a harrowing tale. I remember the twinkle in your eyes when you recalled how you took out a couple of Russians who were in your way during your escape to the West. Here it was 11 years later and you puffed up your burly chest with the pride of the opportunity to rid the world of more Communists—and get paid for it. Your dedication and commitment to your mission and to your fellow soldiers both awed and inspired me...."

Vietnam Conflict

Laszlo Rabel joined the US Army from Minneapolis, Minnesota in 1965, and by November 13, 1968 was serving as a Staff Sergeant in the 74th Infantry Detachment (Long Range Patrol), 173rd Airborne Brigade, MOS 11F-Infantry Operations and Intelligence Specialist.

There were a total of 536,100 U.S. soldiers deployed to Vietnam. Of that number 58,220 or over ten percent lost their lives in the conflict. Sixty-four percent of the survivors were wounded in action. On November 13, 1968 in Binh Dinh Province of the Republic of Vietnam, Laszlo Rabel sacrificed his life as well by smothering the blast of an enemy-thrown hand grenade with his body to protect his fellow soldiers. For this heroic action he was one of 256 American combatants, 170 of them Army, to receive the Medal of Honor, 63% of them posthumously.

Staff Sergeant Rabel's official Medal of Honor citation reads: "For conspicuous gallantry and intrepidity in action at the risk of his life above and beyond the call of duty. S/Sgt. Rabel distinguished himself while serving as leader of Team Delta, 74th Infantry Detachment. At 1000 hours on this date, Team Delta was in a defensive perimeter conducting reconnaissance of enemy trail networks when a member of the team detected enemy movement to the front. As S/Sgt. Rabel and a comrade prepared to clear the area, he heard an incoming grenade as it landed in the midst of the team's perimeter. With complete disregard for his life, S/Sgt. Rabel threw himself on the grenade and, covering it with his body, received the complete impact of the immediate explosion. Through his indomitable courage, complete disregard for his safety and profound concern for his fellow soldiers, S/Sgt. Rabel averted the loss of life and injury to the other members of Team Delta. By his gallantry at the cost of his life in the highest traditions of the military service, S/Sgt. Rabel has reflected great credit upon himself, his unit, and the U.S. Army."

The Medal of Honor was presented to his wife Eva and daughter Eve at the White House by President Richard Nixon on April 7, 1970. In addition to the Medal of Honor Sgt. Rabel was awarded the Bronze Star and the Purple Heart posthumously.

Rabel, aged 31 at his death on November 13, 1968, was buried in Arlington National Cemetery (Section 52, Grave 1326) in Arlington, Virginia. His name is inscribed on Panel 38W, Row 7 on the Vietnam Veterans' Memorial in Washington D.C.

Compiled by June Gossler Anderson
Anoka Chapter NSDAR

Leo Keith Thorsness 1932-

Medal of Honor
Action: North Vietnam
Date: April 19, 1967

Early Years

Born on Valentine's Day, 1932 in Walnut Grove, Redwood County, Minnesota, Leo Keith Thorsness, was the third and last of Emil R. and Bernice Mae *Learned* Thorsness' children. Leo's two older siblings were Donna M., born in 1926 and John L. born in 1929.   His grandfather, John Thorsness, had emigrated from Norway.

Leo grew up on a farm near Walnut Grove, and earned the Distinguished Eagle Scout Award from the Boy Scouts of America, one of nine known Eagle Scouts who also received the Medal of Honor.   He married Gaylee Anderson on December 26, 1953 in Brookings, South Dakota and had a daughter Dawn Tae Thorsness who also served in the United States Air Force. Leo received his Bachelors degree from the University of Omaha, and his Master's degree in Systems Management from the University of Southern California.

Vietnam War Years

Leo enlisted in the United States Air Force 1951-1973 achieving the rank of Colonel. He flew with the 355h Tactical Fighter Wing and the 357th Tactical Fighter Squadron. In 1954 Leo received his commission as an officer and earned his wings with a rating as pilot through the SUAF Aviation Cadet program in Class 54-G. As a Strategic Air Command pilot he completed fighter pilot training and flew both F-86 and F-100 jets. After 1966 he completed F-105 "Wild Weasel" training at George AFB, California. His task was locating and destroying North Vietnamese surface-to-air missile (SAM) sites during the Vietnam War. It meant making himself a target so the SAM sights would give away their positions. Therefore, it was the most dangerous assignment a pilot could get in Vietnam. "Wild Weasel" losses were 2 ½ times greater than any other flight mission in this war.

On April 30, 1967, seven missions short of completing their tours of 100 missions, Major Thorsness, and his "backseat guy" Captain Harold Johnson were shot down by a Mikoya-Gurevich MiG-2 over North Vietnam. After flying his mission in the morning, Major Thorsness as the Wild Weasel leader assigned himself as a spare aircraft for the afternoon mission because of a shortage of crews. While still inbound over North

Vietnam, communications were disrupted. Just as Thorsness got an instrument indication that the flight was being painted by air born radar, he saw an F-105 going down in flames that eventually was identified as his own wingman, shot down by an Atoll missile. Within a minute, his own aircraft was also hit with a heat-seeking missile fired by the MiGs.

Thorsness and Johnson ejected. Separated from each other by a ridge, they were the object of a three-hour rescue effort involving the entire strike force covering. The effort was futile and all the men were captured. Though CSAR helicopter forces were again launched the next day, none of the downed men were located. Thorsness, then age 35, was taken to the infamous prison camp known as "Hanoi Hilton" where he endured three years of torture. In all, he would spend six years as a Prisoner of War.

During his six years of captivity, his "uncooperativeness towards his captors" earned him a year in solitary confinement and severe back injuries due to torture. The Medal of Honor was awarded by the United States Congress during his captivity, but not announced until his release in 1973 to prevent the North Vietnamese from using it against him. He learned he'd been nominated for the Medal of Honor from a coded message tapped on the wall of his prison cell. He was medically disqualified from further flying in the Air Force due to injuries incurred during his ejection and aggravated by the torture, which he was subjected to in captivity. He retired on October 25, 1973.

During the last three years of his captivity, Thorsness' wife, Gaylee, was allowed to send six-line letters a few times a year. Each of her letters was returned with the word "deceased" written on the front. His daughter, Dawn, was age 11 when he was shot down and 18 when he came home.

A Major at the time Thorsness performed the action that earned him the Air Force Medal of Honor on April 19, 1967. This is his citation: "The President of the United

States in the name of the Congress takes pride in presenting the Medal of Honor to LIEUTENANT COLONEL LEO K. THORSNESS UNITED STATES AIR FORCE for service as set forth in the following citation: "For conspicuous gallantry and intrepidity in action at the risk of his life above and beyond the call of duty. As pilot of an F-105 aircraft, Lieutenant Colonel Thorsness was on a surface-to-air missile suppression mission over North Vietnam. Lieutenant Colonel Thorsness and his wingman attacked and silenced a surface-to-air missile site with air-to-ground missiles and then destroyed a second surface-to-air missile site with bombs. In the attack on the second missile site, Lieutenant Colonel Thorsness' wingman was shot down by intensive antiaircraft fire, and the two crewmembers abandoned their aircraft. Lieutenant Colonel Thorsness circled the descending parachutes to keep the crewmembers in sight and relay their position to the Search and Rescue Center. During this maneuver, a MIG-17 was sighted in the area. Lieutenant Colonel Thorsness immediately initiated an attack and destroyed the MIG. Because his aircraft was low on fuel, he was forced to depart the area in search of a tanker. Upon being advised that two helicopters were orbiting over the downed crew's position and that there were hostile MIGs in the area posing a serious threat to the helicopters, Lieutenant Colonel Thorsness, despite his low fuel condition, decided to return alone through a hostile environment of surface-to-air missile and anti-aircraft defenses to the downed crew's position. As he approached the area, he spotted four MIG-17 aircraft and immediately initiated an attack on the MIGs, damaging one and driving the others away from the rescue scene. When it became apparent that an aircraft in the area was critically low on fuel and the crew would have to abandon the aircraft unless they could reach a tanker, Lieutenant Colonel Thorsness, although critically short on fuel himself, helped to avert further possible loss of life and a friendly aircraft by recovering at a forward operating base, thus allowing the aircraft in emergency fuel condition to refuel safely. Lieutenant Colonel Thorsness' extraordinary heroism, self-sacrifice and personal bravery involving conspicuous risk of life were in the highest traditions of the military service, and have reflected great credit upon himself and the U.S. Air Force."

Leo K. Thorsness was the only Medal of Honor recipient credited with an aerial victory in the Vietnam War.

Post War Years
Thorsness served as Director of Civil Affairs for Litton Industries from 1979 to 1985. On November 1988, Leo was elected to the Washington State Senate. He immediately became the Senator from District 11 to serve the unexpired term of Avery Garnett, who died in April 1988. In the state senate, he sponsored a bill dubbed the "Truth Bill" on March 3, 1990. The legislature unanimously passed the measure, SJM8020, urging the Federal government to release information about 30,000 U.S. soldiers listed as either prisoners of war or missing in action in conflicts dating back to World War II. Currently retired, he serves on the Board of directors of the Congressional Medal of Honor

Foundation. In December 2008, Thorsness' autobiography, *Surviving Hell: A POW's Journey* was published. In 2009, he was awarded the Audie Murphy Award.

Based upon his experience as a U.S. Military officer, fighter pilot and Prisoner of War, he has been a frequent motivational speaker for many businesses and groups. During his talks he relates the lessons he learned during those six long years when he was denied his freedom. In 2007, he spoke at the 60th anniversary of the U.S. Air Force.

Compiled by Susan Carleton Jirele
Anthony Wayne Chapter NSDAR

President Richard Nixon, Major Leo K. Thorsness
Leo's mother, Bernice and Leo's wife, Gaylee

Dale Eugene Wayrynen 1947-1967

Medal of Honor awarded posthumously
Action: Duc Pho, Quang Ngai Province,
Republic of Vietnam
Date: May 18, 1967

Early Years

For Dale Wayrynen, being the best at whatever he opted to do was not a choice; it was just understood from the outset. Born on January 18, 1947 in Moose Lake, Minnesota he was the oldest of four brothers in a tight-knit northern Minnesota household. He grew up in tiny McGregor, population 275. Wayrynen was a natural leader and an outstanding athlete by any standard. During his final year at McGregor High School, he was quarter- back and co-captain of the football team, as well as co-captain of the basketball and baseball teams. He was a member of the student counsel, a class officer, and received all-conference honors in football and baseball. The village of McGregor would not soon forget Dale Wayrynen.

During his senior year, he began talking about Vietnam. His father, Eugene, had been a "waist gunner" on a B-17 during WWII. His plane had been shot down and he finished the war in a German POW camp. Now, the younger Wayrynen was feeling the pull to do his part in his war, and after graduation in May 1965, he joined the Army. He applied for jump school and became a proud member of the 82nd Airborne Division at Ft. Bragg, North Carolina. In March 1967, he volunteered to go to Vietnam and was assigned to the 101st Airborne Division, the "Screaming Eagles.

Vietnam War Years

Six weeks later, Wayrynen was beginning to settle into his new unit. He had been assigned to Company B, 2nd Battalion, 502nd Infantry, part of the First Brigade, 101st Airborne and they were stationed near the town of Duc Pho in Quang Ngai Province. Known as "Battlin' Bravo," the company motto was: "They've got us surrounded, the poor bastards."

On 18 May, units of North Vietnamese regular infantry attacked a Bravo Co. patrol near Duc Pho on what was known as Hill 424. When the attack began Dale Wayrynen was several miles away, with other soldiers from his Bravo Co. platoon. They were patrolling separately from the main body of troops and received news of the attack by radio. Wayrynen's squad immediately set out to assist and ran several miles, fighting their way through outlying NVA units as they moved toward Hill 424.

Bill Gunter and Don Singleton were with Dale Wayrynen that day. "When we got to the base of the hill we could hear some gunfire," Gunter said. "And then we walked slowly up the hill until we reached the company. ...There was wounded all over the place and some killed." The NVA had broken off their attack and retreated into the thick jungle growth, taking their own dead and wounded with them.

Among the friendly casualties were a number of Montagnard soldiers who had been helping the Americans. The platoon made stretchers to move the wounded off Hill 424 and started down a jungle path in single file as darkness fell. The path was going in the general direction the platoon leader wanted to go; Bill Gunter was walking point. Directly behind him was Dale Wayrynen, followed by Don Singleton, and the rest of the troop column. That was the night Specialist 4, Dale E. Wayrynen, United States Army, earned the Medal of Honor for conspicuous gallantry and intrepidity in action at the risk of his life above and beyond the call of duty:

On 15 October 1969, Dale Wayrynen's family was flown to Washington, D.C., to receive his Medal of Honor. The Citation Read: "The President of the United States of America, authorized by an Act of Congress, March 3, 1863, has awarded in the name of The Congress the Medal of Honor posthumously to Dale E. Wayrynen, United States Army. Specialist Wayrynen distinguished himself with Company B, 2d Battalion, 502d

Infantry, 1st Brigade, 101st Airborne Division, during combat operations near Duc Pho, Quang Ngai Province, Republic of Vietnam. His platoon was assisting in the night evacuation of the wounded from an earlier enemy contact when the lead man of the unit met face to face with a Viet Cong soldier. The American's shouted warning also alerted the enemy who immediately swept the area with automatic weapons fire from a strongly built bunker close to the trail and threw hand grenades from another nearby fortified position. Almost immediately, the lead man was wounded and knocked from his feet. Specialist Wayrynen, the second man in the formation, leaped beyond his fallen comrade to kill another enemy soldier who appeared on the trail, and he dragged his injured companion back to where the point squad had taken cover. Suddenly, a live

enemy grenade landed in the center of the tightly grouped men. Specialist Wayrynen, quickly assessing the danger to the entire squad as well as to his platoon leader who was nearby, shouted a warning, pushed one soldier out of the way, and threw himself on the grenade at the moment it exploded. He was mortally wounded. His deep and abiding concern for his fellow soldiers was significantly reflected in his supreme and courageous act that preserved the lives of his comrades. Specialist Wayrynen's heroic actions are in keeping with the highest traditions of the service, and they reflect great credit upon himself and the United States Army."
[Signature of President Richard Nixon]

Bill Gunter had additional injuries to his legs and Don Singleton was injured by the same grenade; however Wayrynen, by his selfless act, had spared the rest of his squad. Wayrynen lived for several hours. Then, as the fighting subsided and the sounds of battle were replaced by the moans of the wounded and the hushed tones of those caring for them, Dale Wayrynen died, killed in action in Quang Ngai Province, Vietnam, on May 18, 1967. He was twenty years old.

Post War Years

Dale Wayrynen is buried at Rice River Lutheran Cemetery, McGregor, Aitkin County, Minnesota. In addition to the Congressional Medal of Honor, awarded October 16, 1969, the Dale Walrynen Memorial, McGregor, Minnesota, was dedicated July 4, 1976; the Dale E. Wayrynen Recreation Center at Fort Campbell, Kentucky, was dedicated October 30, 1974: and the Dale Wayrynen Veterans Memorial Gymnasium at the McGregor School in McGregor, Minnesota was dedicated on Aug. 19, 1995.

Dale Wayrynen Memorial, McGregor, Minnesota

The Dale Wayrynen Memorial Highway (formerly Hwy 210/169) that runs 42 miles through Aitkin County, Minnesota, was dedicated on July 4, 1996. Dale was also granted and assigned the distinction of Distinguished Member of the 502nd Infantry.

Compiled by DeAnn Caddy, Captain Robert Orr Chapter NSDAR

PEACETIME - INTERIM

Prior to World War II, the Medal of Honor could not be awarded for actions not involving direct combat with the enemy. That changed after the war. Nationwide 193 men earned the medal in this way, five of them from Minnesota. Most of the peacetime medals were awarded to members of the United States Navy for their actions during boiler explosions, man-overboard incidents, and other hazards of naval service

Interim Awards, 1901-1911; Davis, Raymond E. entry". Medal of Honor recipients. *United States Army Center of Military History.. "Bennington"*. Dictionary of American Naval Fighting Ships. *Naval Historical Center*. February 8, 2006. [b] John Griffith (November 11, 2003). *"Raymond E. Davis"*. Claim to Fame: Medal of Honor recipients. *Find a Grave. Raymond E. Davis"*. Hall of Valor. *Military Times*.

PEACETIME

INTERIM YEARS

Raymond Erwin Davis 1886-1965

Medal of Honor
Interim: 1901 – 1911
Event: U.S.S. Bennington
      San Diego Harbor
      San Diego, California
Date: July 21, 1905

Early Years
Raymond Erwin Davis was born in Mankato,
Blue Earth County, Minnesota,
September 19, 1885/1886

Interim Years Event
Raymond joined the U.S. Navy from Puget
Sound, Washington. He was stationed aboard the
USS Bennington (PG-4) as a Quartermaster Third
Class. On July 21, 1905 while at San Diego, California, a deadly boiler explosion ripped
through the U.S.S. Bennington. Of the ship's 197 officers and crew, 62 were killed and
more than 40 were wounded. Quartermaster Third Class Raymond Davis was one of ten
members of the Bennington's crew who received the Medal of Honor for heroic actions
to rescue comrades and minimize damage in the explosion and resulting fires. He
received the U.S. Navy Peacetime Congressional Medal of Honor for his actions.

The interim award 1899-1910 was presented January
5, 1906. His citation reads: "The President of the
United States of America, in the name of Congress,
takes pleasure in presenting the Medal of Honor to
Quartermaster Third Class Raymond Erwin Davis,
United States Navy, for extraordinary heroism on
board the U.S.S. BENNINGTON, displayed at the time
of the explosion of a boiler of that vessel at San Diego,
California, 21 July 1905."

Calvary Cemetery, Seattle, Washington

Post Event Years
There was very little information to be found on Raymond Irwin Davis despite much
research. He died September 9, 1965 at the age of 79 at the Retsil Veterans Home, Port
Orchard and is buried in Seattle, Washington in Calvary Cemetery, in the St. Paul plot,
section 2, lot 39, site 4.

Compiled by Diana Dickinson Lynch, Monument Chapter NSDAR

Charles Augustus Lindbergh 1902-1974

Medal of Honor
Peacetime Award
Activity: "nonstop flight in his airplane, the Spirit of St. Louis, from New York City to Paris, France
Date: 20-21 May 1927,

Early Years

Charles Augustus Lindbergh was born on February 4, 1902 to Charles Augustus Lindbergh Sr. and Evangeline (Lodge Land) Lindbergh in Detroit, Michigan. The family moved to Little Falls, Minnesota area where Charles grew up on a farm.

In childhood, Lindbergh showed exceptional mechanical ability. At the age of 18 years, he entered the University of Wisconsin to study engineering. However, Lindbergh was more interested in the exciting, young field of aviation than he was in school. After two years, he left school to become a barnstormer, a pilot who performed daredevil stunts at fairs.

Peacetime Event

In 1924, Lindbergh enlisted in the United States Army in Little Falls, Morrison County, Minnesota so that he could be trained as an Army Air Service Reserve pilot. In 1925, he graduated from the Army's flight-training school at Brooks and Kelly fields, near San Antonio, as the best pilot in his class. After Lindbergh completed his Army training, the Robertson Aircraft Corporation of St. Louis hired him to fly the mail between St. Louis and Chicago. He gained a reputation as a cautious and capable pilot.

In 1919, a New York City hotel owner named Raymond Orteig offered $25,000 to the first aviator to fly nonstop from New York to Paris. Several pilots were killed or injured while competing for the Orteig prize. By 1927, it had still not been won. Lindbergh believed he could win it if he had the right airplane. He persuaded nine St. Louis businessmen to help him finance the cost of a plane. Lindbergh chose Ryan Aeronautical Company of San Diego to manufacture a special plane, which he helped design. He named the plane the "Spirit of St. Louis". On May 10-11, 1927, Lindbergh tested the plane by flying from San Diego to New York City, with an overnight stop in St. Louis.

The flight took 20 hours 21 minutes, a transcontinental record. On December 12, 1927, President Calvin

Coolidge presented Captain Charles A. Lindbergh the Medal of Honor and Distinguished Flying Cross. He was awarded for displaying heroic courage and skill as a navigator, at the risk of his life, by his nonstop flight in his airplane, the Spirit of St. Louis, from New York City to Paris, France, 20-21 May 1927, by which Capt. Lindbergh not only achieved the greatest individual triumph of any American citizen but demonstrated that travel across the ocean by aircraft was possible. Lindbergh is the only non-combat Medal of Honor recipient.

Post Event

Lindbergh's transatlantic flight thrust him into the spotlight. He met Anne Spencer Morrow while on a good will mission to Mexico. They married May 27, 1929. Charles and Anne had six children. On March 1, 1932 their son Charles Augustus Lindbergh, Jr. was kidnapped and murdered by Bruno Hauptmann. This event led to the family moving to Europe in search of privacy and safety.

While in Europe, Lindbergh invented an artificial heart, and toured the aircraft industries of France and Germany. In 1938 Lindbergh accepted the German Medal of Honor. This caused an outcry in the United States among critics of Nazism. The Lindbergh family returned to the United States in 1939. He joined the America First Committee becoming their lead spokesman, which opposed voluntary entry into WWII. After the attack on Pearl Harbor he stopped his non-involvement activity and tried to reenlist but was refused. He entered civilian life serving as a test pilot for the Ford Motor Company and United Aircraft Corporation.

In April 1944, Lindbergh went to the Pacific war area as an adviser to the U.S, Navy where he flew about 50 combat missions as a civilian. He developed cruise control techniques that increased the capabilities of American pilots.

After the War, he withdrew from public attention but continued to work as a consultant in the aviation field. His aptitude for mechanics and passion for aeronautics and conservation left an indelible mark in history.

Charles A. Lindbergh died of cancer on August 26, 1974 in his home and is buried in Palapalo Ho'omau Church Cemetery on Maui, Hawaii.

Both during his lifetime and after his death Lindbergh received recognition and many honors. Next to his boyhood home in Little Falls, Minnesota is the Lindbergh Museum and adjacent to it the Lindbergh State Park. Terminal Two at the Minneapolis-St. Paul Airport now bears his name. In 2002, on the 75th Anniversary of his historic flight, Erik Lindbergh recreated his grandfather's transatlantic flight.

Compiled by Susan Duff-Erkel
Captain Robert Orr Chapter NSDAR

Oscar Frederick Nelson 1881–1951

Medal of Honor
Event: U.S.S. Bennington
San Diego Harbor, San Diego, California
Date: July 21, 1905

Early Years
Oscar Frederick Nelson was born 5 November 5, 1881 in Minneapolis, Minnesota to Danish immigrants, Bendt Nelson and Eliza Glemusestad· He joined the Minnesota Branch Navy in 1899.

Interim Years Event
Nelson was awarded a rare peacetime Congressional Medal of Honor in 1908 for his life-saving efforts as a Machinist's Mate First Class in the U.S. Navy aboard the U.S.S. Bennington. While docked off Point Loma in San Diego Bay, two boilers on the ship exploded; the sailors were killed or tossed overboard and the ship began taking on water. Nelson rescued many of his shipmates before the U.S.S. Bennington sank. The disaster killed 66 naval personnel and maimed 49 others. Of about 30 men working below the decks of the ship, Nelson was the sole survivor.

His citation, granted January 5, 1906, reads, "Serving on Board the U.S.S. Bennington, extraordinary heroism on board the U.S.S. Bennington, displayed at the time of the explosion of a boiler of that vessel at San Diego, California, 21 July 1905."

From the magazine, *Our Navy, the Standard Publication of the U.S. Navy*: "On July 21, 1905, a boiler of the gunboat Bennington exploded, while that vessel was lying in the harbor of San Diego, California, killing and wounding more than one-half of the crew. Shortly after the explosion, the survivors of this dreadful accident formed a society, and elected a secretary, Mr. F. J. Schopbach, to who all agreed to write once a year, giving their address at least. An annual directory was then to be published and mailed to each survivor."

The editor of this magazine was one of the survivors and asked for readers knowing the whereabouts of any of the surviving crew whose names were not included to drop him a card. On the list is "Oscar Nelson, Columbia Heights, Minnesota."

Years later as he was due to revisit the harbor, Nelson related how, in the agonizing moments following the explosion, he had jammed a piece of waste into his mouth, breathing through it as he rescued more than half a dozen of his shipmates gulping hot steam as they screamed in pain. He made several trips to the lower decks, making sure of the men (dead or alive) were out. He was one of eleven U.S.S. Bennington crew members to be so honored for their actions that day, and Duluth, Minnesota's first Medal of Honor winner.

Post-Event Years

Oscar Nelson married Anna Dahl, and had one daughter, Beatrice Helen Nelson (Mrs. Edward W. Verbarg), born 7 November 1912, also in Minneapolis. The family later lived in Duluth, Minnesota.

Nelson was discharged in 1911 and later served for 24 years with the U.S. Army Corps of Engineers in Duluth, Minnesota. (His WWII Draft Registration, at age 60, lists a Duluth address.) In fact, a two-room cabin originally built in 1910 by Oscar Nelson on Lake Superior is now home to the Solglimt Bed & Breakfast located on Duluth's Park Point Beach, the name of which means "the sun on the water". One of its suites is named in honor of Nelson, builder of the home. His medal is on display at the Canal Park Marine Museum in Duluth, as part of its Peacetime Collection (Accession Number 99.57.1).

Oscar Nelson died at the age of 70 on September 26, 1951. His wife died in 1981. The Nelsons are buried in Fort Snelling National Cemetery in Minneapolis, Minnesota.

Compiled by Kathleen M. Barrett Huston,
Lake Minnetonka Chapter NSDAR

Thomas Robinson 1837-1915

Medal of Honor
Event: USS Tallapoosa, off New Orleans.
Date: July 15, 1866

Early Years
Of all our Medal of Honor winners the life story of Thomas Robinson has been the most complicated to unravel. After much research little has been gleamed about his life. We know from his death certificate that he was born May 17, 1837 in Norway to his father Christian Johanson, a native of Norway and to his Mother Ingabold Oleson also born in Norway. It is not known if he had any siblings or when he immigrated to the United States. Conflicting Federal Census data gives us an immigration date of 1856 for the 1910 census or an immigration date of 1860 for the 1900 census. We can calculate that at least Mr. Robinson came to America as a young adult and not as a child.

Interim Years Event
Mr. Robinson settled in New York and it was from there that he entered the U.S. Navy. His Soldiers' Home record from Minneapolis, Hennepin County, Minnesota gives his service length as three years. Although no specific dates are given, he is cited as serving from 1865 to 1870. It was while serving on the U.S.S. Tallapoosa that Mr. Robinson saved a man, Wellington Brocar, a landsman, from drowning. For his bravery Thomas Robinson was awarded his Medal of Honor through General Orders 77 on August 1, 1866. Robinson's official Medal of Honor citation reads: "For heroic efforts to save from drowning Wellington Brocar, landsman, of the Tallapoosa, off New Orleans, 15 July 1866." Mr. Robinson left the service after having achieved the rank of Captain of the After Guard.

Post Event Years
On May 17, 1881 in Minneapolis, Minnesota Thomas Robinson entered into holy matrimony with Louise Herlin. She was a 30 year old immigrant from Sweden, fourteen years his junior. Mr. Robinson supported his growing family working as a painter. While living in Minneapolis, Thomas and his wife had three daughters. Pearl was born March 4, 1882 followed by Ruby Louise on March 28, 1885 and finally, Rachael born May 4, 1889. Twelve weeks after her birth Rachael died of cholera on July 27, 1889. A little over two years later, Mr. Robinson would lose his wife. Louise died September 5, 1891 in Minneapolis. She is buried near her daughter Rachael in the Minneapolis Pioneers and Soldiers Memorial Cemetery. Around 1895 Mr. Robinson entered the Soldiers' Home in Minneapolis, Minnesota.

After living in the Soldiers' Home in Minneapolis for 20 years, Thomas Robinson passed away· He died May 12, 1915 from complications suffered from a fall from a second story window while mentally deranged. At the time of his death, Mr. Robinson was 77 years of age. He was buried in Lakewood Cemetery in Minneapolis.

Compiled by Laura Gallup
Anoka Chapter NSDAR

George William Rud 1883-1916

Medal of Honor awarded posthumously
Event: Destruction of USS Memphis
Santo Domingo City
Dominican Republic
Date: August 29, 1916

Early Years
George William Rud was born October 7, 1883, in Minneapolis, Minnesota to Maren Caroline (Halvorsen) Ingebredtson and Martin Ingebredtsen who were both born in Norway. George Rud may have used the Ingebredtsen family name for a time when younger, but then went back to his birth name when he joined the Navy.

In 1901 the family was living in Minneapolis and George Rud was working as an operator for the N.S. Shoe Co. The 1903 Minneapolis City Directory lists George as a machine operator, his sister Olga as a seamstress, and his father, Martin Ingebredtsen, as a "scaler," They were all living at 2818 Aldrich.

The Minnesota State census shows the family residing at 1925 Hillsdale Avenue North in Minneapolis in 1905. It lists Martin, his wife Caroline Ingebredtson, their children, George W. Ingebredtson (21) occupation US Navy, Olga (19), Sine (17), Florence (12), Arthur (14), and Ethel (6).

George Rud is no longer listed in the 1906 Minneapolis City Directory and is probably now stationed on a ship. The rest of the family is still living together. The 1913 Minneapolis City Directory shows Caroline as the widow of Martin who died on November 10, 1912 at age 56.

Interim Years Event
George Rud entered service in the U.S. Navy as Chief Machinist's Mate in 1904. He served aboard the following ships: USS Memphis, USS Franklin, USS Maine, USS Roe, USS Hancock, USS Bagley, USS Minnesota, USS Wenley, and USS Tennessee. On August 20, 1916 George Rud was attached to the U.S.S. Memphis, at a time when that vessel suffered total destruction from a hurricane while anchored off Santo Domingo City, Dominican Republic.

The Minneapolis Morning Tribune published an article regarding the tragic end of the USS Memphis and the loss of many lives: "Washington, Aug. 31.-Reports to the Navy

Department last night said 33 enlisted men were missing, most of them probably drowned; four were known to be dead, two officers and six men seriously injured and 67 others hurt as a result of the armored cruiser Memphis being hit by a hurricane Tuesday in San Domingo City Harbor. Most of the missing were in a small boat overturned by wind and waves while returning to the Memphis. It is believed by the Navy Department perhaps a dozen of these may be alive on shore and will be discovered by a later muster. "The known dead are: J.H. Townsend, fireman, George W. Rud, Minneapolis. A.H. Porter, water tender, W. Copius, coal passer, and L.J. Hemstead.

"The cause of the wreck has not yet been explained fully. The scout cruiser Salem was ordered to San Domingo yesterday to replace the wrecked vessel, which was Admiral Pond's flagship. Early reports from Admiral Pond were taken by navy officials to indicate that the storm was of such force that it created a series of tidal waves which drove the Memphis across a long stretch of shallow water to her present resting place at the foot of the rocky bluff upon which San Domingo City stands. Wrecking companies will be asked to study the vessel's plight and determine whether she may be saved.

"G.W. Rud, chief machinists' mate of the first class, who was drowned when a heavy swell struck the cruiser Memphis in San Domingo harbor, was a Minneapolis man, and is survived by several relatives living in the city. Dispatches concerning his death vary; one stating that he lost his life when a small boat capsized and another stating that he died when a steam pipe burst. He had served 12 years in the navy, and would have been discharged January 1,1917 had he lived. He is survived by his stepmother, Mrs. Caroline Ingebredtsen, four sisters, Mrs. Albert Hanson, Mrs. J. C. Johnson, Mrs. Albert DeBoynton, and Ethel Ingebredtsen, and a brother, Arthur Ingebredtsen, who lives with his mother."

George Rud's funeral notice appeared in the newspaper: "The funeral of George W. Rud, 3110 Morgan Avenue North, who was killed when the cruiser Memphis was driven ashore at San Domingo beach by a tidal wave, was held from the family residence at 2 p. m. yesterday. Services also were said at St. Olaf's Norwegian Lutheran church at 2:30 p. m. The body was taken to the Crystal Lake cemetery wrapped in the naval jack and the United States flag and interred with military honors. Comrades from the navy were the pall bearers. They were Chief Quartermaster Howard Benjamin, Chief Machinist Edward Thompson, Chief Yeoman Leo B. Ketterer,

Chief Gunner's Mate F. A. McClure and Second Class Quartermaster Edward Johnson.

The Medal of Honor was awarded to George William Rud posthumously on August, 1932. The citation read as follows: "For extraordinary heroism in the line of his profession while attached to the U.S.S. Memphis, at a time when that vessel was suffered total destruction from a hurricane while anchored off Santo Domingo City, 29 August 1916. C.M.M. Rud took his station in the engine room and remained at his post amidst scalding steam and the rushing of thousands of tons of water into his department, receiving serious burns from which he immediately died."

Post Event Years

George Rud died on August 29, 1916 at age 32 off Santo Domingo, Dominican Republic. He was buried September 14, 1916 at Crystal Lake Cemetery, Minneapolis, Hennepin County, Minnesota. Rud's mother, Maren Caroline Ingebredtsen, was certified as a Navy Dependent on November 2, 1916. She died at age 86 on September 9, 1943 in Minneapolis, Minnesota.

Compiled by Tracy Moore MacAllister
Maria Sanford Chapter NSDAR

Index

Medal of Honor Recipients and their Minnesota Counties

It may seem at first that some Medal of Honor recipients had multiple personalities—or multiple bodies, because their names may be listed in more than one county, even more that one state. That is because, according to The Congressional Medal of Honor Society, Medal of Honor recipients are claimed by the State of Minnesota based on the following criteria: 1) if they are born in Minnesota; 2) if they enlisted into service in Minnesota; 3) if they died in Minnesota; 4) if they are buried in Minnesota. The following table shows the Minnesota counties that can claim MOH recipients according to these criteria:

County	City/Town	MOH recipient	Criteria
Anoka	Columbia Heights	LaBelle, James	Born
Anoka	Anoka	Sorenson, Richard	Born, Enlisted
Aitkin	McGregor	Wayrynen, Dale	Buried
Blue Earth	Mankato	Davis, Raymond	Born
Blue Earth	Mankato	Hanna, Milton	Buried
Blue Earth	Mankato	Holmes, Lovilo	Enlisted, Died, Buried
Blue Earth	Mankato	Pay, Byon	Enlisted
Brown	New Ulm	Bianchi, Willibald	Born, Enlisted
Brown	Sleepy Eye	Pickle, Alonzo	Died, Buried
Carlton	Moose Lake	Wayrynen, Dale	Born
Dodge	Wasioja	Cilley, Clinton	Enlisted
Goodhue	Hay Creek	Burkard, Oscar	Enlisted
Hennepin	Minneapolis	Blanchfield, Michael	Born
Hennepin	Crystal Lake	Burger, Joseph	Enlisted
Hennepin	Minneapolis	Chandler, Stephen	Died
Hennepin	Minneapolis	Cukela, Louis	Enlisted
Hennepin	Minneapolis	Fleming, Richard	Buried*
Hennepin	Minneapolis	Frantz, Aloysius	Enlisted
Hennepin	Minneapolis	Grant, Lewis	Died, Buried
Hennepin	Minneapolis	Hanna, Milton	Died
Hennepin	Minneapolis	Kraus, Richard	Enlisted, Buried*
Hennepin	Minneapolis	LaBelle, James	Enlisted, Buried*
Hennepin	Minneapolis	Mallon, George	Buried*
Hennepin	Minneapolis	Morgan, George	Enlisted
Hennepin	Minneapolis	Nelson, Oscar	Born, Enlisted, Died, Buried*
Hennepin	Minneapolis	O'Brien, Henry	Enlisted
Hennepin	Minneapolis	Olson, Arlo	Buried*
Hennepin	Minneapolis	Olson, Kenneth	Enlisted
Hennepin	Minneapolis	Pruden, Robert	Enlisted, Buried*
Hennepin	Minneapolis	Rabel, Laszio	Enlisted
Hennepin	Minneapolis	Robinson, Thomas	Died, Buried
Hennepin	Minneapolis	Rud, George	Born, Enlisted, Buried
Hennepin	Minneapolis	Rudolph, Donald	Enlisted, Buried*
Hennepin	Minneapolis	Schmidt, William	Died, Buried

County	City/Town	MOH recipient	Criteria
Stearns	St. Cloud	Mallon, George	Died
Todd	Long Prairie	Davis, Charles	Born
Todd	Staples	McKay, Charles	Died
Washington	Stillwater	McMillian, Albert	Born
Wilkin	Breckenridge	Boehler, Otto	Died, Buried
Winona	Winona	Hawthorne, LeRoy	Born
Winona	St. Charles	Pickle, Alonzo	Enlisted
Winona	Winona	Shepard, Irwin	Died, Buried
Wright	Unknown	May, William	Died
Wright	Monticello	McCornack, Andrew	Died, Buried
Wright	South Haven	Rudolph, Donald	Born
Wright	Maple Lake	Vlug, Dirk	Born

*Buried at Fort Snelling National Cemetery

SOURCES & DOCUMENTATION

CIVIL WAR
DR. JAMES MCPHERSON: HTTP://WWW.CIVILWAR.ORG/EDUCATION/HISTORY/CIVIL-WAR-OVERVIEW/OVERVIEW.HTML
ALLEN, JAMES
Allen, H. Merian, America's Victoria Cross, *The Bellman*, January 6, 1917, Minneapolis, Minnesota, Volume XXII, Number 547 p. 691;"Badges of Daring," *St. Paul Globe*, St. Paul, Minnesota, September 4, 1896. p5; James Allen Grave Marker courtesy of Don Morfe, www.findagrave.com; James Allen Portrait found in the *Story of American Heroism,* Springfield, Ohio, J.W. Jones, 1897, p 138; Minnesota Historical Society, Death Certificate Susan Blanchard Morgan Allen, Death Certificate, Burton E. Allen, Death Certificate Benton O. Allen;, Soldiers'Home Record, 06 E 11 2 F-1, James Allen.*Story of American Heroism,* Springfield, Ohio, J.W. Jones, 1897, p 137-139;United States Federal census records and Minnesota State census records.Wilna, Watertown Re-Union The, September 6, 1913, Column 4.

BARRICK, JESSE T.
Ancestry.com/search;Ancestry.com/tree; CivilWarArchives.com. *Civil War Union Regimental Histories – MN;* Findagrave.com; Homeofheros.com ;Minnesota Adjutant General's Report of 1866 p.22;*Minnesota in the Civil War and Indian Wars 1861-1865, Vol II*. pp 336-337;Seattletimes.com/ *News from the Past Sept 7, 2000*;United States of America's Congressional Medal of Honor Recipients & Their Official Citations. 2nd edition. P. 770;U.S. Federal Census – 1850 & 1900.

BURGER, JOSEPH
Ancestry.com/search; Ancestry.com/tree;CivilWarArchives.com. *Civil War Union Regimental Histories – MN;*Dairystar.com; Fischenich, Mark. Mankato Free Press; *Young Civil War soldier made lasting impression.* April 24, 2011;Homeofheros.comMankato Free Press. April 24, 2011. *Boy soldier's diary details battles,hunger,misery;* Minnesota Legislative Reference Library; Legislators Past & Present. Burger, Joseph. www.leg.state.mnus;Missouri History. State Legislators 1820-2000. www.SOS.mo.gov/archives/history/historicallistings;Rolston, Les. *Home of the Brave*. Revival Waves of Glory Books. 2015; United States of America's Congressional Medal of Honor Recipients & Their Official Citations. 2nd edition. P. 792; U.S. Federal Census – 1880 **Note:** Great-great granddaughter, Sara Burger-Edwards, has a copy of Joseph's diary and provided the entries in the Mankato Free Press article. Burger-Edwards is a lawyer, like her great-great-grandfather, and is an adjunct professor at Bethany Luther College in Mankato, Minnesota.

CAMPBELL, JAMES
References: 1 Book "New York in the War of Rebellion 1861-1865 Vol 1 p 437 by Frederick Phisterer 1912;2 Ancestry.com U.S. Civil War Soldier Records and Profiles 1861-1865; 3 NY Report of the Adjutant General Deeds of Valor p 362; 4 Find a Grave Memorial Alma W & Blanche. I

CHANDLER, STEPHEN
George Chandler, *"The Family Of William And Annis Chandler; Who Settled In Roxbury, Mass 1637"*; printed for the family on the press of George Hamilton of Worcester, Mass; 311 Main Street, 1883; p. 549, 948 Kent Scriber, *"Three Oswego County Brothers in the Civil War and After: A Review of the Scriber Family and the 24th, 110th, and 184th NYSV Infantry"*; Published by Danby Press, Ithaca, NY, 3 January 2014, p. 19; Civil War Research Database; US Army Quartermaster Foundation; Bert Dunkerly, *"Cavalry Action at Painesville: 150 Years Ago"*,
National Park Service Civil War website, online at; Deeds of Valor, p. 524, Edmund F. Slafter, *"Memorial of John Slafter: with a genealogical account of his descendants, including eight generations"*; Published by H. W. Dutton & Son, Boston, MA, 1869; p. 70; Edmund F. Slafter, *"Memorial of John Slafter: with a genealogical account of his descendants, including eight generations"*; Published by H. W. Dutton & Son, Boston, MA, 1869; p. 70;; Homestead Land Office Records, www.ancestry.com; Stephen E. Chandler memorial at findagrave;Bio Photo Courtesy of Gregory Speciale, findagrave.com Contributor;Gravestone Photo by Don Morfe, findagrave.com Contributor Both online at:Find a Grave.com.

CILLEY, CLINTON
J. P. Cilley. *The Cilley Family*. Augusta, ME: n.pub., 1878; Paul D. Escott, "Clinton A. Cilley, Yankee War Hero in the Postwar South: A Study in the Compatibility of Regional Values", *The North Carolina Historical Review*, Vol. 68, No. 4 (OCTOBER 1991), p. 406-408, Published by: North Carolina Office of Archives and History; http://www.cilley.net/thecilleypages; NSSAR Profile, Compatriot Medal of Honor Recipients; Michael Eckers, *The Boys of Wasioja: Dodge County Men in Company C, Second Minnesota Volunteer Infantry,* published by Community News Corp., 2009, back cover; Dodge County Historical Society, Civil War Recruiting Station findagrave.com; Minnesota Historical Society, The Second Minnesota Volunteer Infantry; *Reports of the Committees of the Senate of the United States for the Second Session of the Forty-eighth Congress and Special Session,* March 1885; Government Printing Office, Washington, D.C., 1885; Report No. 1089, p. 1 Biographical Directory of the United States Congress, 1774-Present; The University of North Carolina, Chapel Hill, *Bluecoats and Tar Heels: The Transition from War to Peace in North Carolina, 1865—1877*; Published by ProQuest, 2006, p. 88; Paul D. Escott, "; Catawba Museum

http://catawbahistory.org/museum-of-history. ; Bio Photo NSSAR Profile,;Gravestone Photo courtesy of Robert Cilley, descendant of MOH recipient.

CLARK, WILLIAM

Adjutant General, O. O. (1866, December 1). *Internet Archive.* R 5). Willian Andrews Clark.*Congressional Medal of Honor Recipients.*).Home of Heroes. (n.d.). *Home of Heroes..* Family Papers. (R. Carlson, Interviewer)Schrader, J. H. The Heritage of Blue Earth County.Wikipedia. (n.d.). *Wikepedia the free Encyclopedia.*

FLANNIGAN, JAMES

Genealogical and Family History of Northern New York: A Record of the Achievements of Her People in the Making of a Commonwealth and the Founding of a Nation, Volume 3; Lewis historical publishing Company, 1910 - Clinton County (N.Y.); edited by William Richard Cutter; Pp 1158-1159;Canadian Medal of Honor Website; *Scott County's Civil War Veterans remembered*, by Scott Stone. Medal of Honor Recipients, 1863-2013; *The War of the Rebellion: A Compilation of the Official Records of the Union and Confederate Armies*. 70 vols. in 128 parts. Washington, D.C.: Government Printing Office, 1880–1901. Reprint: Harrisburg: National Historical Society, 1971. (Series 1, vols. 7, 30 and 31.); *The Story of a Regiment: Being a Narrative of the Service of the Second Regiment, Minnesota Veteran Volunteer Infantry, in the Civil War of 1861-1865* by Judson Wade Bishop, 1890 - United States. Pp. 215, 216*Watertown Daily Times*; *"*Flanagan: Louisville's Medal of Honor Recipient"; PUBLISHED: THURSDAY, JUNE 5, 2014 AT 2:03 AM; http://www.watertowndailytimes.com "New York Deaths and Burials, 1795-1952," database, FamilySearch.Find A Grave; Photo by Alan Brownsten; Created by: Don Morfe; Obituary 1: *The Massena observer*. (Massena, St. Lawrence County,N.Y.18971989, October 12, 1905,; Obituary *The Ogdensburg advance and St. Lawrence weekly Democrat.* (Ogdensburg, N.Y.)

FRANTZ ALOYSIUS JOSEPH

War Hero Recognized 140 Years Later, Jun 14, 2003 northfieldnews.com;;The Northfield News, Sept 22, 1894, p.1;http://newspapers.mnhs.org/

"Indiana Marriages, 1780-1992," database, *FamilySearch* 1880; Census Place: Northfield, Rice, Minnesota; Roll: 632;1900; Census Place: Northfield Ward 1, Rice, Minnesota;;Rice County City Directory and Rice County Farmers Directory ;Northfield News, 1903 as transcribed at dalbydata.com. http://www.dalbydata.com.Northfield News; Friday, Oct. 24, 1913, p. 3Northfield News blog, "Cheers...06/18/03"

GERE, THOMAS PARK

Military Order of the Loyal Legion of the United States Minnesota Commandery. In Memoriam Circular No 7 Series 1912 Whole No 439;Thomas Gere: "19 Years old and in charge of a fort". Allies Newsletter for Members and Friends of the Military History Society of Minnesota' Summer, 2013, Vol XXI, No.3;"Thomas Parke Gere, First Lieutenant, United States ArmtArlingtoncemetery.net;Findagrave.com;"Thomas Parke Gere, First :Lieutenant and Adjutant with the Fifth Minnesota Volunteer Infantry. **GRANT, LEWIS ADDISON**

"Lewis A. Grant" Wikipedia, the free encyclopedia"Major-General Lewis Addison Grant" Iowa History Annals of Iowa by Charles Keyes, January 1921;"Lewis Addison Grant" Findagrave.com.;"Colonel Lewis Addison Grant" NSSAR National Society of the American Revolution.

HANNA, MILTON

"Answered His Last Roll Cali," Mankato Review, 22 Jan 1913. "Death Summons Mr. Hanna," Mankato Review, 10 Aug 1913 "First Church Services and Pioneer School Class, Held in James Hanna Home, 1853," Mankato Free Press, 21 Jun 1927. 'The Grand Review of Armies," Civil War Trust;1865" Shotguns' home of the American Civil War;Thomas, *History of Blue Earth County,* Volume 2, page 419. *"Marking their mettle with honor," Mankato Free Press,* 31 *Mar 1999.* "Milton Hanna, Civil War Hero, Cited On Field For Bravery" Mankato Free Press, 11 Mar 1936: 19:2 "Mrs. W. A. Beach Dies Here Today', Services Saturday." Mankato Free Press, Q9 Oct ~ 952 'Taps Are Sounded for Milton Hanna, Veteran," Mankato Free Press, 22 Jan 1913 US and State Census records.

HOLMES, LOVILO N.

KELLY, ANDREW JOHN

Congressional Medal of Honor Society Gray, Kristina Torkelson, *Legendary Locals of Crookston*, Arcadia Publishing, Charleston, South Carolina, 2014.United States of America, Bureau of the Census. *Seventhh Census of the United States, 1850*. Washington, D.C.: National Archives and Records Administration, 1900...

McCORNACK, ANDREW

News From the Past; Monticello, Minnesota, May 6, 1920: Death of a Gallant Veteran of 611; Obituary: Monticello, Minnesota, May 6, 1920; Idaho, Death Index, 1890-1964. for Effie Myrtle Moulton; 1860 FC Rutland, Kane, Illinois, Roll: M653_191; Page 685; Family History Library Film: 803191;.Web: Illinois, Databases of Illinois Veterans Index, 1775-1995; Web:FindaGrave.com; Minnesota, Death Index, 1908-2002.

McKAY, CHARLES WESLEY

Cattaraugus Co Medal of Honor Recipients by Mark H Dunkelman; A Regiment Redeemed, The New York Times, Mark H. Dunkelman,

May 9, 2014;Deeds of Valor; Report of the Adjutant General;Ancestry.com.;Newspapers.com. Find-a-GraveMinnesota Historical Society;

Special thank you to Mark H. Dunkelman of the 154th New York Volunteer Infantry reunion organization.

MERRITT, JOHN G.

Find A Grave; Home of Heroes;US Army Center of Military History; Photos of grave markers courtesy of Don Morfe, "Find A Grave" contributor who researches and photographs Medal Of Honor Recipient gravesites.

OBRIEN, HENRY

Find A Grave; Fold 3; Home of Heroes.

PAY, BRYON EDWARD

American Civil War Research Database. Copyright © 2016, by Alexander Street Press, LLC. American Civil War Research Database™. Copyright 1997-2016 Historical Data Systems, Inc. Soldier Data. History: by Lovilo H. Holmes, Nolensville, TN., 02'15'63. "Byron E. Pay (Union) Born Oct 21 1844 in LeRoy [sic] Twp., Jefferson Co., NY . . Enlisted on July 15 [sic], 1861 at Watonwan County [sic], Minnesota." ; Arlington Sun, Arlington, Kingsbury County, South Dakota, February 27, 1906, Front page, Pioneer Passes Away [sic], Byron E. Pay Dies Monday morning. One of South Dakota's Best Known Pioneers . . . Photocopy of front page, Frank Crisler e-mail via Sharon Pay to author July 5, 2016; Baldwin, Thomas J. and Thomas J. (M.D.). A NEW AND COMPLETE GAZETTEER OF THE UNITED STATES:;Philadelphia: Lippincott, Grambo & Co. 1854. Page 596: "Le Ray, a township in the central part of Jefferson county, New York. Pop. 3654.;Le Roy, a township of Genesee County, New York. Population, 3473. Le Roy, a village of Otsego county, New York, at the outlet of Canadarago Lake"; Brookings County History Book Committee, Brookings County History Book, Brookings, South Dakota, In the Year of the South Dakota State Centennial, Pine Hill Press, Freeman, South Dakota. Copyright 1989, pages 27, 34, 35, 36, 37,71, and 160. Original book owned by Grace Linn, Brooking, SD 57106; photocopy of pages in possession of author. (Page 27: "Byron E. Pay, who later settled at Oakwood Lakes, traveled through the area in September 1858 [sic] . . .");E-mail: May 24, 2016 from Nancy Anderson, Kingsbury County Genealogy Society (KCGS);Brookings County History Book, Pioneer Life 1861-1889. "This collection of stories was published in one or more of the county publications ---Brookings County Press: The Brookings Register: Elkton Record: Volga Tribune: White Leader and the Arlington Sun." Brookings, South Dakota, 7 September, 1879, original owned by Grace Linn, Brooking, SD 57106; photocopy in possession of author. E-mail: May 24, 2016 from Nancy Anderson, Kingsbury Co. Gen. Soc;Brookings County Press, Brookings, South Dakota, Newspaper clippings. Originals owned by Grace Linn, Brooking, SD 57106; photocopies of the articles in possession of author; Newspaper clipping from Thursday, Sept. 4, 1879 and reprinted on July 18, 1929, Romantic Oakwood, the story of the first July 4th and the naming of Oakwood. Newspaper clipping: W. W. Pay Oakwood Settler in Year 1873, Pay brothers attending court in Pembina. Newspaper clippings: Thursday, May 15, 1879, Byron Pay grand jury; Thursday, May 29, 1879, Mail routes; Thursday, Sept. 4, 1879, Oakwood businesses; No date – Pettigrew Surveys Oakwood; Breyer & Keydel editors, DEEDS OF VALOR, From records in the archives of the United States Government. How American Heroes won the Medal of Honor. Volume I, The Perrien-Keydel Company, Detroit, Mich. USA, 1907. Pages 137-140. National Park Service Website. Page 137, three images at the top of the page are of Lovilo H. Holmes on left, Milton Hanna on right and on the center of the page, Byron E. Pay with wings and ribbon around his image. Title, "THE "D__D YANKS" DIDN'T BEG FOR MERCY". Civil War Draft Registrations Records, 1863-1865. Web, Ancestry.com U.S., Civil War Draft Registrations Records, 1863-1865 Provo, UT, USA. Ancestty.com Operations, Inc., 2010. Original date: Consolidated Lists of Civil War Draft Registrations, 1863-1865. NH-65, entry 172, 620 volumes. NAI: 4213514. Records of the Provost Marshal General's Bureau (Civil War). Record Group 110. National Archives at Washington D.C. "Residence: Vernon Center, Entry #7. Pay, Byron (no information for age, white or colored, married or single, or place of birth) Former Military Service: 2nd MN Regt; (Author's note - This record was for counties: Olmsted, Winona, Nicollet and Rice, State of Minnesota, but Vernon Center was, and still is, in Blue Earth County, Minnesota.); Crisler, Frank, editor, Arlington Sun, Arlington, South Dakota, Volga Tribune, Volga, South Dakota, November 9, 2006, Page 13. Volga Civil War vet to be honored. (100 years after Byron E. Pay died). E-mailed by Frank Crisler to Sharon Pay on Monday, November 14, 2011; Daily Deadwood Pioneer-Times (Deadwood, South Dakota) - Thursday March 1, 1906, Page 5. BYRON E. PAY, Old Soldier Resident of Brookings County Passes Away. Printed May 22, 2016 from Newspapers.com. by Leslie Sprott and e-mailed to author on May 23, 2016; Daily Plainsman from Huron, South Dakota, Tuesday, June 24, 1930, page 34. Lake Byron in South Dakota named after Byron E. Pay after Indians named it Lake Byo after him in fall of 1866 as they called him "Byo"; Brother Asher F. Pay worked for the Huronite Newspaper, Huron, S.D. and wrote story; Find A Grave - Byron E. Pay. Arlington Cemetery, Arlington, Brookings County, South Dakota. Plot: Block 4, Lot 15, Grave 16; Fold3 by Ancestry.com. Medal of Honor Recipients, 1863-2013.. Home of Heroes. Web "Hometown Heroes of the North Star State: Minnesota. Civil War. Pay. Byron E.; Army; LeRoy [sic] Township, NY; MOH accredited to Mankato, Minnesota."; Illinois, Databases of Illinois Veterans Index, 1775-1995. Residence Place: Marengo, McHenry CO, IL. Record Source: Illinois Civil War Muster and Descriptive Rolls.; Minnesota, Civil War Records, 1861-1865 Web. Civil War Records, 1861-1865. Provo, UT, USA: Ancestry.com, Operations, Inc., 2011. Original data: Minnesota Civil War Muster Rolls. St. Paul, Minnesota: Minnesota Historical Society. "Name: Byron E. Pay, Birth Year: 1843 [sic]; Enlistment Date: 22 Jun 1861; Enlistment Location: Mankato; Age 18 [sic]; Regiment: 2nd Minnesota Volunteer Infantry Regiment; Minnesota, Civil War Records, 1861-1865. Name: Byron Z [sic] Pay, (MUSTER-OUT ROLL of Captain John B. Beatty.) Regiment: 2nd Minnesota Volunteer Infantry Regiment. Ancestry.com. Minnesota, Civil War Records, 1861-1865 Provo, UT, USA: Ancestry.com, Operations, Inc., 2011. Original data: Minnesota Civil

War Muster Rolls. St. Paul, Minnesota: Minnesota Historical Society. Cite Discharge dates - Date of July 15, 1863; Minnesota Civil War Soldiers. Dalby, John, Minnesota Civil War Soldiers Provo, UT, USA: Ancestry.com Operations Inc. 1999. Biron [sic] E. Pvt Pay, Mustered In: 15/JUL/1861 [sic] (June 11, 1861), County Wattonwan [sic] (Blue Earth); Minnesota, Marriages Index, 1849-1950 Provo, UT, USA: Ancestry.com Operations, Inc., 2011. Original data: "Minnesota Marriages, 1849–1950." Index. FamilySearch, Salt Lake City, Utah, 2009, 2010;Minnesota Historical Society, St. Paul, Minnesota, Kane, Lucile M., New Light on the Northwestern Fur Company, Winter 1955, pages 325-329; New York, Passenger and Immigration Lists, 1820-1850. Web. Ancestry.com. New York, Passenger and Immigration Lists, 1820-1850 . Provo, UT, USA: Ancestry.com Operations Inc, 2003. Original data: Registers of Vessels Arriving at the Port of New York from Foreign Ports, 1789-1919. Microfilm Publication M237, rolls 1-95. National Archives at Washington, D.C; New York State Census, 1855: E.D. 1, Watertown, Jefferson County, New York, William Pay, hh# 300. Web "New York State Census, 1855," database with images, Family Search, William Pay, E.D. 1, Watertown, Jefferson, New York, United States; count clerk offices, New York; Plat map of Oakwood Homestead Township Map, Township 111 N, Range 51 W, ??, original owned by Grace Linn, 108 7th St., Brooking, SD 57106; photocopy in possession of author. "South Dakota, Grand Army of the Republic Membership Records, 1861-1941," database with images, FamilySearch Byron E Pay, 1882-1932; citing Oakwood, Brookings County, South Dakota, United States, (and later citing Volga, Brookings County, South Dakota) box #Box 3387 Adjutant and quartermaster reports and muster rolls, posts 55-95, 1882-1891, line #2, South Dakota State Historical Society, Pierre; FHL microfilm 2,400,704; Sterner, C. Douglas. "Home of Heroes". Hometown Heroes of the North Star State Minnesota. Medal Of Honor Individual Citations: Pay, Byron E. Web. (Byron E. Pay was born in Le Ray Township, Jefferson County, New York not Le Roy) U.S., Civil War Pension Index: General Index to Pension Files, 1861-1934; National Archives and Records Administration. U.S., Civil War Pension Index: General Index to Pension Files, 1861-1934 Provo, UT, USA: Ancestry.com Operations Inc, 2000. Original data: General Index to Pension Files, 1861-1934. Washington, D.C.: National Archives and Records Administration. T288, 546 rolls; U.S., Civil War Soldier Records and Profiles, 1861-1865. Historical Data Systems, comp. U.S., Civil War Soldier Records and Profiles, 1861-1865. Provo, UT, USA: Ancestry.com Operations Inc, 2009. Original data: Data compiled by Historical Data Systems of Kingston, MA from the following list of works. Copyright 1997-2009 Historical Data Systems, Inc. PO Box 35 Duxbury, MA 02331; U.S., Civil War Soldier Records and Profiles, 1861-1865. Roster & Record of Iowa Soldiers in the War of Rebellion. Historical Data Systems, comp. U.S., Civil War Soldier Records and Profiles, 1861-1865 Provo, UT, USA: Ancestry.com Operations Inc, 2009. Original data: Data compiled by Historical Data Systems of Kingston, MA from the following list of works. Copyright 1997-2009. Historical Data Systems, Inc., PO Box 35, Duxbury, MA 02331; Asher Foster Pay. U.S., Register of Civil, Military, and Naval Service, 1863-Name: B. E. Pay, Residence Date: 30 Sep 1875, Station or Residence Place: Brookings, Dakota Territory. Year: 1875. Title: Register of Officers and Agents, Civil, Military, and Naval in the Service of the United States. Volume: Volume 1. Page 750. Post-Office Department. Source Information Ancestry.com. U.S., Register of Civil, Military, and Naval Service, 1863-1959. Provo, UT, USA: Ancestry.com Operations, Inc., 2014. U.S. Post Office Information Post-Office Oakwood, County Bookings, B. E. Pay, from April 1, Salary $5.49; UNITED STATES GENERAL INDEX TO PENSION FILES, 1861-1934; Affiliate Publication Number T288. Affiliate Publication Title. General Index to Pension Files, 1861-1934. Affiliate Film Number 365. GS Film Number 000541121; Veterans Schedule, 1890 - Web. "United States Census of Union Veterans and Widows of the Civil War, 1890," database with images, South Dakota, Brookings County, Oakwood. FamilySearchByron E Pay, 1890; citing NARA microfilm publication M123 (Washington, D.C.: National Archives and Records Administration, n.d.); FHL microfilm 338,253. 1860 United States Federal Census. Ceresco, Blue Earth, Minnesota;1870 United States Federal Census, Mankato Ward 4, Blue Earth, Minnesota; 1880 United States Federal Census, Brookings, Dakota Territory;1900 United States Federal Census, Volga, Brookings, South Dakota 1910 United States Federal Census, West Lincoln, Lancaster, Nebraska (Hattie Pay) 1920 United States Federal Census, (Hattie Pay not found) 1930 United States Federal Census, Enid, Garfield, Oklahoma (Hattie Pay)

PICKLE, ALONZO

Alonzo Pickle's gr-gr-grandson, Lee Skold provided the photo of Alonzo as an older man and the quote from Alonzo Pickle about Gettysburg; Armstrong, Bart, *Canada's Medal of Honor Recipients* ;Fritsche, L. A., M. D., *History of Brown County, Minnesota: Its People, Industries and Institutions*, vol. 2, Indianapolis: B. F. Bowen & Company, Inc., 1916, 425-28;Historical Marker Project; *Minnesota in the civil and Indian wars, 1861-1865* , two volumes/ prepared and published under the supervision of the Board of Commissioners appointed by the act of the Legislature of Minnesota of April 16, 1889;United States Federal census records and Minnesota State census records.

REED, AXEL HAYFORD

Reed, Axel Hayford; *Genealogical Record of the Reads, Reeds, the Bisbees, the Bradfords of the United States of America in the line of Esdras Read of Boston and England, 1635-1915. Thomas Besbedge or Bisbee of Scituate, Mass., and England, 1634 to 1915. Governor William Bradford of Plymouth, Mass., and England, 1620 to 1915. And their connections, with biographical sketches, illustrations, military services, etc,* Published 1915.Historical Marker Project: Home of Heroes Medal of Honor winners: United States Federal census records and Minnesota State census recordsMinnesota Legislators Past and Present http:findagrave.com; http://valor.militarytimes.com/recipient. Mayflower SocietyReed, Sam (gr-gr-grandson of Axel Hayford Reed, member of Sons of Union Veterans of the Civil War: http://suvcw.org/past/axelhreed.htm

SCHMIDT, WILLIAM

Photo of Lakewood Cemetery, Grand Army of the Republic Lot (G.A.R.), Section 8 from: .findagrave.com courtesy of "JC", "Find A Grave" contributor; Print of Missionary Ridge www.fold3.com. The print made with compliments of the McCormick Harvesting Machine Company/Cosack & Co. lith., Buffalo & Chicago Newspaper Announcement: The evening bulletin., November 07, 1895, Image 1 The evening bulletin. (Maysville, Ky.) 1887-1905 Page 1, Column 4; Records of the Grand Army of the Republic, H.S. Crocker and Co. Publishers, San Francisco, 1886, page 466; Deeds of Valor. How our Soldier-heroes won the Medal of Honor, Publisher Detroit, Mich., The Perrien-Keydel Company, 1905, Page 289; information obtained from office of Lakewood Cemetery, Minneapolis, Hennepin Co., MN;

SHEPARD, DR. IRWIN

Obtained at Winona County Historical Society Archives South Fourth Street Winona, Minnesota: Personal account of Dr. Irwin Shepard's life, probably dictated by Dr. Shepard but finished by someone else because he talks about his death in the first person. The Winona Daily Republican, April 19, 1918, p. 12. "Noted Educator Pays High Tribute to Dr. Irwin Shepard." The Winona Area Post, Vol. 7, No.9, February 29, 1984, "Irwin Shepard, educator" History of Winona County (MN), Volume 2, pp. 681-2, published 1913 ; History & Heritage, Winona Daily News, July 22, 2001, "Medal of Honor marker 84 years late to Shepard" The Daily Republican Herald, April 17, 1916, page 2, "Dr. Irwin Shepard, Prominent Educator Died in City Today" . "The Early Years", The Winona Daily News, (no date) p. 21, by Jerome Christenson; Irwin Shepard: Medal of Honor Winner" Winona Daily News, May 16, 2000, "Veteran's Grave to be Honored for Civil War Heroics" Progressive Men of Minnesota, 1897, page 47; Winona State Normal School, p. 191, biographical sketch of President Shepard.

SHERMAN, MARSHALL

Photos: Marshall Sherman in front of flag, page 1 & Marshall Sherman with artificial leg, page 2 collections.mnhs.org.MNHistoryMagazine/articles/; Photo of Headstone: http://vermontcivilwar.org http://1stminnesota.net/;Marshall https://www.fold3.com/;marshall_sherman/stories;http://collections.mnhs.org/cms/displayhttp://1stminnesota.net/Marshall Menof Minnesota, A Collection of Men Prominent in Business and Professions, Page 350, MHShttp://1stminnesota.net/Marshall R.L. Polk & Co., St. Paul Directory, 1895 MHS, book K-Z, page 1249Burial Record Marshall Sherman, Saint Paul's Historic Oakland Cemetery Association record; http://collections.mnhs.org/MNHistoryMagazine/articles.

VALE, JOHN

The Story of a Regiment Service of the 2nd Regiment, Minnesota Veteran Volunteer Infantry, In the Civil War of 1861 to 1865, by Judson W. Bishop, pages 1-6 Minnesota in the Civil War and Indian Wars, page 141, published 1890; John Vale biography on Wikipedia; History of Scott County, Iowa, page 923, published 1882; The Davenport Daily Times, September 30, 1897, "Mr. Vale Honored, An Honor Deservedly Conferred by the War Department" Davenport Sunday Democrat, September 19,1897, page 1, "A Medal of Honor" Davenport Democrat, February 5, 1909, obituary, "John Vale, Soldier and Good Citizen."

WRIGHT, SAMUEL

Personal communication with granddaughter. Lois Nixon, doukabil@gmaiLcom; BiliionGraves ; 1850 census, District 45, Harrison Co, Indiana 1880 census, Posey Twsp, Harrison Co, Indiana ; 1850 census, District 45, Harrison Co, Indiana ; 1900 census, Grant Twsp, Sedgwick Co, Kansas
Minnesota, Territorial and State Censuses, 1857 ; 1860 Census, Nicollet Twsp, Nicollet Co, Minnesota page 70 ; Dalby, John, Minnesota Civil War Soldiers, online ; Muster out roll of Captain Beaty ;) Family Search Research Wiki Minnesota Civil War Records, 1861-1865 ; 2nd Minnesota Volunteer Infantry ;) "Marking their mettle with honor." Mankato Free Press, 31 Mar 1999. Minnesota Civil War Records, 1861-1865 " Obituary of Samuel Wright," The Wichita Daily Eagle, Wichita, Kansas, 9 July 1918 "Obituary of Samuel Wright," The Wichita Beacon, Wichita, Kansas, 9 July 1918

INDIAN CAMPAIGNS
ALBEE, GEORGE EMERSON

Photos George E. Albee: page 1- https://www.fold3.com;Photos of Indian War Medal and Medal of Honor: http://jamesdjulia.com/item/lot-1220-rare-volcanic-arms-no2-navy-lever-action-pistol-with-history-to-indian-wars-medal-of-honor-winner-george-e-albee-46815/"
Grave Marker: photo courtesy of M.R. Patterson; United State Census 1860 MariaUhl/; http://www.secondwi.com/wisconsinregiments/ Berdans ; The Story of American Heroism: Thrilling Narratives of Personal Adventures by Lew Wallace, Pub. St.Louis, Riverside Pub., 1897, page 749-750;.findagrave.com; United State Census, 1900 1890/ photo of Albee's Diary cover

BURKARD, OSCAR

Photos of grave markers courtesy of Don Morfe, "Find A Grave" contributor King, Steven C. Seeds of War. Bloomington, Indiana: Author House, 2007. (pg. 83) ;Owens, Ron. Medal of Honor: Historical Facts & Figures. Paducah, Kentucky: Turner Publishing Company, 2004. (pg. 57)

"Chronological List 1832 through 1898, Indian War And U.S. Cavalry". USMilitaryHistory.com. 1989."Medal of Honor: Oscar Burkard". Office of Medical History. 2002.Photo of Grave site of MOH Recipient Oscar Burkard". Retrieved October 4, 2010."Oscar Burkard". Claim to Fame: Medal of Honor recipients. Find a Grave. Retrieved April 17, 2008.Home of Heroes.com

BYRNE, DENNIS

1900 USC for Melville, Renville, MN, p. 178A, line 3, HH #1; online Army, Register of Enlistments, 1798-1914 Denis Byrne, 16 March 1858, New York, New York; Civil War Pension Application of Dennis Byrne,; Service Company G 5th U.S. Infantry; online in U.S. Civil War Wikipedia.org.;ancestry.com; Kansas State Historical Society, Fort Hays Don Russell, *The Lives and Legends of Buffalo Bill*; University of Oklahoma Press, 1979; p. 84-87;U.S.; Bio Photo Montana Memory Project, Billings Public Library Historic Collection, 1880 USC for Fort Custer, Custer County, Montana Territory; South Tipperary Military History Society Forum; Homestead Land Office Records, www.ancestry.com; 1895 Minnesota State and Territorial Census for Melville, Renville, MN;1900 USC for Melville, Renville, MN, p. 178A #1 Gravestone Photo by Dick H., findagrave.com Contributor

HAWTHORNE, HARRY LEROY

Alchetron, The Free Social Encyclopedia: alchetron.com; Harry-L-HawthorneArlington National Cemetery Website:.Congressional Medal of Honor Society/recipientsEncyclopedia of Northern Kentucky; Findagrave.com; Medal of Honor;Harry LeRoy Hawthorne, *Song of the Bullet* Munsey's Magazine, Vol. 15, p.254 Lakota-Wounded Knee: A Campaign to Rescind Medals: https//www.fold3.com ; Military Times Hall of Valor: valor.militarytimes.com; Wikipedia: List of Medal of Honor recipients for the Indian Wars;

HUGGINS, ELI LUNDY

Aktalakota.stjo.org/;Ancestry.com/search; Ancestry.com/treeCivilWarArchives.com. *Civil War Union Regimental Histories - MN* Foreman, Carolyn Thomas. *Chronicles of Oklahoma,* Volume 13, No. 3. September 1935. *General Eli Lundy Huggins.*goantiques.com/eli-lundy-huggins-;Holbrook, Franklin F. *Minnesota in the Spanish American War and the Philippine Insurrection.*Homeofheros.com;*Minnesota Adjutant General's Report of 1866.* p. 201Mohconvention.com. ;*United States of America's Congressional Medal of Honor Recipients & Their Official Citations.* 2nd edition. p. 727.U.S. Federal Census – 192 worldcat. **Note: Hunkpapa Chief, Rain-in-the- Face, fought at the Battle of Little Big Horn and is alleged to have cut out the heart of Thomas Custer, a feat that was popularized in the Longfellow poem, The *Revenge of Rain in the Face.* Later in life, he denied this.**

McMILLAN, ALBERT WALTER

The article contained detailed researched information and much was used in the above biography: by Samuel L. Russell, "Sergeant Albert Walter McMillan, E Troop, 7th Cavalry – Conspicuous Gallantry", *Army at Wounded Knee* (Sumter, SC: Russell Martial Research, 2013-2015,http://wp.me/p3NoJy-d4), updated 7 Dec 2014, accessed date. https://armyatwoundedknee.com/2014/10/29/sergeant-albert-walter-mcmillan-e-troop-7th-cavalry-conspicuous-gallantry;/Ancestry.com;Newspapers.com;Find-a-Grave;Minnesota Historical Society

MONTROSE, CHARLES H.

Oath of Enlistment and Allegiance/National Archives and Records Administration; Ancestry.Com ;Wikipedia re: Indian Campaign.

MORGAN, GEORGE

Arlingtoncemetery.net; ;Findagrave.com;Geni.com/people/Colonel-George-Horace-Morgan; George Horace Morgan: Wikipedia.org; Homeofheros.com/photos1_indian/Morgan;Westpointaog.org/memorials/article/2848.

PHILLIPS, SAMUEL D.

State of Minnesota, death certificate; Military information from pension application and certificate. Samuel D. Phillips, (Private, Co. H, 2nd U.S. Cavalry), veterans invalid pension, Department of Veterans Affairs; National Archives, Washington, D.C; 1850 U. S. census, Butler County, Ohio, *Ancestry.com* ancestry.com ; *Ancestry.com* (http://www.ancestry.com; John Phillips; digital image, *Ancestry.com* 1900 U.S. census, Ramsey County, Minnesota, Samuel D. Phillips; digital image, *Ancestry.com* State of Minnesota, death certificate Margaret Jane Phillips; Oakland Cemetery Association Office (St. Paul, Minnesota), Interment Record, Samuel D. Phillips and wife Margaret Phillips; copy of records provided by staff to author.

TAYLOR, WILBUR NELSON

1850 and 1860 U.S. Federal Census, Family of Thomas Taylor, Hampden, Penobscot, Maine. Ancestry.com; Information provided by Dave Flewelling of the Penobscot County Genealogical Society (PCGS) in an email message dated 5Jun2016.Harold G. Taylor, "The Taylor Family," memoirs and family history written by Wilbur Nelson Taylor's son in 1966 and provided to this DAR member by his descendants.;Maine Wills and Probate Records, Thomas Taylor, 1584-1999. Ancestry.com "Honor and Courage: Organizational History 3rd Squadron 8th U.S. Cavalry,"; Senate Documents, 66th Congress, May 19-November 19, 1919, lst Session, page 443,; U.S. Sons of the American Revolution Membership Application, 1889-1970, #56588. Ancestry.com Cook County, Illinois, Marriages Index, 1871-1920. Ancestry.com

WELCH, CHARLES HENRY

Find-a-grave photo by Paul. M Branum.;"Record of Funeral, Charles H. Welch,"Allnut Funeral Records, 1914-1915, page 283, copy provided by Weld County Genealogical Society, Greeley, CO;.U.S.; Army Register of Enlistments, 1798-1914, image 428. Ancestry.com ;"7th Cavalry Regiment," from Wikipedia.org. "Battle of Little Big Horn articles," from Historynet.com.;E. A. Brininstool and J. W. Vaughn, *Troopers with Custer: Incidents of the Battle of the Little Big Horn*. Chapter 14; *Around and About*

LaSalle, by LaSalle (CO) History Book Committee, Carol Connell and Helen Connell, editors, 1988, page 27,115; The Welch family apparently arrived after 1870 as none is listed among Weld County residents in the 1870 U.S. Federal Census. U.S. Army Register of Enlistments, 1798-1914; 1880 U.S. Federal Census, Household of Holon Godfrey, Weld County, Colorado. Ancestry.com 1900 and 1910 U.S. Federal Census, Household of Charles H. Welch, LaSalle, Weld County, Colorado, Ancestry.com; Photo of gravesite-www.Homeofheroes.com.

WILSON, WILLIAM OTHELLO

http://buffalosoldiers-washington.com/MajorHenrySep24.html;Buffalo Soldier by the National Park Brochure for the state of California on Buffalo Soldiers. – Wikipedia,. Indian Wars, *Buffalo Soldier*;. Find A Grave, FamilySearchElsie M. Comer, 2001; Burial, Hagerstown, Washington, Maryland, United States of America, Cedar Lawn Memorial Park; National Historic Site, National Park Service, U.S. Department of the Interior, Black Recipients of the Medal of Honor From the Frontier Indian Wars Fort McKinney (Wyoming); Greater Los Angeles Chapter of the Ninth & Tenth (Horse) Cavalry Association. History, Culture, Economy & facts; Flagpole dedicated at memorial to Hagerstown Buffalo Soldier, May 28, 2011 by Don Aines, dona@herald-mail.com;HAGERSTOWN; Home of Heroes; Maryland Memories, Hagerstown, Washington County News and Blog. February 9 Tuesday; Famous Hagerstown Medal of Honor Recipient Honored With New Museum Gallery in Wyoming. (Photo of William O. Wilson in uniform) Information from CVB's African American Heritage Guide of Washington County, MD;. Maryland Military Heroes, Medal of Honor Recipients; Military Times, Hall of Valor, William O. Wilson;. Nebraska State Historical Society. Article Title: Ten Troopers: Buffalo Soldier Medal of Honor Men Who Served at Fort Robinson. Full Citation: Frank N Schubert, ";Remington, Frederic. *"A Scout with the Buffalo Soldiers"* from The Century: a popular quarterly, Volume 37, Issue 6, April 1889. From the discontinued periodical, Discover Arizona. http://www.discoverseaz.com/History/BufSold.html.Schubert, Frank N. *"Buffalo Soldiers, Braves and the Brass: the Story of Fort Robinson, Nebraska* (Shippensburg, PA: White Mane, 1993); Schubert, Black Valor: Buffalo Soldiers and the Medal of Honor, 1870-1898 (Wilmington, DE: SR Books, 1997). United States Census, 1900," database with images; History of Leitersburg District, Washington Co., Md ; William O. Wilson Historical Marker. The Journey Through Hallowed Ground, Gettysburg to Monticello; National Park Service. Fort Davis National Historic Site. "Black recipients of the Medal of Honor"; Wikipedia. 9thCavalry regiment (United States) Drexel Mission Fight. 1910 Census Place: Hagerstown Ward 5, Washington, Maryland. 1910 United States Federal Census Provo, UT, USA: Ancestry.com Operations Inc,

SPANISH-AMERICAN WAR-PHILLIPINES INSURRECTION

Wikipedia and http://www.history.com/topics/spanish-american-war.)

BELL, HARRY

"Iowa, County Marriages, 1838-1934", Harry Bell and Kate Reimers, 1904."Iowa, County Births, 1880-1935,", 1910 U. S. census, Leavenworth County, Kansas, Fort Leavenworth Military Reservation, Enumeration District /www.ancestry.com The National Archives at College Park, College Park, Maryland;1920 U. S. census, Leavenworth County; 1930 U. S. census, Franklin County, Ohio, pop. sch., Columbus City, p. 8-B; Elizabeth Ertley; digital image, *Ancestry.com*; "U.S. National Cemetery Interment Control Forms, 1928-1962, Kate Bell wife of Harry Bell; The National Archives at College Park, College Park, Maryland; 1930 U.S. census, Leavenworth County, Kansas, pop. sch., Leavenworth City Ward 3, p. 8-A, Kate Bell; digital image; *Ancestry.com*. "Illinois Deaths and Stillbirths, 1916-1947,"."U.S. National Cemetery Interment Control Forms, 1928-1962.

BOEHLER, OSCAR R.

"Photo of Grave site of MOH Recipient Otto Boehler at www.homeofheroes.com ;Home of Heroes";"Otto Boehler". Claim to Fame: Medal of Honor recipients. Find a Grave. United States Federal census records and Minnesota State census records; Congressional Medal of Honor,

DAVIS, CHARLES

Backes, Brian, Find A Grave. Tombstone photo and Cemetery photo, Giffith, findagrave.com; Congressional Medal of Honor Society,.cmohs.org; http: Military Times: Hall of Valor, valor.militarytimes.com;United States Federal Census: 1880, 1910, 1920, 1930, and 1940;Wikipedia: Charles P. Davis; Excerpted from http://2001-2009.state.gov.

MEXICAN EXPEDITION

Wikipedia

CATLIN, ALBERTUS

This article incorporates public domain material from websites or documents of the United StatesMarine Corps. and public domain material from websites or documents of the United States Navy."Catlin, Albertus W., Brigadier General, USMC, (1868-1933)". Naval History and Heritage Command. Catlin, Albertus Wright; Dyer, Walter Alden (1919). *"With the Help of God and a Few Marines"*. Garden City, New York: Doubleday, Page and Company United States Navy Department (1893). *Annual Report of the Secretary of the Navy.* U.S. Government Printing Office. pp. 585–586. "Catlin House dedicated to Marine hero". *Guantanamo Bay Gazette*63 (49): 1-4. "Maine Spectrelike in Green, Slimy Pool". *New-York Tribune* (New York, NY). June 21, 1911. p. 2. "Col. A. W. Catlin Wounded in Action". *Evening Star* (Washington, DC). June 13, 1918. p. 2. Simmons, Edwin H. (Spring 1993). "Catlin of the 6th Marine Regiment" (PDF). *Fortitudine* XXII (4): 3– 12. "List of Expeditions 1901-1929". Naval History and Heritage Command.Yates, Jr., John R.; Yates, Thomas (2015). *The*

Boston Marine Barracks: A Hist01y, 1799–1974. Jefferson, North Carolina: McFarland & Co. "Brigadier General Albertus W. Catlin, USMC". *Who's Who in Marine Corps History.* History Division, United States Marine Corps. "Forming the Regiments". *1st Marine Division.* United States Marine Corps. "Navy and Marine Corps Officer to Advance in Rank". *Evening Star* (Washington, DC). February 7, 1917. p. 7. Albertus W. Catlin *"George Washington If'.* *Dictionary of American Naval Fighting Ships. Navy Department, Naval Hi*story &Heritage Command.

DYER, JESSE FARLEY

Photo of Brigadier General Jesse Farley Dyer from: navylog.navymemorial.org; Grave Marker photo courtesy of ssgrove, Find A Grave contributor;, 1895 Oakland Tribune, Oakland California, 20 March 1910; valor.militarytimes.com; Census of the Virgin Islands of the United States 1920 Report of Joint commission appointed under authority of the concurrent resolution passed by the Congress of the United States. January, 1920 Government Printing Office; Census of the United States, 1930; 1940; .mca marines.org/leatherneck/1937/08/parris-island.

WORLD WAR I

Excerpts from Wikipedia and http://history1900s.about.com/od/worldwari/p/World-War-I.htm

CUKELA, LOUIS

Arlington National Cemetery; Find a Grave; Congressional Medal of Honor Society: : http://burnpit.us/2014/07/gunnery-sergeant-louis-cukela-receives-medal-honor-twice; Home of Heroes: Burnpit.US Serbia America website: http://www.eserbia.org/people/military/123-louis-cukela;USMC History website:

MALLON, GEORGE HENRY

ALLIES, Newsletter for Members and Friends of the Military Historical Society of Minnesota. Spring 2009, Vol. XVII, No. 2. Page 6, Curator Notes by Doug Bekke; Briggs, H. B. R., Former Editor of the St. Paul Daily News. Newspaper Archive of Farmers Independent, Bagley, Minnesota, July 29, 1920, page 1 of 8. With Both Fists!;. Brotherhood of Locomotive Firemen and Enginemen's Magazine, Volumes 70-71. (1921) Page 5, last three paragraphs: Capt. Mallon. Minnesota Historical Society, St. Paul, Minnesota;. Brotherhood of Railroad Trainmen (author) book, The Railroad Trainman, 1922, Volume 39, page 648, Candidates Endorsed By The Legislative Board, Brotherhood Of Railroad Trainmen And The Working People's Non-Partisan Political League Of Minnesota . . Minnesota Historical Society, St. Paul, Minnesota; Congressional Medal of Honor, Kansapedia, Kansas Historical Society; Death Certificate Index ,Minnesota Historical Society, St. Paul, MN; Find A Grave.com Fold3 by Ancestry; 1796-1969, George H. Mallon, Army, Company M, Pvt., 22 Kansas Infantry; .fold3.com/image/3338130 Page 1: Investigative Case Files of the Bureau of Investigation 1908-1922; Holt, Dean W., American Military Cemeteries, 2d ed. Part I, VA National Cemeteries – Fort Snelling. McFarland & Co., Inc. Publishers. Page 146. First burial, One of General John J. Pershing's outstanding solders of WWI. Remains were reinterred Section B DS 1-S;Hometown Heroes of the North Star State: Minnesota; Jenkins, Nate, Salina Journal, Salina, Kansas, posted online under Snowbizz.com at 7:38 AM on Sunday, May 28, 2009. Salinan won Congessional Medal of Honor for World War I heroics;The search by Bruce Powell to find the list of General Pershing's 100. www.snowbizz.com; Kansas City Kansan newspaper, Kansas City, Kansas, Wednesday, March 26, 1919, Page 1. Captain George H. Mallon , General John J. Pershing; Kansas Marriages, 1840-1935, database, Mallon, George H; Lansing, Michael J. author, Insurgent Democracy. chapter 5, page 206. The Non partisan League in North American Politics; Lundeen, Ernest, U.S. Senator, Speech before Congress, August 15, 1940. The Farmer Labor Party-A Political Pattern for America, speech detailing the history of the Minnesota Farmer Labor Party on August 15, 1940.) Congressional Record – Senate, August 15, 1940. Page 7-8 of 17; Military Times, Hall of Valor. George H. Mallon, WWI; Minnneapolis: Campaign Committee, [1920] Includes sample Republican ballot; George H. Mallon, candidate for lieutenant governor / issued by Campaign Committee, C. Z. Nelson, Secretary. Minnesota Historical Society, St. Paul, MN; Minneapolis Sunday Tribune, Minneapolis, Minnesota, November 11, 1956, page 18A. Valor is Written in Minnesota's History. Minnesota Historical Society, St. Paul, MN; Minneapolis Tribune, Minneapolis, Minnesota, Saturday, August 4, 1934, page 2. Obituary. MALLON RITES TO BE MONDAY. and Sunday, August 5, 1934, page 2. MALLON RITES TO BE MONDAY. MN Historical Society, St. Paul, Minnesota; Minnesota, Death Index, 1908-2002, Ancestry.com. Minnesota, Death Index, 1908-2002 Provo, UT, USA: Ancestry.com Operations Inc, 2001. Original data: State of Minnesota. Minnesota Death Index, 1908-2002. Minneapolis, MN, USA: Minnesota Department of Health;Minnesota Family History Research, Thursday, May 16, 2013. "National Cemeteries: Remembering Those Who Have Served Our Country;Minnesota Historical Society, St. Paul, Minnesota: Page 61, Minnesota War Records Commission; Minnesota History Bulletin, Vol. 4, No. ½ (Feb. – May, 1921), pp. 76-104. Published by: Minnesota Historical Society Press. Web. June 2016. WAR HISTORY ACTIVITIES, Page 101; Minnesota History Magazine, Review and Short Features: Vol. 04/ 1-2 (1921), page 99, War History Activities. Page 101, second paragraph; Minnesota Secretary of State Election Division. An Inventory of Its Nomination Petitions;New Ulm Review Newspaper, New Ulm, Brown County, Minnesota, Wednesday, June 16, 1920, CAPT. MALLON AT LAMBERTONNewspaper Archive of Farmers Independent, Bagley, Minnesota. August 19, 1920; May 20, 1920, page 4 of 8. FARMER-LABOR TICKET. Powell, Bruce, Once Lost and Almost Forgotten, But Retrieved from the National Archives, "A List of One Hundred Individual Acts of Extraordinary Heroism Performed by Soldiers of the American Expeditionary Forces". Presented by Worldwar1.com. Pershing's 100. (#55 Mallon, George H.) ; U.S. Department of Veterans Affairs, VA » National Cemetery Administration » Fort Snelling; Captain George H. Mallon, (World War I), 132rd Infantry, 33rd Division, U.S. Army. Bois-de-Forges, France, Sept. 26, 1918 (Section DS, Grave 1-S);. U.S. National Cemetery

Interment Control Forms, 1928-1962, Ancestry.com. Provo, UT, USA: Ancestry.com Operations, Inc., 2012. U.S., Social Security Applications and Claims Index, 1936-2007, Ancestry.com. U.S., Social Security Applications and Claims Index, 1936-2007 Social Security Applications and Claims, 1936-2007. George H. Mallon. . United States Civil War and Later Pension Index, 1861-1917, database,FamilySearch; United States General Index to Pension Files, 1861-1934, database with images, FamilySearch; United States Index to Service Records, War with Spain, 1898", database with images, FamilySearch, familysearch.org/ United States Registers of Enlistments in the U.S. Army, 1798-1914," database with images, FamilySearc Wikipedia, George H. Mallon; Wikipedia, Meuse-Argonne Offensive; Wikipedia, Nonpartisan League; Willbanks, James H. Editor, America's Heroes: Medal of Honor Recipients from the Civil War to Afghanistan. ABC-CLIO,LLC, Santa Barbara, CA, 2011, Pages 199-200; Willmar Tribune, Willmar, MN, Wednesday, June 9, 1920, Front page: "YELLOW PAINT BOYS FLAYED BY MALLON "Scabs" Might Have Painted "No Man's Land," Candidate Says;World War I bonus file, warrant number 41588: Mallon, George H. Minnesota Historical Society, St. Paul, Minnesota. World War I military service questionnaire: Mallon, George Henry (Minneapolis, Minn.); WORLD WAR VETERANS (1918-192X) organizational history. MARCH; "Letter to Frank B. O'Connell, Department Adjutant, The American Legion, in Lincoln, Nebraska, from Harrison Fuller, Commander, Department of Minnesota, American Legion, in St. Paul, Minnesota, March 15, 1920;1870, 1870 & 1900 – United States Federal Census Ogden, Riley County, Kansas;1895 Kansas State Census Record, Ogden, Riley County, Kansas. 1900 United States Federal Census – Momada, Philippine Islands, Military & Naval Forces;

WOLD, NELS

Congressional Medal of Honor Society official website; *Crookston Times*, 1 Feb 2011, obituary for Ione Ostgarden;*Crookston Times*, 25 Jul 2013, "Kristina Gray series: Nels T. Wold's story continues," Gray, Kristina Torkelson, *Legendary Locals of Crookston*, Arcadia Publishing, Charleston, South Carolina, 2014.Missouri History Museum Archives, American Expeditionary Force, 35th Division, 138th Infantry, Company I, Records, 1917-1976. Wentsel, C. E., *Polk County Minnesota in The World War*, Ada, Minnesota, 1922.

WORLD WAR II

Excerpts from: *http://www.nationalww2museum.org; http://www.u-s-history.com*

BIANCHI, WILLIALD C.

Excerpts from the "Military Press Release "For Immediate Release with Army Forces Western Pacific 29th Replacement Depot Near Manila" – author unknown; Cpt Willibald C. Bianchi Congressional Medal of Honor Recipient Monument Dedication Program at South Dakota State University (SDSU), Brookings, SD, on September 22, 2000; Excerpts taken from various sources such as official military correspondence and various local newspapers;"On Veterans Day, …WWII heroism of Lt Bianchi", Minneapolis Tribune (Gail Tollin/AP) 11-12-1979 "SDSU Honors Bianchi with Monument, Scholarship", New Ulm Journal (Dan Robrish) 7-15-1997 "New Ulm Legion to Add Name of Medal of Honor Recipient Bianchi", New Ulm Journal (Marge Excerpts from a story "Bill Bianchi, Bataan Fighter, In the Tuol River Pocket, Bataan, February 3, 1942" – author unknown; Excerpts from Iverson)

COLALILLO, MICHAEL

COURTNEY, HENRY ALEXIUS

FLEMING, RICHARD EUGENE

Delta Kappa Epsilon; Flemingfield.com/ history;Marinemedals.com; Military.wikia.com/ Missing Marines: Captain Richard Eugene Fleming April 13, 2012;Mn.gov/gov state/images/Medal-of-Honor-Day.pdf;Vachon, Duane A. PH.D hawaiireporter.com/you-cant-test-courage-cautiously-captain-richard-e-fleming-us-marine-corps-wwii-battle-of-Midway-medal-of-honor-1917-1942/123

HAUGE, LOUIS JR.

Corporal Louis James Hauge Jr.", *Who's Who in Marine Corps History*.;Louis J. Hauge Medal of Honor citation, *Marines Awarded the Medal of Honor.'MSC Ship Inventory* 2002.;*U.S. Navy Ships* 1999; *U.S. Navy Fact File* 2005;Findagrave.com;United States Federal census records and Minnesota State census records.

KRAUS RICHARD E.

1930 United States Federal Census; www.mcu.usmc.mil/historydivision/Pages;www.militaryhallofhonor.com/honoree-record; www.militaryhallofhonor.com /honoree-record[1]
http://theirfinesthour.net/2014/10/richardkrauswww.facebook.com/ParrisIslandMarinesPage

LaBELLE JAMES D.

Find A Grave;Wikipedia; United States Marine Corps History Division

OLSON, ARLO LAVERNE

Iowa, County Births, 1880-1935; *FamilySearch*), Delva Veryle Olson, 04 Aug 1922; citing Greenville, Clay, Iowa, United States; county districtcourts,Iowa1930; U.S.census, Deuel County, South Dakota, *Ancestry.com*[1] *South Dakota Department of Veterans Affairs* Memorials>Medal of Honor Recipients>Captain Arlo L. Olson.

RUDOLPH, DONALD EUGENE

Medal of Honor Society www.cmohs.org; Find a grave

SORENSON, NELS CHRISTIANSON

Findagrave.com Memorial for Nels Christian Sorenson 1920 USC for Duluth, St. Louis, MN District 0106, Frank Mox, p 18 A-B, line 48-55; 1930 USC for Flint, Genesee, MI District 14, Carl Sorenson, p 12 –A, line 1-5; Anoka Hennepin, Minnesota School District, Nick Del Calzo and Peter Collier, *Medal of Honor: Portraits of Valor Beyond the Call of Duty; Taking the Impact: Richard K. Sorenson* Anoka County Historical Society Interview with Richard K. Sorenson, conducted by Pat Schwabik May 28, 1991: Naval History and Heritage Command ; Captain John C. Chapin, U.S. Marine Corps Reserve (Ret.), "Breaking the Outer Ring: Marine Landings in the Marshall Islands", Marines in World War II Commemorative Series, p. 15 Nick Del Calzo and Peter Collier, *Medal of Honor: Portraits of Valor Beyond the Call of Duty,* Published in collaboration with the Congressional Medal of Honor Foundation by Artisan/Workman Publishing Co., Inc., New York, New York, 2003; p. 242-243;"Pvt Richard K. Sorenson, Medal of Honor, 1944, 4th MarDiv, Namur Island, Kwajalein Atoll [Medal of Honor citation]". *Marines Awarded the Medal of Honor*. United States Marine Corps ;Naval History and Heritage Command Website;AR15, Home of the Black Rifle, Obituary of Richard K. Sorenson, online at http://www.ar15.com/archive/ The Marine Corps Medal of Honor Recipients, U.S. Marines Home of the Heroes: Bio Photos: wikipedia.org/wiki/ Richard_K._SorensonGravestone Photo courtesy of Christina, findagrave.com Contributor

VAN VALKENBURGH, FRANKLIN

photo : U.S. Naval Historical Center; .wikipedia.org/FranklinVan Valkenburgh_; Wikipedia: The Arizona

VLUG, DIRK JAN

Headstone Photo courtesy of Jeff Machiele posted on findagrave.com Greenwood Cemetery in Grand Rapids, Michigan; Dirk Vlug with Truman photo courtesy of Ron Moody, .findagrave.com; Koonce, Richard S., "State's Top Military Honor Will Go to World War II Vet," *Grand Rapids Press*, Grand Rapids, Michigan, November 4, 1992; Michigan Marriage Records, 1867-1952;Minnesota Historical Society, Birth Certificate Index; Angie Vlug Obituary, *Grand Rapids Press*, Grand Rapids, Michigan, January 8, 2013;"City Honors Veteran", *Grand Rapids Press*, Grand Rapids, Michigan, October 27, 1999; Revere, C. T., "Friends Say Humility Characterized Life of Medal of Honor Winner Dirk Vlug", *Grand Rapids Press*, Grand Rapids, Michigan, June 27, 1996; "One GI Destroys Five Jap Tanks. Gets Medal of Honor", *Escanaba Daily Press*, Escanaba, Michigan, May 24, 1946; United States, Department of Verterans Affairs BIRLS Death File 1850-2010;United States Federal census records and Minnesota State census records; United States World War II Army Enlistment Records, 1938-1946; Vlug, Dirk, Michigan Department of Military and Veteran Affairs

KOREAN WAR

militaryhistory.about.com/od/battleswars1900s/tp/The-Korean-War.

PAGE, JOHN UPSHUR DENNIS

wikipedia.org/wiki/John_U._D._Page;www.findagrave.com

VIETNAM WAR

The Vietnam War:ushistory.org

BLANCHFIELD, MICHAEL REINERT

Medal of Honor Society;Wikipedia; Ancestry.com; Newspapers.com;Find-a-Grave; Minnesota Historical Society.

OLSON, KENNETH

Brodin, Rodger. *Kenneth L. Olson Memorial."* n.d. Bronze. University of Minnesota St. Paul Student Center Minnesota Commons Room, Falcon Heights, MN.; *Congressional Medal of Honor Society*, database (http://www.cmohs.org: accessed 21 Jul 2016), recipient page for Kenneth L. Olson; *Find A Grave*, database and images , memorial page for Kenneth L. Olson (1945-1968); Find a Grave Memorial no. 7861505, citing Paynesville Cemetery, Paynesville, Stearns County, Minnesota; accompanying photograph provided by Don Morfe; Jacobson, Michael. "Medal of Honor recipient honored posthumously as distinguished PAHS alumni." *Paynesville (MN) Press* .5 May 2004.. Accompanying photograph uncredited; Stelling, Linda. "Legion rededicated Olson memorial plaque at open house." *Paynesville (MN) Press*. 24 May 2000.

PRUDEN, ROBERT JOSEPH

Ben Bartenstein, "St. Paul East Side police herald fallen Vietnam War soldier," St. Paul Pioneer Press, July 5, 2015Charles W. Bailey, "2 state GIs posthumously cited for heroic service," Minneapolis Tribune, April 23, 1971, page 14A.; "Genealogy home page for Lawerence [sic] Gilbert Pruden," "The Virtual Wall," Vietnam Veterans Memorial Wall; U.S. Army Center of Military History, Medal of Honor Recipients, Vietnam War, "Wall of Faces," Vietnam Veterans Memorial Wall; Bio photo taken from "Wall of Faces."
Gravestone photos from Findagrave (Front by Christina, Reverse by Devon)

RABEL, LASZLO

A Veterans' Day Remembrance; Immigrant MOH Records: USCIS.gov; Laszlo Rabel: militarywikia.com; Laszlo Rabel: mishalov.com; MOH Citations for Laszlo: homeofheroes.com; Specialforcesmoh.com;Virtual Vietnam Veterans' Wall of Faces Laszlo Rabel/Army:.vvmf.org/Wall-of-faces.

THORSNESS, LEO

Amazon.com,Inc. Leo K. Thorsness; Congressional Medal of Honor Society. Thorsness, Leo K.
DecaturDaily.com "Spirit honoree is ex-POW, Medal of Honor winner, more. June 21, 2009. Web July, 2016; Find A Grave Westbrook Cemetery, Westbrook, Cottonwood County, Minnesota, USA , Bernice Mae Thorsness Thompson, Peder Emil

Thorsness; Encounter Books, Author Leo Thorsness. Humana-military, biography of Leo K. Thorsness; Iowa State Census, 1915FamilySearch; Emil Thorsness, 1915; citing , Woodbury, Iowa, United States; Iowa State Historical Department, Des Moines; FHL microfilm 1,487,314.Minnesota Historical Society Birth Record Minnesota Official Marriage System MOMS ;United States Census, 1910 Emil Thorsness in household of John Thorsness, Sioux Ward 3, Woodbury, Iowa, United States; United States Census, 1920," database with images, FamilySearch Emil Thorsness in household of Oscar A Bakke, Westbrook, Cottonwood, Minnesota, United States; citing sheet 8A, NARA microfilm publication T625 (Washington D.C.: National Archives and Records AdministrationUnited States; 1940 Census. United States Public Records, 1970-2009, database; FamilySearch(Donna M Martinson, Residence, Hector, Minnesota, United States; a third party aggregator of publicly available information.; Wikia, The Home of the Fandom. Military. Leo K. Thorsness; WikipediaLeo K. Thorsness.

WAYRYNEN, DALE EUGENE

Findagrave.com ; "Vietnam vets remember Dale Wayryene's sacrifice" by Mark Steil, Minnesota Public Radio News, 2007 For more information and an oral history about Dale Eugene Wayrynen, please go to: http://minnesota.publicradio.org/display/web; Department of the Army General Order #66, 27 October 1969 (vvmf.org) ; The Road to Remembrance--There's no time like the last weekend in May to start the journey down Dale Wayrynen Memorial Highway"by Kathleen Pakarinen; County's Most Decorated Hero Fought in County's Most Controversial War."; Medal of Honor recipients" Medal of honor citations. United States Army Center of Military History.

SPECIAL/INTERIM

DAVIS, RAYMOND

Interim Awards, 1901-1911; Davis, Raymond E. entry". Medal of Honor recipients. *United States Army Center of Military History.. "Bennington".* Dictionary of American Naval Fighting Ships. *Naval Historical Center.* February 8, 2006. [b] John Griffith (November 11, 2003). *"Raymond E. Davis".* Claim to Fame: Medal of Honor recipients. *Find a Grave. Raymond E. Davis".* Hall of Valor. *Military Times.*

LINDBURGH, CHARLES A.

Congressional Medal of Honor Society: Charles A. "Lucky Lindy" Lands at the Navy Tissue Bank photo; Spirit of St. Louis 2 Project: Charles A. Lindbergh, An American Aviator. Medal of Honor: Lindbergh, Charles A; Certificate of Marriage, Englewood, Bergen, New Jersey, May 1929

Spirit of St. Louis 2 Project: Erik. Lindbergh, Biography.

NELSON, OSCAR F.

Social Security Index; Veterans Memorial Hall; Social Security IndexBeatrice Helen Nelson Verbarg (daughter); Oscar F. Nelson Obituary, online at: http://www.homeofheroes.com/photos Military Times, Hall of Valor; http://valor.militarytimes.com/recipient.php?recipientid=2496U.S. Navy, Record *of Medals of Honor Issued to the Officers and Enlisted Men of the United States Navy, Marine Corps, and Coast Guard, 1862-1917;* U.S. Government Printing Office, 1917; p. 8; U.S. Navy, *"Our Navy, the Standard Publication of the U.S. Navy",* Vol. 4, October 10, 1910, No. 6, p. 19; published monthly at the Naval Training Station, San Francisco, CA; USS Bennington; Veterans Memorial Hall; WWII Draft Registrations; Photo of Medal and Story appear at http://www.vets-hall.org. U.S.National Cemetery Interment Control Forms, 1928-1962 at ancestry.com https://en.wikipedia.org.

Bio Photo from Veterans Memorial Hall; Gravestone Photo courtesy of Findagrave Contributor Chris H.

ROBINSON, THOMAS

Grave Photo of Thomas Robinson by Dave Vangsness, findagrave.com. "Civil War Veteran Buried," *Minneapolis Morning Tribune,* Minneapolis, Minnesota, May 15, 1915, p 20.Commonwealth of Virginia, Certificate of Death, October 22, 1940, Ruby Robinson Reid.

Minnesota Historical Society, Death Certificate Index; Minnesota Historical Society, Marriage License and Certificate, Hennepin County, May 17, 1881, Thomas Robinson and Louise Herlin; Minnesota Historical Society, Marriage License and Certificate, Hennepin County, March 19, 1909, Hugh Sutton Reid and Ruby Louise Robinson;Minnesota Historical Society, Return of a Death: July 27, 1889, Rachael Robinson;Minnesota Historical Society, Report of a Birth: May 4, 1889, Rachael Robinson.

RUD, GEORGE WILLIAM

Birth information for Sine Nellie Ingebredtsen; Ancestry.corn. Minnesota, Births and Christenings Index, 1840- Provo, UT, USA: Ancestry.corn Operations, Inc., 2011_;Original Data: "Minnesota Births and Christenings, 1840-1980." Index.;FamilySearch, Salt Lake City, Utah, 2009, 2010;, *FamilySearch* https:/familysearch.org/; Minneapolis City Directories 1905 Minnesota State Census ;*Minneapolis Man A Victim* of *Disaster to Cruiser Memphis;The* Minneapolis morning tribune. Pub. Date 1916-08-31 *Hospital Ship Solace Brings Memphis Dead;* Evening star. (Washington, D_C_) 1854-1972, September 09,1916, Page 4*"Sailor Killed on US Ship buried nere";* The Minneapolis Moming Tribune September 15,1916, p.8 ;U.S_ Army Center of Military History Minnesota Death Index, 1908-2002April 2016), Maren Caroline Ingebredtsen, 09 Sep 1943; from "Minnesota Death Index, 1908-2002; Find A Grave; Originally Created by: Don Morfe

35229724R00134

Made in the USA
Middletown, DE
25 September 2016